Women and Slavery in the French Antilles, 1635–1848

D1081697

BLACKS IN THE DIASPORA

Darlene Clark Hine, John McCluskey, Jr., and David Barry Gaspar,

general editors

Women and Slavery in the French Antilles, 1635-1848

Bernard Moitt

Indiana University Press

Bloomington and Indianapolis

This book is a publication of

Indiana University Press
601 North Morton Street
Bloomington, IN 47404-3797 USA

http://iupress.indiana.edu

Telephone orders   800-842-6796
Fax orders   812-855-7931
Orders by e-mail   iuporder@indiana.edu

Library of Congress Cataloging-in-Publication Data

Moitt, Bernard.
    Women and slavery in the French Antilles, 1635–1848 / Bernard
Moitt.
        p.   cm. — (Blacks in the diaspora)
    Includes bibliographical references and index.
    ISBN 0-253-33913-8 (cl : alk. paper) — ISBN 0-253-21452-1
(pa : alk. paper)
        1. Women slaves—West Indies, French—History. 2. Women,
Black—West Indies, French—History.   I. Title.   II. Series.

HT1079 .W48 M65 2001
305.48'9625'09729—dc21

                                                        00-143858

1 2 3 4 5   06 05 04 03 02 01

For
Cynthelia (Tia),
Kojenwa,
and
Thandika Moitt,
and
to the memory of Mama
(the late Pearl Agusta Moitt)

Contents

Preface

THIS BOOK WAS written with relatively little funding, much institutional support and goodwill, and assistance and encouragement from friends and colleagues in many places. It has not been developed from a Ph.D. thesis. Indeed, it grew out of my interest in Atlantic slavery and my determination to fill a significant gap in the historiography of the French Caribbean. While teaching Caribbean history at the University of Toronto in the 1980s, I was faced with the lack of material in both English and French specifically about slave women and decided to make gender and slavery a major focus of my research. This was not a difficult decision. The neglect of gender issues in the historical literature of both Africa (my major field of specialization) and the Caribbean (a minor field) was telling and disturbing, but I considered the lacuna in French Caribbean historiography particularly urgent, in spite of Arlette Gautier's pioneering study in French. After publishing several articles on various aspects of slavery in Africa and the Caribbean, some dealing with gender, my focus on slave women intensified. To date *Women and Slavery in the French Antilles, 1635-1848* is the primary result of this concentration.

In spite of good intentions, dedication, and hard work, the task of illuminating the role that enslaved black women played in the French West Indies was difficult, time consuming, and even at times paralyzing. This is mostly due to the fact that the data are highly fragmented, spotty, and often in poor condition. Since gender was not a preoccupation of slaveowners, French administrators, and contemporary observers, research on slave women entails looking in every nook and cranny for information about their lives, which I did. Also, the archival sources are hard to read and decipher, especially the seventeenth- and eighteenth-century manuscripts on microfilm. Consequently, I spent hours on end (often with the aid of a magnifying glass) poring over illegible words and phrases, even paragraphs and pages written in arcane French, so as to get at the specificity of the slave woman's condition and not misrepresent her experience. In probing this experience, I hope that I have done justice to the multitude of women whose lives were shaped by slavery, but who responded, at every turn and in multidimensional ways, to the assault it unleashed on them with vigor, fortitude, a sense of self, and a will to prevail over adversity.

The circumstances under which I researched and wrote this book made it inevitable that I would accumulate many debts, especially to individuals. While it is not possible to acknowledge them all, I must thank the Humanities and Social Sciences Committee of the University of Toronto for awarding me a small grant that permitted me to do research in France in the initial stages of the study. Thanks are also due to the grant-in-aid program of Virginia Commonwealth University (VCU) in Richmond, Virginia, from which I obtained a modest research grant at a critical stage in the book's development. Other branches of the university were supportive as well. In the advanced stages of my work, help from the history department enabled me to consult archival and other sources in France that I had previously overlooked. Critical to the successful completion of the book was a semester free from teaching, which the College of Humanities and Sciences at VCU made possible. Being able to dedicate blocks of time to writing accelerated the pace of the study immeasurably. I am therefore grateful to Stephen Gottfredson, dean of the college, and to Susan Kennedy, chair of the history department, for their support in this and other instances.

The staffs of the archives and libraries where I conducted research should know that I appreciate the help they provided and the patience they exercised. The archives include the following: the Archives Nationales de France in Paris, the Archives d'Outre-Mer in Aix-en-Provence, the Archives Nationales d'Haïti, the Archives Départementales de la Martinique, and the Archives Départementales de la Guadeloupe. In Martinique the archival staff was particularly cordial and helpful. Liliane Chauleau, who recently retired as director, took an interest in my work and guided me to sources that I might otherwise have missed. For this I am grateful.

Most of the secondary sources I used were acquired through interlibrary loans. In this regard, the staffs at the Robarts Library in Toronto and the Cabell Library at Virginia Commonwealth University provided invaluable service. I wish to express my thanks to the staffs of the following libraries as well: in Toronto, the Royal Ontario Museum; in Washington, D.C., the Library of Congress; in Paris, the Bibliothèque Nationale; and in Haiti, the Bibliothèque Nationale, the Bibliothèque des Pères du Saint-Esprit (formerly the Bibliothèque du Petit-Séminaire Collège Saint-Martial), and the Bibliothèque des Frères de Saint-Louis de Gonzague.

I owe a great deal to friends and colleagues who went out of their way to make my visits to France and the Caribbean lively and productive, and to those who did their utmost to keep me focused. They provided generous support when needed, and applied constructive pressure, however subtle, in my best interest. At the risk of exclusion, I must thank Frederick Case, Keren Krathwaite, Egya Sangmuah, and Lamin Jabbi—former colleagues at the University of Toronto—as well as Sada Niang of the University of Victoria, British

Columbia, Barry Gaspar of Duke University, and Howard Johnson of the University of Delaware, for their moral support and constant encouragement. In Paris José Robelot, and Pierre Lacroix of the Aumônerie Antilles-Guyane, provided accommodations and a unique opening to the French West Indian community from which I benefited. In Martinique the Anneville family from Schoelcher, particularly Christiane, Marcel, and Jean-Michel, gave of themselves in ways that made my experience there very pleasant. Added to this was the help provided by Lucien Abénon and Jean Bernabé of the Université des Antilles et de la Guyane, which made the university more accessible to me while creating greater opportunities to do research. The location of the Archives Départementales at Gourbeyre in Basse-Terre (Guadeloupe) makes the generosity of Freddy Alexis—who provided hospitality and drove there from his home in Morne-à-l'Eau daily without complaint—very special indeed. This level of generosity was also forthcoming from my good friends Asselin Charles, who took care of me in Haiti and made sure that I got to the research institutions regardless of traffic conditions in Port-au-Prince, and Thomas Gabriel, who looked after me in Antigua on my stopovers to and from Martinique and Guadeloupe. Many thanks are also due to those whose names do not appear here but who made other valuable contributions to this study.

Of the help I received, none was more generous, precious, and steadfast than that of my wife, Tia Moitt. She accompanied me on some of my research trips and witnessed firsthand both the agony and exhilaration that I experienced along the way. The sacrifices that she, along with my children, have made cannot of course ever be adequately compensated. The only thanks I can offer is to have produced, I hope, a book that specialists and laypeople alike could read—her sole request. Because she insisted, all along, on reading a published book and not a manuscript, I especially acknowledge my indebtedness to her with gratitude and love.

Introduction

INTELLECTUAL INQUIRY into slavery in the Caribbean has pointed up the need for historical studies of slave women in all linguistic areas of the region, especially in the French Antilles or Caribbean, where slavery was a major and enduring institution. The word "Caribbean" appears in the title or subtitle of some current studies on women and slavery, giving the impression of a broad, pan-Caribbean treatment, when in fact the works concentrate almost exclusively on particular linguistic regions—the British and French Caribbean. This applies not only to Barbara Bush's *Slave Women in Caribbean Society* but also to Arlette Gautier's *Les Soeurs de solitude* and Marrietta Morrissey's *Slave Women in the New World.* Morrissey's book is the most comparative in approach, but most of the examples in it are drawn from the British Caribbean, as Bridget Brereton has keenly observed.[1] This tendency should not be considered intellectual dishonesty, however. There is little doubt that scholars are attempting to fill a legitimate gap in Caribbean historiography for which they deserve credit, given the neglect of gender issues in the historical literature to which Lucille Mathurin-Mair, Bridget Brereton, Verene Shepherd, Hilary Beckles, and others have called attention.[2] But comparative studies of slave women in the Caribbean—if they are to be truly comparative—require greater effort and a more serious attempt to draw upon data from across linguistic frontiers than we have seen so far. Such studies may have to await the publication of more studies of individual colonies and specific regions, however.

This study of enslaved black women in the French Caribbean is a contribution to ongoing efforts to expand the parameters of gender history. It takes gender to be a component in the social relations between males and females through which differences were created, enacted, reproduced, and perpetuated over time. It follows that gender identities were sometimes socially constructed.[3] As gender underlay all social and institutional relations, this study shows the magnitude of its effects in French Caribbean society and will serve, it is hoped, to provide a greater understanding and appreciation of the role of women during slavery. Based on French archival data and secondary sources, it details and analyzes the social condition of enslaved black women in the plantation societies of Martinique, Guadeloupe, Saint-Domingue, and French Guiana. But it also deals with the early period of slavery in the island of Saint Christopher (now Saint Kitts), which had important historical connections with the other French colonies in the seventeenth century and remained, in part, a French colony until the early eighteenth century. The inclusion of Saint Christopher—as opposed to Saint Lucia, Saint Croix, Grenada, or other colonies that were under the hegemony of France at one time or other—is important because French activities there turned out to be a rehearsal for the development of slavery in the French Caribbean. Thus, although this study takes 1635 (when Martinique and Guadeloupe were colonized by the French) to 1848 (when slavery was abolished in the French colonial empire) as its chronological boundaries, events dating back to the period of French settlement in the 1620s are discussed. As slaves in Saint-Domingue fought for and achieved their independence several decades before the end of French slavery, the 1790s constitute the outer limits of the chronological boundaries in this case.

This study is really an examination of the lives of enslaved black women —of the impact slavery had on them and how they dealt with it. In some ways, though not all, slavery was different for black men than for black women. What did it mean to be a female slave in the French Caribbean? Since we have no direct slave testimonies, answering this question requires probing, as much as possible, the economic, political, cultural, legal, psychological, sexual, racial, and other aspects of slave women's lives, to get at the specificity of their condition. While doing so, this study also highlights women's individual and collective responses to bondage from their own perspective. As such, it focuses primarily on the organization of slave labor and explores the relationship between the allocation of tasks and women's resistance to slavery in the French colonies. In this respect, it reinforces my previous research findings and confirms the labor patterns outlined by Hilary Beckles, Barbara Bush, and others, which indicate that the fortunes of the slave plantations were accumulated largely on the backs of enslaved black women, who performed a disproportionate amount of hard labor.[4] As this labor was sometimes (though not always) gender specific, women's roles often permitted them to engage in specific forms of resistance. These, in addition to other forms of resistance that complemented male resistance, are explored in detail here. Together, then, labor and resistance form the core of this study, which also deals with gender relations and their interplay with race.

This study concentrates on specific aspects of gender as they relate to slavery, thereby demonstrating how gender made slavery different for women than for men. One such aspect is the interplay of gender and labor. Although gender was obliterated under slavery in the French Antilles, where sexual differentiation gave way to the demand for hard, intensive labor, it played a role in the allocation of tasks. Black women entered the plantation system at the bottom of the slave-labor hierarchy and spent most of their lives performing field work, while men monopolized the specialized tasks, such as carpentry or blacksmithing. As they were outnumbered by men on most French Caribbean plantations before 1800, slave women performed proportionately more hard labor than slave men.

In the French Antilles the allocation of tasks based on gender conditioned women's responses to slavery. Thus, although slave women resisted slavery in the same ways that men did, there was a correlation between the gender basis of labor and resistance. Most of the altercations which occurred between slave women and members of the planter class and their representatives involved field hands who refused to perform plantation labor. Some midwives were killed by slaveowners, who consistently clashed with them over low birth rates and accused them of infanticide. The majority of slaves accused of poisoning slaveowners were also women. Slave men, like women, served as cooks on the plantations, but the association of women with acts of poisoning is aptly demonstrated by a significant number of charges brought against slave women by their owners. These cases suggest that women were perceived as slaves who utilized their access to the kitchen in different ways than men did.

In probing the social condition of slave women, this study goes beyond the gender basis of work and resistance to explore the continuum along which women resisted slavery, and which included armed resistance and *marronnage* (flight). Women's participation in the Saint-Domingue revolution, and in the struggle against the reestablishment of slavery in Guadeloupe in 1802, is viewed in a multi-dimensional manner which casts them in roles previously ignored. Certainly, the penalties imposed upon slave women in Guadeloupe and Martinique by military tribunals for their participation in anti-slavery struggles show that their roles went beyond the ones to which they have been traditionally ascribed. As for *marronnage,* it was a form of resistance in which more women participated than historians have previously acknowledged. While the pattern of *marronnage* in the French colonies conforms to that in the British colonies in that more men became maroons than women, the variety of woman maroons, the periods they remained at large, and the many advertisements of women maroons in colonial prisons show that *marronnage* was a very important dimension of female resistance. *Marronnage* was sometimes combined with other forms of resistance, but in any case women were penalized for it in ways that males were not. To be sure, the historian can gain valuable insights into resistance by exploring the prison experience of women maroons, a worthy scholarly pursuit that requires attention.

This study also probes gender relations between women and men of all races, relations among women, and women's experiences with the law. Scholars have neglected the issue of gender and race with regard to the establishment of liaisons and conjugal relations between slave women and white males.

The fact that the data are not easily accessible may explain why little light has so far been shed on the slave woman's relations with white men in the French Antilles. Yet these relationships were part of everyday life in slave society. That the Code Noir attempted to legislate concubinage between slaveowners and slaves suggests that they were a factor as early as 1685.[5] In theory, the law penalized slaveowners who had children by their slaves, but in reality it was the women and children who suffered most for their owners' actions. In any case, the law obviously carried little weight, as evidenced by the number of mixed-race people in the colonies—twenty-eight thousand in Saint-Domingue in 1789. Profiles of the black slave family are also rare, which may come as a surprise to many, as there is a popular misconception that the Code Noir promoted family unity by placing restrictions on the sale of family members owned by the same individual. What needs to be highlighted is the fact that it was slave women, not men, who litigated to keep their families intact, an issue that this study explores.

The question of sisterhood is perhaps easier to document. In the French Antilles, there were several European women plantation owners, most of whom inherited estates from their husbands. Morrissey has questioned whether female slaveowners were more abusive to their female slaves than male slaveowners, and, if so, what implications this had for the relationship between free and slave women.[6] This aspect of gender relations is beginning to gain greater ascendancy and deserves exposure. This study will show that women slaves were treated in much the same manner by male and female slaveowners. For example, besides being accomplices in their mistreatment, female slaveowners themselves tortured and brutalized women slaves, as did their male counterparts.

By examining court cases, this study demonstrates that slave women used the law, as outlined in the Code Noir of 1685 and in later ordinances, to combat slavery. Although there is no indication that the women who engaged in litigation were literate, it is evident that they were aware both of the laws in the Code Noir and of changes in the law down to the last years of slavery. At that time, the slaves engaged in a strict interpretation of the laws. They expected their owners to honor the laws, even though they had not done so in previous times. The actions of the slaves in the post-1830 period point to a heightened sense of change and a more vulnerable planter class.

This study is divided into eight chapters. Chapter 1 deals with the black woman's early presence in the slave societies of the French Caribbean. It focuses mostly on her presence during the period of European indentureship, when the colonies were largely male in composition. It shows how she was viewed in society and draws a relationship between the construction of her image and changes in French immigration policy. As slaves from Africa began to arrive in larger numbers in the late seventeenth century, black women were outnumbered by black men on the plantations. Only in the early nineteenth century did sex ratios even out, and the consequences of this demographic pattern are examined in chapter 2. Chapter 3 offers an analysis of the gender basis of the allocation of tasks while focusing on women in field labor, household production, petty trade, and marketing. Chapter 4 discusses labor in the domestic sphere, which includes not just cooks and household staff but doctors, nurses, midwives, seamstresses, and slave women engaged in other pursuits.

How women functioned as mothers, wives, concubines, and prostitutes, how they lived and died, constitute the subject matter of chapter 5. Because mortality rates were extraordinarily high in the French Antilles—where, as in the rest of the Caribbean except Barbados, slave births did not exceed slave deaths—issues of nutrition, health, and reproduction are probed in this chapter. In focusing on discipline, physical abuse, and assault, chapter 6 details the brutality, mostly physical, to which slave women were subjected by slaveowners and other plantation personnel in positions of power. Women were accused of committing crimes, and were convicted and punished for them, often on very slim evidence. So corporal punishment, execution, and deportation or transportation are documented. But the ways in which slave women drew upon the judicial system and used other means at their disposal to combat abuse are an important aspect of this chapter as well.

Slave resistance is taken up in chapter 7, which examines women's multidimensional responses to slavery in detail. It probes patterns of resistance such as armed revolt, *marronnage,* acts of poisoning, work slowdowns, and work stoppages, and documents penalties that women suffered for their resistance. Discussion of how slave women acquired freedom, including the status of *libre de savane* (liberty of the savanna) or *libre de faite* (liberty of action)—both unofficial forms of freedom—and of the protracted struggles they waged at all levels of the judiciary to free their children in particular from the shackles of slavery constitutes the bulk of chapter 8, which is followed by a conclusion that highlights the enduring legacy of slave women.

The women who spring from these chapters faced formidable odds in their struggle against all forms of oppression on the sugar plantations of the French Caribbean from the seventeenth to the mid-nineteenth century. French Caribbean society was not the "playground" it is now considered to be, paradoxical as it may seem. It was a tough and brutal society, so brutal that is often difficult to grapple with some of the more degrading aspects of the slave woman's experience. However, slave women responded to the complex institution of slavery in diverse ways that merit careful analysis. They were ingenious and inventive in using the resources at their disposal, and they exhibited courage, strength of character, bravery, and resilience. I have tried to capture their strengths in this study, keeping in mind their human frailties as well as the limitations imposed by the data. Slave women on coffee, cocoa, indigo, and other plantations deserve as much attention, but the predominance of the sugar economy during slavery made slave women on sugar plantations more accessible to the historian.

Dissecting the lives of slave women in the French Caribbean, where slavery had very distinctive features, requires overcoming major conceptual and methodological problems brought by the lack of studies on the French Caribbean and the paucity and fragmented state of the existing data. Even with the best of circumstances and intentions, the scholar comes up against hurdles that can be immobilizing. In this study, therefore, I have tried to present and analyze evidence as creatively and as critically as possible, thereby allowing the slave women of the French Antilles to speak for themselves.

Women and Slavery in the French Antilles, 1635-1848

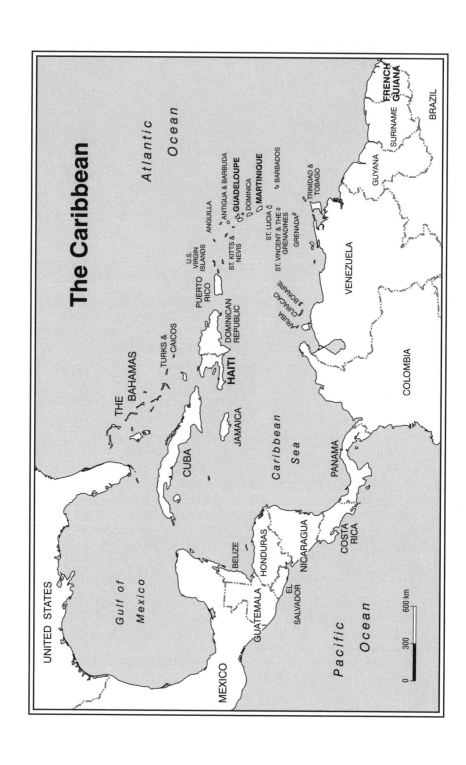

The Caribbean

UNITED STATES

Gulf of Mexico

MEXICO

Atlantic Ocean

THE BAHAMAS

TURKS & CAICOS

PUERTO RICO

U.S. VIRGIN ISLANDS

ANGUILLA

ST. KITTS & NEVIS

ANTIGUA & BARBUDA

GUADELOUPE

DOMINICA

MARTINIQUE

ST. LUCIA

BARBADOS

ST. VINCENT & THE GRENADINES

GRENADA

TRINIDAD & TOBAGO

DOMINICAN REPUBLIC

HAITI

CUBA

JAMAICA

Caribbean Sea

BELIZE

GUATEMALA

HONDURAS

EL SALVADOR

NICARAGUA

COSTA RICA

PANAMA

ARUBA

CURAÇAO

BONAIRE

COLOMBIA

VENEZUELA

GUYANA

SURINAME

FRENCH GUIANA

BRAZIL

Pacific Ocean

0   300   600 km

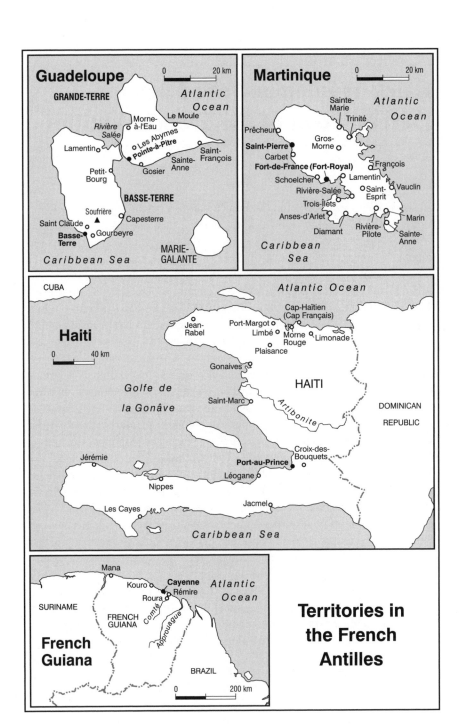

Guadeloupe

GRANDE-TERRE

Atlantic Ocean

0   20 km

Morne-à-l'Eau
Le Moule
Rivière Salée
Les Abymes
Pointe-à-Pitre
Lamentin
Saint-François
Sainte-Anne
Gosier
Petit-Bourg

BASSE-TERRE

Soufrière
Capesterre
Saint Claude
Basse-Terre
Gourbeyre

Caribbean Sea

MARIE-GALANTE

Martinique

0   20 km

Atlantic Ocean

Sainte-Marie
Trinité
Prêcheur
Gros-Morne
Saint-Pierre
Carbet
François
Fort-de-France (Fort-Royal)
Schoelcher
Lamentin
Rivière-Salée
Saint-Esprit
Vauclin
Trois-Îlets
Anses-d'Arlet
Marin
Diamant
Rivière-Pilote
Sainte-Anne

Caribbean Sea

Haiti

0   40 km

CUBA

Atlantic Ocean

Cap-Haïtien
(Cap Français)
Jean-Rabel
Port-Margot
Limbé
Morne Rouge
Limonade
Plaisance
Gonaives

HAITI

Golfe de la Gonâve

Saint-Marc

Artibonite

DOMINICAN
REPUBLIC

Jérémie
Croix-des-Bouquets
Port-au-Prince
Léogane
Nippes
Les Cayes
Jacmel

Caribbean Sea

Mana
Kourou
Cayenne
Roura
Rémire
Atlantic Ocean

SURINAME
FRENCH
GUIANA
Comté
Approuague

French Guiana

BRAZIL

0   200 km

Territories in the French Antilles

1

Black Women and the Early Development of the French Antilles

BLACK WOMEN were present in the French Antilles beginning in the early decades of the seventeenth century, when the French occupied part of Saint Christopher. As French hegemony spread in the region in the 1630s, so did the number of black women, most of them slaves. However, their numbers remained small for many decades thereafter, and the paucity of French and other historical sources permits us only fleeting glimpses into their lives. Though deficient, the sources reveal that these black women worked alongside white male and female *engagés* or indentured servants, married, and entered into concubinage with both black and white males and produced mixed-race offspring—the product of their relations with European males—who were among the first freed slaves in the French colonies. Since conjugal relations between enslaved black males and white females were rare (though not unheard of), the emergence of a mixed-race grouping in the seventeenth century testifies to the presence of black women. As the sugar plantation economy developed in the second half of the century and indentureship gave way to slavery, first in Martinique and Guadeloupe and later in Saint-Domingue and French Guiana, the number of black women increased, but information about their lives remained scanty until well into the eighteenth century. In spite of the absence of hard data for Saint Christopher and other Leeward Islands like Antigua and Montserrat in the seventeenth century, the French presence on Saint Christopher provides an important starting point for examining the development of slavery in the French Antilles during the early colonial period.

Scholars are at variance as to the date when the French first began to inhabit Saint Christopher. Some suggest that it was prior to 1624 when the English arrived.[1] What appears certain is that in 1625 a French party led by Belain d'Esnambuc (whose name decorates some of the ferries that today run between Fort-de-France and Trois-Ilets in Martinique), and his companion Urbain de Roissey, arrived on Saint Christopher, where they encountered a small band of Frenchmen. Père Du Tertre recounted how these men virtually worshipped d'Esnambuc as "an angel from heaven" and obeyed him as their master. After a brief stay, in which he apparently surveyed the situation and assessed the prospects of settling the island permanently, he returned to

France, where he promoted the idea of colonization among French authorities.[2]

D'Esnambuc's timing could hardly have been better. This was a period when the establishment of colonies overseas, especially at the expense of other European powers, was seen as a means of enhancing the glory of France. The result was a favorable audience with Cardinal Richelieu, who gave him permission to form a joint-stock company—the Compagnie de Saint Christophe —in October 1626. So it was that d'Esnambuc and de Roissey rounded up settlers in France and in February 1627 set sail once again for Saint Christopher.[3] As the English governor, Sir Thomas Warner, was apparently too weak to resist the French intrusion, he agreed to let the French occupy the two ends of the island, the English remaining in the middle.[4] From their strategic positions, the English and French pursued a course of action that dispossessed the Caribs, a Native American population whom they soon wiped out in a joint endeavor.

In a mercantilist era characterized by greed and fortune seekers intent on making quick profits, the English and French may well have wished to secure the island for themselves. But the elimination of the Native Americans in the process is troubling. Given that the prevailing view of the Carib in seventeenth-century European accounts was that of the noble savage, the motivation behind the attack on them ought not to be ignored. Indeed, Gordon K. Lewis wrote of "a curious ambivalence, the schizoid character of early European attitudes towards native America, oscillating inconclusively between the utopian theme of the noble savage and the Christian view of the benighted pagan. There is at once fascination and repulsion."[5] Evidently, the Europeans on Saint Christopher must not have regarded the Native Americans as potential labor units, even though the royal *cédula* (edict) of 1508 legitimized the enslavement of the Caribs.[6] With the Caribs eliminated, the Europeans would have to look elsewhere if they intended to coerce labor.

CONFLICT, SETTLEMENT, AND ACQUISITION OF SLAVES

Some sources suggest that when d'Esnambuc arrived on Saint Christopher in 1625, slaves were already on the island, forty of them owned by Levasseur, a Huguenot.[7] According to Lucien Peytraud, these were the first slaves owned by the French in the Antilles.[8] A code of bylaws for living together, which the French and English signed in 1627, lends credence to Peytraud's assertion and can be used to speculate on slavery. Under this agreement, both parties promised not to confiscate each other's men or slaves.[9] Also, an official document of the Compagnie de Saint Christophe, signed by Urbain de Roissey and others in 1628, mentioned that male and female slaves on Saint Christopher were to be considered chattel, and could be worked by their owners in any manner necessary for the first three years, after which they could be trans-ported elsewhere or sold. In the interest of the company, their owners could not grant them liberty without the permission of the governor.[10] Taken to-gether, these documents suggest that male and female slaves were among the early inhabitants of Saint Christopher.

The source of these slaves is in doubt as they were not direct French im-ports from Africa. In the first half of the seventeenth century, the French usu-ally obtained most of their slaves from other European traders, mainly the Dutch. The Dutch were the major suppliers of slaves in the region, while French ships carried *engagés*.[11] From their depot in Curaçao, the Dutch shipped slaves to the French Antilles.[12] However, it is likely that the early slaves on Saint Christopher were acquired through raids or purchase from the Spanish, whose association with Africans in the Caribbean goes back to the late fifteenth century. In 1518, as Franklin Knight noted, the Spanish king, Charles V, "sanc-tioned the monopolistic commerce of non-Spanish-speaking Africans shipped directly to the Antilles"—an act which gave Spanish traders the right to en-gage officially in the Atlantic slave trade.[13] The result of this act was that "af-ter 1518, approximately 75,000 Africans had been shipped to the Spanish Americas, accounting for about 60 percent of the total transatlantic slave trade before 1600."[14] As Spanish hegemony weakened in the early seventeenth century, other Europeans raided their territories for slaves. In 1635 the French on Saint Christopher bought slaves from Pitre, a resident French captain who acquired them in raids on Spanish colonies.[15] Indeed, under regulations of the Compagnie de Saint Christophe, slaves taken in raids or pirated slaves could be sold by ship captains, the price to be divided between the company and ship captains and their cohorts.[16]

Conflicts and open warfare between the English and French were also a source of slaves. One such conflict broke out in 1635, but the details of it are unclear. Many scholars have accepted unchallenged Du Tertre's account of how d'Esnambuc armed five to six hundred slaves with cutlasses and bill hooks and used them, on the promise of liberty, to keep the English within their borders and force them to accept French conditions.[17] Regarded as "de-mons" who terrified English women in particular, these slaves were valued, so Du Tertre noted, for their fighting spirit.[18] Thus Peytraud credited them with saving the colony for the French. Had they been conscious of their strength, he believed they might have made themselves "masters of the island."[19]

It is unlikely, however, that a decade after they arrived, the French would already have had 500–600 slaves. This was, after all, the tobacco era, the era of European indentureship, when Barbados, the best example of a planta-tion society in the Caribbean, had few slaves—10 in 1627, a handful more by 1638.[20] It is difficult to deal with statistics from the Leeward Islands, given

Table 1.1. Slave Population of (French) Saint Christopher

Year	Adult Males	Adult Females	Boys	Girls
1671	1,527	1,614	1,140	–
1682	1,575	1,563	636	527
1686	1,635	1,528	1,185*	

Source: Abdoulaye Ly, *La Compagnie du Sénégal* (Paris: Présence africaine, 1968), 49.
*The figure 1,185 represents a combined total of boys and girls.

that, as Curtin points out, "Import records for the four major islands [Antigua, Montserrat, Saint Christopher, and Nevis] are available for less than twenty years out of more than a century and a half during which they imported slaves."[21] Thus one should be skeptical of the slave population statistics given by Abdoulaye Ly and outlined in table 1.1. They show that by 1671 the French had about 4,281 slaves, more adult females than adult males at a time when, as we shall see in the next chapter, the Atlantic slave trade focused on male slaves. The high proportion of the child slave population is highly improbable as well since slave deaths exceeded slave births in the Caribbean.

Drawing upon British census data for the Leeward Islands in 1678, Dunn gave a total of 1,436 slaves for Saint Christopher, of which 550 were adult males, 500 were adult females, and 386 were children of both sexes. These figures do not include slaves held by the French. It may well be that the French had as many slaves as the English. This would appear to be the case, in fact, since Curtin's population figure for the Leeward Islands as a whole in 1672 is 4,200.[22]

As the slave population grew, so did the prospect of conflict. Indeed, the altercation of 1635 was a mere beginning. To be sure, joint occupancy of Saint Christopher was fraught with difficulties, as European wars spilled over into the Antilles, resulting in constant confrontations between the French and English that lasted from the 1630s to around 1713, when the French ceded their part of the island to the English.[23] During this period both parties pillaged, raided, and destroyed each other's property. In a war fought in Saint Christopher in 1666, for example, the French captured four hundred slaves from the English. In a subsequent raid on Antigua and Montserrat, where they burned sugar works, the French carried off another thousand slaves from the English planters there. As in Saint Christopher, the accumulation of African slaves in the other French colonies was slow at first. For example, the French presence in Cayenne, French Guiana, dates back to 1626. After attempts by private French traders resulted in the establishment of a colony there in 1643, the French could boast only about 420 slaves—male and female—in 1665. As the colony passed back and forth between the Dutch and the French during the seventeenth century, when the latter were formidable traders, it seems reasonable to assume that some slaves were brought there by Dutch traders. Others were taken in raids. By 1674 the Jesuits were listed as slaveowners in the colony. However, French Guiana was never a priority for slave traders, and during the seventeenth century there was little such activity.[24]

The other colonies—Saint-Domingue, Martinique, and Guadeloupe—were settled largely from Saint Christopher, and fared somewhat better. In 1629 some Frenchmen who had been chased from Saint Christopher by the Spanish took refuge in Tortuga. Filibusters and buccaneers, they moved into northern Hispaniola some years later, where they became small-scale slaveholders. Under the Treaty of Ryswick in 1697, the Spanish ceded the western third of Hispaniola to the French, who named it Saint-Domingue (the Spanish section became Santo Domingo) and turned it into the most prosperous slave colony in the Americas in the eighteenth century.

As for Martinique, it was d'Esnambuc who gathered about a hundred French colonists from Saint Christopher, provisioned a ship, and sailed with them to settle the island in 1635. There is no mention of slaves among the party, but d'Esnambuc was already knowledgeable about African servitude in the Caribbean, as were two of his former French compatriots from his first Saint Christopher expedition—Pierre de l'Olive and Jean Duplessis; these two left Dieppe in France that same year to settle Guadeloupe in the name of the newly formed Compagnie des Iles d'Amérique, which had just replaced the Compagnie de Saint Christophe. De L'Olive and Duplessis arrived in Martinique on June 25 but departed hastily for Guadeloupe, arriving there on June 28. In both Martinique and Guadeloupe, the settlers were beset by serious problems, not unlike those faced by others in frontier communities. In Martinique they fought one another and the Native Americans, who burned their food crops, forcing them to sue for peace. A similar rivalry took place in Guadeloupe, where the colonists suffered death by famine, turned to cannibalism, and engaged in wars with the Native Americans which lasted until 1641. In 1641 the Compagnie des Iles d'Amérique sent one of its officers, Charles Houël, to head the colony in Guadeloupe. He named himself governor, but the proprietorship of Guadeloupe, like that of the other French colonies, changed in the ensuing years until 1664, when Colbert, Louis XIV's main minister, put the French Antilles under the control of the Compagnie des Indes Occidentales.[25]

Contrary to the opinion that all French colonies had slaves from the inception of French colonization,[26] there were no African slaves in either Martinique or Guadeloupe in 1635. Around 1638 the Compagnie des Isles d'Amérique requested slaves from Cap-Vert;[27] but even in 1643 only rich planters and those who had the backing of merchants in Dieppe, Nantes, and La

Rochelle could afford what Maurice Satineau called "exorbitant prices" for slaves, which resulted in their numbers remaining low.[28] As in the case of Saint Christopher, Martinique and Guadeloupe sometimes benefited from the odd war booty, as during the Anglo-French war of 1689–97. Barry Gaspar's research shows that during this period, and into the eighteenth century, some fugitives from Antigua escaped to French colonies. But fugitives from the French colonies also headed for Antigua, although their loyalty to the British appears to have been fickle. This may well have been the case in 1704, when Governor Charles-François de Marchault of Martinique sold a female slave, who, along with twelve male slaves owned by French planters once living in Saint Christopher, escaped to Antigua. The group subsequently made their way to Guadeloupe in hopes of rejoining their owners. He turned the male slaves over to their owners upon proof of ownership, rather than confiscating them in the name of the king—an accepted practice during wartime. But he sold the "English" slave woman for 400 *livres*[29] and put the proceeds in the treasury to support the hospital at Fort-Royal. No details were given about the sale but it is possible that gender played a role, in that sexual or reproductive labor could be extracted from her that was not typically sought from slave men.[30]

In light of the limited number of slaves at the outset of colonization in Martinique and Guadeloupe, European indentureship was very important for several decades as *engagés* filled a labor need that Native Americans did not and could not meet. Instead, they resisted European encroachment and died in large numbers from European diseases like smallpox from which they had no immunity. De l'Olive and Duplessis brought a number of *engagés* from France with them to Guadeloupe in 1635, but the task of settling the colonies effectively proved daunting and required more than a handful of men. The need for labor to clear land and establish farms was primary, and was provided mostly by white indentured servants for many years. In spite of the bickering which characterized the relationship between French settlers and administrators in the early years of settlement, they soon managed to accelerate the process of European immigration while importing slaves from Africa. Limited in number, however, *engagés* were incapable of satisfying the insatiable demand for labor as economic activity, based on the development of the sugar plantation, expanded. The French colonists looked to Africa, as did others in the region, and found the solution to the labor shortage that had eluded Europeans involved in plantation agriculture since medieval times. During the period of indentureship, which lasted from the 1640s to the 1690s and beyond, the black woman's presence in the French Antilles was marginal, as the large-scale forced migration of Africans to the Americas had not yet hit its stride. Even so, her social presence was important and was a catalyst for social change. French colonial society focused on her sexuality and on changes brought about by her presence—not that of the black man—while demonizing both sexes in law and custom.

IMMIGRATION AND INDENTURESHIP

In the seventeenth century, black women came into a rugged society of small farmers dominated by white males. Thus, Arlette Gautier's characterization of seventeenth-century Caribbean societies as "masculine" is apt. There were only 2 women in Saint Christopher in 1631. The male population of Martinique between 1678 and 1687 was twice that of the female. In Guadeloupe in 1671, there were 2.5 men to every woman, whereas in Saint-Domingue, there were 8 males to every female in 1681, 4.4 in 1686, and 2 in 1700.[31] Not only was French Antillean society overwhelmingly male in composition but it was also a patriarchal society in which women of all ethnicities were considered subordinate. In addition, it was a hierarchical society based on race and social ranking. Gautier has argued convincingly that in seventeenth-century French society, women were considered inferior under law, and were required by church doctrines to accept subordination to men. In essence, women were treated as minors, irrespective of the social class of their fathers or husbands.[32] In the French Antilles, however, the black woman was to become the most subordinate of all women, subjected to what Barbara Bush referred to as "triple oppression," that is, "to both black and white patriarchy, in addition to experiencing class exploitation [and] . . . racism."[33] Although there has not yet been a specific study of the French Antillean planter class on the magnitude of Richard Dunn's *Sugar and Slaves* (which chronicles the rise of the planter class in the British West Indies), the works of Liliane Chauleau, Jacques Petit Jean Roget, and Lucien Abénon, among others, help us to understand the formation of social groupings in the French Antilles during the seventeenth century.[34] These works show that ranking occurred in the French colonies from the outset. Chauleau argued that Martinique was not a class society in the seventeenth century;[35] Jacques Petit Jean Roget called it a "*société d'habitations,*" suggesting that the mere existence of plantations cannot be taken to mean that a plantation society, characterized by power and influence, had already developed.[36] However, the existence of slavery in the colonies made class differentiation inevitable even then. From 1635, there were a small number of nobles among the colonists in Martinique and Guadeloupe. There were also large and small planters, *engagés*, and Africans, slave and free.

Large tracts of land and sufficient capital enabled the *grands blancs*, the large planters, to make the transition from small farming to large sugar plantations without much difficulty. Even in the seventeenth century, some *grands blancs* sent their children to France to be educated. The *petits blancs,* small planters or *habitacos,* as they were sometimes called, had less land and capital. Some were artisans and merchants struggling to make ends meet. Consequently, they were generally despised by the *grands blancs* to whom they were often indebted. Indeed, Gaston-Martin has noted that the *grands blancs* became a virtual caste, choosing to socialize with people of the same economic standing. Gabriel Debien also indicated that lower-class whites turned against blacks as intense rivalry developed between both groups at the end of the seventeenth century, more so than in the British Caribbean.[37]

Lower in status than the *grands blancs* and *petits blancs* were the white *engagés,* many of whom came from the lower rungs of French society. From the 1640s down to the early years of the eighteenth century, the French state, merchants, and ship captains made serious efforts to attract *engagés,* but they were not altogether successful. The *engagés* performed field, domestic, and artisanal labor on three-year contracts—hence their designation as *les trente-six mois* (thirty-six months)—and often under adverse conditions. There was a demand for both male and female *engagés,* but colonial officials placed greater emphasis on the immigration of white females.

The slaves were at the lowest end of the social hierarchy, viewed by whites as inferior, lacking in intelligence, lazy, and "happy-go-lucky" but a better investment than the *engagés* whose contracts were temporary, whereas the condition of slavery lasted a lifetime in most cases. Black and mixed-race women appealed to the senses in the view of contemporary observers. Indeed, mixed-race women were depicted as pleasure-seekers whose entire being was given over to sensual delight. Ironically, white creole women—those born in the colonies—were also deemed to be lazy, but their idleness, according to Moreau de Saint-Méry, was a result of complacency, the hot climate, and the fact that they were not brought up as laborers. White women were also depicted as elements of stability and continuity to be protected, however lowly their status. As early as 1641, an ordinance of the Compagnie des Iles d'Amérique forbade passengers or crew aboard ships leaving France for the colonies from exploiting women and young girls, who were considered to be under the protection of the captain.[38]

The concerted efforts that state and civilian bodies made to recruit *engagés* is worth probing, for had they been successful, the shape and character of the black presence in the French Antilles would have been radically altered. In the mid-seventeenth century, French authorities made it obligatory for ships leaving France for the Antilles to carry at least two to four servants depending on tonnage. But recruitment was a difficult undertaking from the start. As early as 1656, Governor Houël of Guadeloupe wrote to the king of France complaining that for several years the *engagés* who had been sent to the colonies were recruited only at French ports, and he asked that recruitment be carried out on a broader scale. These were years when forced recruitment of vagabonds and prostitutes was common.[39]

On November 14, 1680, 128 young women of ill repute aged fifteen to twenty-two were rounded up on the streets of Paris and shipped to Martinique. The state paid for passage and expenses for old clothing amounting to about 17–18 *livres* each. A similar contingent of 50 women from Paris were shipped on September 13, 1682.[40] Young women were also recruited from hostels to satisfy requests made by officials in the colonies. Arlette Gautier indicated that the king of France consciously chose these women, as they were expected to be proper and well raised from infancy. However, few such women came.[41] In 1669 Lieutenant Governor Jean-Charles de Baas of Martinique requested young men of fourteen years and young girls of ten from French hospitals for colonists to use as *engagés* for a period of four years.[42] In 1681 Pouancay, governor of Saint-Domingue, wrote to the Minister of Marine and Colonies in Paris requesting 150 young women a year for three years, as they were considered necessary to attract settlers and promote the development of families. In response, the minister appealed to the general hospital in La Rochelle, whose administrators reportedly found young women there willing to emigrate. There were young, poor girls at several hospitals in France. Some were orphans and others were homeless juveniles.[43] To this so-called "love trade" the state contributed 12 *livres* for each woman, and the hospital added a variety of gifts including sandals, amber necklaces, red skirts, stockings, and other items of clothing valued at 15–20 *livres*. This was supposedly voluntary migration, but the list of items given to the women makes coercion a distinct possibility. In any case, 29 of them were shipped to the governor of French Guiana on March 29, 1681, nine days after the women had signed contracts.[44] In 1685 the hospital responded positively to additional demands from the state to provide women as wives for French settlers in Saint-Domingue. Authorities in that colony requested 50 young women at first, but later held out the hope that 100 could be recruited. How many of these the hospital was able to provide is not clear, but the need was certainly pressing in this case as the king offered 24 *livres* to each woman—twice the regular offering.[45] These inducements did not entice enough people to migrate to the colonies, however.

The colonies continued to request *engagés* with the hope of attracting white women primarily. In 1695 Governor Pontchartrain of Saint-Domingue wrote to Minister du Hardy in Paris with an urgent request for 100 young women, aged fifteen to thirty years, "to marry colonists who are obliged to take black women as wives, and 150 young people who will be sent directly to the planters."[46] Thus, the number of black women, though statistically small in the seventeenth century, was enough to cause concern about the consequences of racial mixing. And their presence brought about social change in that it influenced an immigration policy that focused on increasing the number of white women.

Concern over racial imbalance was an outgrowth of this immigration policy. For example, a royal ordinance of September 30, 1686, required that colonists keep a balance between the number of *engagés* and slaves. The fact that slaves in excess of the number of *engagés* would be confiscated by the state indicates that there was concern about blacks outnumbering whites.[47] However, the ordinance was not enforced, which suggests that slave labor was already gaining ascendancy.[48] An ordinance of February 19, 1698, had a similar objective in that it required colonists to maintain a ratio of *engagés* to slaves of 1:20, with the exception of the slave driver.[49] French sources claim that the concern over racial imbalance stemmed from the planters' fear of slave revolts,[50] but the large number of Africans who were imported in later years raises questions about the legitimacy of this claim. Resistance was an ongoing concern, but fear of the social and economic consequences of miscegenation, which involved black women, whether willing participants or not, was more paramount at this time and remained so. This fear made white women desirable. When white female *engagés* were betrothed, they were normally released from their contract. Also, colonists easily bought out their contracts to marry them.[51] However desirable they may have been, the harsh reality was that the rugged frontier societies of the Caribbean were viewed as unsuitable for them, but not for black women whose economic viability carried the day.

After 1690 few *engagés* came. Departures from France were more tightly scrutinized at this time, as settlers became more sensitized to concerns about the health and conduct of vagabonds, beggars, and prostitutes. Some colonial officials were still willing to resort to desperate means to recruit white immigrants, but it was too late to round up such labor from France at the end of the century. By 1700 the pool of white indentured laborers virtually dried up while imports of African slaves mounted. Between 1686 and 1702, no more than fifty *engagés* a year arrived in Guadeloupe. By 1706 Governor Hancelin of Guadeloupe reported that the movement of servants from France had ceased. And yet in 1710, King Louis XIV gave authorization to send vagabonds of twenty years and older from the Hôpital de la Manufacture de Bordeaux to serve as *engagés* in the colonies. With greater resistance in France to forced recruitment in the early eighteenth century, transportation of vagabonds did not last, however.[52]

THE BLACK PRESENCE IN THE ERA OF INDENTURESHIP

One might well ask whether black women posed a real threat to the maintenance of white families or to society, as they were relatively few in number, isolated, and dependent. In the late 1630s, the Compagnie des Iles d'Amérique gave a bonus of twenty *livres* of tobacco to males who brought wives to Saint Christopher with them and established households, and to men who married white, black, or Native American women. In addition, men who married in Saint Christopher were exempted from paying taxes to the company for the first year if their wives remained in the colony during that period. The likelihood that white males would find Native American women in Saint Christopher to marry (if they so desired) was slim, but relationships with black women, who were obtained from many sources, were probable on however small a scale. Cases of black women *engagés* are rare, but Gabriel Debien mentioned the black woman Marie-Anne, who apparently wanted to return to the colonies from France and who in 1660 was indentured to Courselles, a lieutenant in Martinique. The provisions of her contract were unclear, but Debien believed that Marie-Anne received 300 *livres* of tobacco—the usual payment for a three-year contract.[53]

Early census data from Martinique and Guadeloupe also point to a limited if growing presence of black women by the 1660s, the result of both direct and indirect imports from Africa. A partial census of Martinique in 1660 hints at this presence. In drawing upon this census, Jacques Petit Jean Roget noted that it does not list slaves by sex unless all of the slaves were women, in which case the designation *"négresse"* was used. He thus resorted to the use of the gender-neutral categories *"Nègres"* (adult slaves) and *"petits nègres"* (child slaves)—that is, those under the age of ten years.[54] The 1660 census is useful in showing the total number of slaves in relation to *engagés* and the districts where they were concentrated, but not much more. The census put the slave population at around 2,683, compared to 2,580 whites. There were around 100 *engagés* for about 331 slaves—a 3:1 ratio of slaves to servants. Even so, the French colonists possessed relatively few slaves in 1660. At his death, Pierre Baillardel from Saint-Pierre, Martinique, left four estates to his wife and children. To his three sons, he left 4 slaves each; his wife, Jeanne Bonhomme, received 11 slaves. By 1664, two of his sons had 5 slaves each; his remaining son had 7 slaves. These estates were therefore worked by a small number of slaves, in addition to a few *engagés* in the service of two of Baillardel's sons.[55]

A 1664 census of Martinique is more revealing. It offers a clearer picture of the black presence than the 1660 census, and suggests that the slave-servant ratio had increased in favor of the slaves. The census lists a number of households and their occupants, and indicates that most colonists were still small holders engaged in cash-crop production, and that a significant number of them owned equal numbers of male and female slaves. Among those who held the most slaves was forty-seven-year-old François Rolles Escuyer, a captain in the service of one of the French chartered companies. He had about 7 *engagés* aged between twenty and thirty years, as well as 15 male slaves, 10 female slaves, and 13 slave children, boys and girls. Similarly, forty-five-year-old Claud Colard had 4 servants, 10 male slaves, 10 females, 1 boy, and 1 girl. Forty-five-year-old Jan des Lauviers, a sergeant in a French chartered firm, along with his wife, owned 6 slaves equally divided between males and females, both adults and children. Jacques Carnel, twenty-four, and his wife, Catherine Rally, had a male and female slave. Women, usually widows, also owned black women. Madame Jeanne Herault, thirty-seven, owned 26 male slaves, 25 females, and 20 boys and girls. Enslaved black women were dominant in some households. Two female slaves constituted the number of chattel owned by Jan Robullare, fifty, and his wife, Catherine, forty. This was also the case of Louis Bonualler, thirty-six, and his wife, Rachel, thirty-four. Laurene Peiné, thirty-five, and his twenty-year-old wife owned 4 female slaves and 1 male.[56] Arlette Gautier used these and other census data to argue that 22.6 percent of the estates in Martinique in 1664 were the domain of female slaves only and 22.4 percent in Guadeloupe. In 1671, 15.5 percent of the estates in Guadeloupe were still female-only estates. This led Gautier to conclude that these estates were stud farms.[57] There is no doubt that some slaveowners had only female slaves. Whether they made a conscious decision to purchase only women to use as breeding stock remains an open question, however.

Of statistical importance is the fact that in 1664 the town of Saint-Pierre, Martinique, had 166 black males, 147 black females, and 178 mixed-race children.[58] It is conceivable that some of these urban blacks may already have acquired freedom, if only by unofficial means, but the majority would have been slaves. The significant number of mixed-race children also points to active social intermingling between black women and white males in the era of indentureship. This is a revealing phenomenon given the early and strong emphasis on morality in the French colonies, and the equality of the sex ratio among the blacks that could have led to the development of the black family in slavery. Indeed, Moreau de Saint-Méry noted that a distinctive characteristic of African-born slave women in Saint-Domingue was their "indomitable propensity for black men. Neither their dealings with white males nor the advantages they gain thereby, which often lead to liberty for them and their children; neither the fear of severe punishment that can result from pride and jealousy, are capable of restraining them in this endeavour."[59]

In Guadeloupe the black presence can be determined from sources that date back to the mid-seventeenth century, and from censuses that appeared later. Classen, a wealthy colonist who led a Dutch party that arrived in Guadeloupe in 1654, established himself in Capesterre and owned 57 black males, 54 black females, 6 boys, and 6 girls. Hubert de Looure, a member of the same group, owned six lots of land, a mansion located at Montagne de l'Espérance, and a sugar plantation with 8 servants, 18 male slaves, 14 females, 6 boys, and 8 girls. Data from a 1671 census of Guadeloupe reinforce the presence of

Table 1.2. Slave Population of Guadeloupe by Sex

	Male	Female
1671	1,677	1,513
1699	2,038	2,054
1790	31,614	28,913

Source: Guy Lasserie, *La Guadeloupe, étude géographique,* 2 vols. (Bordeaux: CNRS, 1961), 1:293.

blacks in the years after colonization, and mirror other trends in the 1664 census of Martinique. They show that both *petits blancs* and *grand blancs* owned slaves, and that there were almost as many female slaves as male slaves. Thus the black woman's presence was just as notable as that of the black man. Lucien Abénon used this census to study the demography of Guadeloupe. He indicated that the number of slaves was 4,267, of which 1,677 were adult males, 1,513 adult females, and the remainder, 1,077, children.[60] Guy Lasserie arrived at the same figures but left out the slave child population, as table 1.2 shows.

Table 1.2 also shows that by 1699 there was an equilibrium in the adult slave population of Guadeloupe. But Abdoylaye Ly pointed to a female majority by 1696, when, according to him, there were 1,533 male slaves and 1,819 female slaves.[61] It is tempting to conclude that there was little difference in the sex ratios of Guadeloupe during slavery, but the data in table 1.2 are too limited to be conclusive, in spite of Lucien Abénon's assertion that they show that "from the outset, a large number of women were transported by slavers. There seems to have been no preference for males among slavers." The inclination to endorse Abénon's assertion is strong, given what appears to be an equilibrium in sex ratios among the slave force on small holdings and plantations in Guadeloupe from the 1650s onward. Certainly, the early presence of the black woman is supported by the evidence. The 1671 census showed that François Rigollet, a *petit blanc* and martial from La Montagne de l'Espérance, had a labor force comprising a white male, one Julien Boulanger, two black women, and a black boy. According to Abénon, it is likely that one of these slave women was his concubine, as "European women were still rare and many *petits blancs* created households, more or less legitimate, with mixed-race women. When the sexual equilibrium in the white population came into balance, such households became rare, even though they never disappeared completely."[62]

Further investigation into the conditions under which black women lived point to mixed marriages and concubinage, which suggest that society frowned upon but turned a blind eye to racial mingling and that authorities took no action at this stage. The 1671 census shows that Mathieu Pasquet, a *petit blanc* and owner of two slaves, was married to "Marie négresse" and had a son by her. Florent Commère was married to Luce Sarisse, a black woman from

Goyaves. Suzanne, another black woman, was married to Jacques Cramilly from the district of Citronniers in Grande-Terre.[63]

As in Martinique, there were widows in Guadeloupe in 1671 who owned slaves. One of them was Françoise Benoist of La Montagne Saint-Robert, the head of a religious sect whose household consisted of 5 children (4 boys and 1 girl, who may well have been her own biological children), an artisan, 5 white servants, and 25 slaves—6 adult males, 7 adult females, 8 boys, and 4 mixed-race children of both sexes. A member of the social elite because of her economic standing, Benoist also owned a number of animals. Léonore Ramírez from La Montagne Saint-Louis was another widow of standing who held 3 white servants and 6 black slaves, 3 male and 3 female. These widows were sought after by bachelors, who by marrying them made their fortune. As for the *petits blancs,* they were often poor and depressed, but some, from Montagne Saint-Louis, owned 2 black women, 2 boys, 3 cows, and 3 calves.[64]

Slave ownership in Guadeloupe spread in the years after 1671, particularly among large landowners. By 1677, when labor was at a premium, Governor Hancelin, a *grand blanc,* owned a commercial establishment, a sugar plantation, and 29 adult male slaves, 19 adult female slaves, 5 boys, 6 girls, and a mixed-race boy. In 1687, when another census was taken in Guadeloupe, the total population had declined, but the mixed-race child population showed an increase over 1671.[65] Thus there was an acceleration in conjugal relations between black women and white males. However, the status of their mixed-race offspring would become and remain an issue in slave society.

As the era of indentureship came to a close, there is evidence that black women in Guadeloupe had established a lasting presence. In 1696 French authorities in Guadeloupe complained that a group of bandits from Antigua pillaged the home of the de Verdure family in Grande-Terre on October 27, seized six black and mixed-race individuals, and sold them as slaves in the British colony. The captured individuals were females, all but one—four- or five-year-old Marg (Margueritte)—free. The oldest among them was seventy-year-old Simonne Négresse. The others ranged in age from twenty-nine to forty years. The status and age of the women indicate that they had been in Guadeloupe for some time, enough to have achieved freedom.[66] Thus by the end of the seventeenth century, black women in the French Antilles were more visible than at the outset, but they remained as vulnerable as ever.

The fragility of the black woman's position can be gauged from the sustained attack on her character and womanhood. She was held responsible for the existence of mixed-race individuals, as if reproduction was a one-way affair. Indeed, the seventeenth century was a precursor of what lay in store. In the French colonies, there was a tendency among Europeans to attribute promiscuity and prostitution to black women, and to view these elements as being responsible for low fertility rates. This was the case despite the lack of knowledge among Europeans about Africans and the cultures from which they came. Barbara Bush wrote about the damaging stereotypes to which European attitudes gave rise, noting correctly that the attributions that were "particularly damaging to black women characteristically fell into the realm of sexual morality."[67] A good example of the prevailing view is Lucien Peytraud's statement: "[O]ne must remember that as the climate was hot, slave women were only partially clad. Also, they were women of easy virtue who had no control over their person. At the outset, no legislative measures were taken to protect them."[68] Thus, the low morals attributed to slave women were seen as a factor in the sexual exploitation they suffered. Indeed, the white male *engagé* has been painted as a victim of the slave woman's alleged promiscuity, which made him "more than a demi-slave, a servile thing, a dependent person."[69] In other words, association with the black woman lowered his status even further. Indeed, in the early years of the seventeenth century it was assumed that the filibusters and buccaneers who inhabited that part of Hispaniola that later became Saint-Domingue were enticed to condescend to the level of slave women only because of the lack of white women.[70] Here Bush's assessment of "the impact of contemporary stereotyping upon the projected image of the black woman" is solid. The black woman "came to represent the delights of forbidden sex and in consequence her sexual attributes were highly and sensationally exaggerated."[71]

For a time, slaves and *engagés* lived under very similar conditions. Some shared slave huts; others lived side by side. They did the same work and were treated in similar ways by their owners; hence the tendency to view the *engagés* as white slaves.[72] However, *engagés* could not ordinarily be whipped or punished as severely as slaves.[73] But concern over sexual mores and the breakdown of order—not the protection of black women—led de Tracy, lieutenant général of the French Antilles, to prohibit those who were responsible for disciplining slaves and *engagés* from engaging in debauchery with them, which was considered a misdemeanor. Debien argued that, in this instance, the term "debauchery" is vague and could have applied to anyone who harbored slave women who were maroons, or who had illegitimate children with black women.[74] *Marronnage* was considered a heinous crime from the outset, as later chapters will show, but the emphasis on morality in the documentation leaves little doubt that sensual indulgence was the issue. A first offense carried twenty strokes with the *liane* (liana), a second, forty strokes, and a third, fifty strokes, in addition to branding with the fleur-de-lis on the cheek.[75] By taking this ruling a step further in 1669, Lieutenant Governor Jean-Charles de Baas, who put great emphasis on the need to avoid moral decay, revealed that mixed unions were a source of concern. He dropped "drivers of *engagés*" from the regulation and added "slaveowners," who, if found in contravention of the new law, suffered confiscation of the woman slave to the benefit of the poor, and deprivation of her children, who would be freed. For unmarried slave drivers, the penalty was four thousand *livres* of sugar for the first offense, and the same amount for a second offense, in addition to an "exemplary punishment." De Baas went further. Similar penalties were to be imposed upon male valets working in the slaveowner's household but living with women slaves.[76] Mixed unions were seen as sinful. According to Debien, a white male living openly with a slave woman drew little sympathy irrespective of his profession or the desires of slaveowners. As he noted, "When a slave woman's owner filed a grievance against an *engagé,* it was like a torrent of blows falling upon the head of the accused. However, this became a weekly event once slaves became numerous."[77]

Punishment associated with "debauchery" appeared stringent but was seldom carried out, which points up contradictions in French policy—a common problem both in the French Antilles and in French West Africa, where slavery existed up to the first years of the twentieth century. In 1687, almost two decades after Governor de Baas's ruling, the Catholic priest Saint-Gilles lamented that in French Guiana, "licentiousness and disregard for morals reigns everywhere, and debauchery is widespread, principally among women slaves and Indian women." Saint-Gilles believed that black women turned to prostitution as their owners deprived them of food and shelter. And in 1695, Du Maitz, the intendant governor of Martinique, proposed a motion to prevent white "boys" from keeping young black women at their abode. "Unless there is a strong royal ruling against this," he warned, "we will never be able to remedy the disorder that this causes."[78]

The existence of double standards and the disregard for black women were all too real, as the following cases demonstrate. In 1687 Pierre François and Vincent Verger were severely punished for seducing and raping a young white girl, probably a minor. They were condemned to have their heads shaved—a common symbol of enslavement, according to Orlando Patterson—to make supplications in front of a church, to be exposed in iron collars with written inscriptions in front of and behind them attesting to their crime, and to serve in the galleys for five years. In addition, all their belongings were to be confiscated and sold by the state, the proceeds going toward the ten thousand *livres* in compensation for the victim. But in 1697 when the mixed-race slaveowner Jean Boury of Martinique was condemned to pay a fine of two thousand *livres* of sugar for having a child with a mixed-race slave woman, the Conseil Souverain (Sovereign Council) of Martinique, which made the laws, canceled the fine. The king of France overturned the council's decision and upheld Article 9 of the Code Noir of 1685, which called for a fine of two thousand *livres* of sugar, confiscation of the slave woman and her child or children in cases where the deed was done by the slave woman's owner, and compulsory marriage in the Catholic Church to the slave woman if her owner was unmarried at the time the act was committed. In the end, the Intendant Robert let Boury go free on the grounds that he did not provide sufficient proof that the child was his. Besides, Martinique needed his artisanal skills. In 1706 Toussaint Labbé, a white male accused of having a child with his slave woman, Catherine Rose, was also freed pending proof. Catherine was not as fortunate as her owner, however, for while he escaped punishment she was condemned to thirty lashes for debauchery. The outcomes of these cases show that although race may have been a factor in the treatment of the black women, gender was the more important variable. The two males who exploited these women were of different phenotypes, but they were exonerated while the women were left to carry the burden and the pain of societal censure. Thus Governor de Baas's ordinances and Article 9 of the Code Noir were toothless when it came to slave women and worked against them rather than protecting them.[79]

When slavery took a firm hold in the French Antilles, the number of black women increased significantly. Debien has argued that the advantage of having slaves was that planters could purchase not only men but women and children, and that it was easier to provide a wife to a male slave than to an *engagé*. Furthermore, the presence of female slaves on the plantations was a guarantee of stability to the slave system. Most of all, the black woman could perform hard labor.[80] This argument has a ring of inevitability about it and can be contested, for greater and more generous incentives could have been provided to attract *engagés* in sufficient numbers if there was consensus that white laborers were preferable to black. The fact is that the African alternative was cheaper, but it was not inevitable. As Kenneth Stampp has rightly stated, the "rise of slavery in the South was inevitable only in the sense that every event in history seems inevitable after it has occurred."[81] In the Caribbean, slavery was also a deliberate choice. However, the selection of Africans for the Atlantic slave trade was not under the control of Caribbean planters.

2

The Atlantic Slave Trade, Black Women, and the Development of the Plantations

BLACK WOMEN were outnumbered by black men in the Atlantic slave trade, but their presence in the trade and their socioeconomic impact on the plantations are very significant factors in the study of Caribbean slavery. The black woman's presence in the Atlantic slave trade has usually been examined as part of the larger issue of how the trade affected Africa and Africans. Thus the quantitative impact of the slave trade, its effects on fertility patterns and family structure, as well as on demography and agricultural production, have drawn the most interest.[1] If we are to better understand the multidimensional nature of black women's experience in the slave plantation societies of the French Antilles, however, we must examine their presence in this trade with a view to determining, first, the extent to which the French colonies fell into traditional import patterns of fewer females than males and, second, the overall effects of unbalanced sex ratios on the lives of slave women. This requires going beyond statistics on export data of slaves from Africa to the Caribbean. Equally if not more revealing are the data on sex ratios on the plantations themselves.

THE EARLIEST IMPORTS

Before the Atlantic slave trade began to supply the French Antilles in earnest starting in the 1660s, the French had already acquired a limited number of slaves from other Europeans through purchase and plunder. By the 1660s, sugar planters outfitted large boats and enlisted the help of former indentured servants, who used axes, spears, and pikes to raid English and Spanish vessels in Caribbean waters for slaves. Such predatory methods could only yield a limited number of slaves, however. For several decades after the colonization of Martinique and Guadeloupe in 1635, the supply of slaves to the French colonies was sporadic because the French chartered companies, notably the Compagnie des Indes Occidentales, the Compagnie du Sénégal, and the Compagnie de Guinée were unable to supply the colonies with sufficient slaves, despite preferential treatment and tax exemptions given by the French state. To a large degree, the French became dependent upon Dutch traders for slaves. Indeed, by 1665 Dutch traders had supplied Martinique and Guadeloupe with 1,200–1,300 slaves.[2] In the 1660s, Jean-Baptiste Colbert, the French minister, hoped that the Compagnie des Indes Occidentales could furnish 2,000 slaves per year to the French colonies and a further 2,000 to the Spanish colonies, but the company failed to live up to expectations, and neither the other chartered companies nor private French traders were successful. Thus there was a chronic need for slaves in the French colonies well into the eighteenth century. In response to calls by plantation owners in Saint-Domingue for more and cheaper slaves, the French king, Louis XIV, authorized the establishment of a slave-trading company—the Compagnie de Saint-Domingue —in 1698, but the problem of shortage remained.[3]

There is no agreement as to when the slave trade to the French Antilles began, but Maurice Satineau has argued that the French colonists felt the need for slaves as early as 1638, when it became clear that the Native Americans could not be successfully enslaved. In 1643 the Compagnie des Isles d'Amérique granted Captain Montabalar of Rouen, France, the right to commandeer Spanish slave vessels coming from Africa to Guadeloupe and Martinique. That year the General Assembly in Paris authorized a loan of 8,000 *livres* so that the company could pay a Dutch captain, Durant, for forty slaves he sold in Guadeloupe. In 1647 Governor Hoüel of Guadeloupe asked the French king for slaves to augment the work force or, better yet, to replace indentured servants. But he complained that Dutch merchants sold slaves at rates so exorbitant that even rich planters could not purchase them. Hoüel no doubt hoped that the state would make it possible for French traders to take up the slave business and sell slaves more cheaply. However, he inadvertently benefited from the misfortune of a group of Dutch Jews who were expelled from Brazil by the Portuguese in 1654. Along with other possessions, the Dutch brought slaves with them to Martinique and Guadeloupe.[4]

Over the course of the Atlantic slave trade, the French colonies received well over a million and a half slaves, more than half of them going to Saint-Domingue. Not all of these were delivered by French slavers, even though the French sent out more than three thousand ships to Africa and began delivering slaves to their colonies soon after they were settled. The nature of record keeping in an often clandestine business, as well as the absence of data for some periods of the trade, have created huge gaps in the historical demography of the slave trade. The numbers game, as it is sometimes called, has therefore been the source of ongoing debate. In this debate, Robert Stein has posited that the eighteenth-century French slave trade was 21.4 percent higher than Philip Curtin estimated in his 1969 census of the Atlantic slave trade. This and other such responses have led to an upward revision of Curtin's estimates.

Even so, Paul Lovejoy has found Curtin's projection of total imports "to have been remarkably accurate." Lovejoy estimated that the number of slaves imported into the Americas from Africa was 9,778,500 and arrived at a global export figure of 9,913,000. Scholars will always be at variance over the volume of the slave trade, but besides demography, other factors such as geography, location, access to resources, gender, and labor regime had a bearing on the slave woman's condition in the Caribbean, as later chapters demonstrate.[5]

Up to the 1780s, that is, for most of the slave trade, the majority of the slaves imported went to Martinique and Saint-Domingue, putting Guadeloupe and French Guiana at a competitive disadvantage that was compounded by scarcity. Of the two colonies, Martinique was the overwhelming favorite, but it was eventually overtaken by the larger and more prosperous Saint-Domingue. Du Tertre attributed Martinique's special position in the French Antilles to the good graces of its governors and inhabitants, as well as to its geographic location, which made it less susceptible to hurricanes than the other French colonies. But Martinique was favored by the existence of a fort, which could be used for defensive purposes, as well as by attractive harbors that were suitable for commerce. In other words, it was Martinique's economic prowess more than any other factor that accounted for its special status. Martinique was also the administrative capital of the French Antilles until 1714, when it was replaced by Saint-Domingue, but it still remained head of the Windward Islands.[6] Even after 1714, it still played a crucial role in the slave distribution network. As Robert Stein explained, not only was Martinique the richest French colony, but

> it also served as an obligatory depot for slaves destined for Guadeloupe. Until the Seven Year's War, direct commerce between Africa and Guadeloupe was illegal, and Martinique merchants had a monopoly of trade with the island. Thus any slaver wishing to deal with Guadeloupe had to deliver his slaves first to Martinique and use the services of a local businessman; the slaves were then carried to Guadeloupe aboard a small craft for local services.[7]

The bias toward Martinique meant that planters in Guadeloupe often had to turn to contraband practices to obtain slaves—not too difficult an endeavor, given the many inlets that characterize Caribbean coastlines. With a slave mortality rate as high as one third, and given that many slaves failed to survive their first year in captivity, fresh supplies were constantly needed. Contraband slaves came from Saint Eustatius (a veritable slave market), Curaçao, as well as Antigua and Montserrat.

Martinique's special status was one thing; its ability to obtain slaves from Africa in sufficient quantities was quite another. Examination of early shipments from Africa reveals that a breakdown of the slave cargoes by sex was seldom given. However, it is possible to extrapolate from the efforts that colonists made to obtain slaves, from the pattern of the trade itself, and from sex ratios on plantations in the Antilles. Women formed part of virtually every group of slaves that arrived in the Caribbean colonies, but the central question has always been how many. Can the bias toward Martinique in the trade enlighten us? A good example of this bias is the distribution of the cargo of the slave ship *La Justice* owned by the Compagnie des Indes Occidentales. It left the West African coast on March 13, 1670, with 434 slaves and arrived at Saint-Pierre, Martinique, on June 7 that year. In correspondence to Minister Colbert regarding the cargo, Governor de Baas of Martinique wrote, "I gave orders for an equal distribution to be made between the three islands, Martinique, Guadeloupe and St. Christopher. Two-thirds were set aside for the last named islands, but as captain Delbrée assured the general clerk [of the company] that there would be a cargo of slaves for each island, and that his own was meant for Martinique, the whole cargo was sold there."[8]

A little more than three months later, on September 22, another company ship, *La Concorde,* having left West Africa some months earlier with almost 600 slaves, arrived at Martinique with 443 slaves. There is no mention of the sex of the slaves or the manner in which they were distributed, but no slave cargo of that or any other size was ever exclusively male. Thus it is not far-fetched to suggest that at least one-third of the cargo of these two vessels was female, as was generally the case in the eighteenth century. It appears that the Compagnie du Sénégal also followed the traditional pattern of favoring Martinique, but favoritism was not enough to satisfy the needs of the colony. In 1684 Governor Charles de Courbon, Comte (Count) de Blénac complained that the company "shipped only 950 slaves last year, all of whom were sold at Martinique, the cargo having arrived during the hurricane season. As a result, we could not risk sending slaves on to the other islands, even though they have had very few imports for the last three years."[9]

Blénac also complained about the infrequent arrival of slave ships. In 1684 he learned, from the captain of one such ship which arrived in Martinique, that there were three slave ships on the African coast procuring slaves for Martinique. But he lamented the fact that, as in previous years, they were scheduled to arrive late in the season and would therefore be subject to the same "success" as the others. "We must impress upon His Majesty," he wrote, "the need for the company to fulfil its mandate punctually and bring in at least 2,000 slaves who are sure to be sold at good prices. Slaves will make the colonies flourish; without them, we will amount to nothing in these islands." Blénac pleaded with the French government to ease the monopolistic restrictions which forbade local trading in slaves. He noted that "a slave or two" could be bought from Native Americans in the neighboring islands of Dominica and Saint Vincent, a trade that would make it possible for French colonists from Martinique to retrieve runaway slaves from among them. This "insignificant" trade would not hurt the company either, Blénac believed. "Your Majesty should know," he continued, "that the majority of the slaves whom the Native Americans sell to our traders, have been stolen from the British with whom they are at war." At the same time Blénac hoped that the French could chase the Dutch from their lucrative slave-trading post at Saint Eustatius.[10]

It was not long before Blénac acted. An administrative report of 1689 noted that the governor left Martinique on March 28 accompanied by three ships mounted with cannon, several smaller vessels, and 200 militia men to attack Saint Eustatius. The year 1689 was indeed eventful in the search for slaves. In August filibusters brought 38 male and female slaves to Martinique. In November Blénac reported that Monsieur du Casse returned from Barbados with three shipments of slaves, flour, and other provisions, as well as a considerable amount of gunpowder. This was also the year that an official administrative accounting showed that the colonial treasury had taken in 117,500 *livres* from the sale of runaway slaves from Barbados, and well over a million *livres* from the sale of 196 slaves, most taken in the successful attack on Saint Eustatius.[11]

The century ended as it began, however, with limited numbers of slaves arriving and demands from the colonies mounting. In 1690 the Compagnie du Sénégal shipped only 100 slaves to Martinique; the Compagnie de Guinée shipped 711. In 1700 they shipped 108 and 1,000 respectively. The Compagnie du Sénégal captured a Dutch ship trading off limits in 1699 and seized its cargo of 152 slaves. On this occasion, the ship's logs revealed that the slaves were bound for Martinique. Martinique was also the destination of the ship *Polly,* owned by the French naval squadron, which left the coast of Senegal in 1696 with 330 slaves. Thus Martinique still had the edge on the West African coast but could do nothing to influence supply patterns. Governor after governor could only express frustration as they watched the economic prospects of the colonies increase and awaited the arrival of slave ships from Africa.[12]

The intendant governor, Vaucresson, pressed the Minister of Marine and Colonies in Paris for slaves in 1709. In his turn, Governor Phélypeaux voiced his concerns in the same manner and language as one his predecessors— Governor Blénac. In 1713 he complained that the promise the state made to supply 2,000–2,500 slaves had not materialized, and that without slaves the sugar economy would collapse. In the three years he had been in office, only 800 slaves had arrived in Martinique. "In the last three months," he wrote, "two company ships brought in no more than 200 slaves. Indeed, there has not been a single ship in the 13 preceding months, as a result of which the island is so desolate that it is difficult to explain. This is the reason why, Monsieur, you must make a serious attempt to bring order to this business in the future."

It would be easy to accuse Phélypeaux of exaggerating the needs of Martinique, all the more so since he did not criticize the traditional practice of governors, lieutenants, and other officials, who had the right to pick a designated number of slaves from arriving cargoes and pay very low prices. But the story he told the minister about a transaction that Captain Joseph Traharn Anglais carried out in 1713 was probably a true reflection of the planters' plight. That year inclement weather forced Captain Anglais and his cargo of 200 slaves bound for Barbados to dock at Martinique. Phélypeaux appealed to him to sell the slaves there, but the captain requested time to consult authorities in Barbados, who graciously obliged "for the good of Martinique." This was also the year when the governor gave permission to two Barbados merchants, Mr. Gordon and Mr. Lindal, to sell 275 slaves and thirty barrels of flour, "which we need while awaiting ships from France." As there was an equilibrium in the Barbados slave population in the eighteenth century, there is every likelihood that female slaves were part of this cargo. This was a period when Martinique and Barbados enjoyed good commercial relations. Phélypeaux could only bemoan the fact that while slaves were dying in Martinique at the rate of about 2,000 per year, mostly as a result of famine, the Barbadians were being well provisioned by the British.[13]

The conditions that prevailed in Martinique in the early eighteenth century could also be witnessed in Guadeloupe, where there was an acute shortage of slaves. During the Seven Years' War (1756–1763), the English, who occupied Guadeloupe from 1759 until the Peace of Paris, brought in 25,000 slaves. When the colony was returned to France, however, the English repatriated the slaves the French could not purchase. Shortage of slaves was still the complaint in 1765, a time when, according to observers, the colony could easily have accommodated 120,000 slaves but had only 40,000. The shortage was even more acute in French Guiana, which was hampered by inaccessible ports, poor colonists who could scarcely afford slaves, and limited prospects for the development of a strong sugar plantation economy. Saint-Domingue was more fortunate in that it drew in large numbers of slaves in the eighteenth century, but apparently never enough. In 1777 Madame Desclos de la Fonchais of France, daughter of a plantation owner in Saint-Domingue, wrote to her nephew, Lory, an administrator on the plantation who wanted to increase the slave force. She instructed him to purchase 40–50 slaves and to feed them adequately: "If you cannot find creole slaves to purchase, as predicted," she wrote, "buy them from the Gold Coast, and be sure to buy young women." Lory was asked not to purchase either creole or African slaves from the Congo, whose mortality rate was said to be high. However, he ignored his orders and bought, among other slaves, "a big woman, and she is a Congo."[14]

In spite of having relatively few slaves in the initial stages of their development as plantation societies, the French colonies underwent significant demographic change in the eighteenth century, largely as a result of the importation of African slaves. Table 2.1 shows that the most dramatic shift occurred in Saint-Domingue, where the slave population moved from 2,000 in 1681 to 117,400 by 1739, and to almost 500,000 by the French Revolution of 1789. Saint-Domingue used up slaves at a rapid rate and depended on the African trade to replenish its stock. In response to the declaration of the abolition of slavery by the French National Convention in 1794, a Saint-Domingue planter suggested that "after chasing . . . useless Europeans who are attracted by a thirst for gold from our shores," French authorities should take advantage of wars on the West African coast to import large numbers of slaves and distribute them to planters on a pay-later plan.[15]

WOMEN IN THE ATLANTIC SLAVE TRADE

The statistics in table 2.1 offer a global demographic picture of the slave populations of the French Antilles and are very similar to the ones given by Moreau de Jonnès, but there is no breakdown of the population by sex. Nevertheless, Curtin is correct in asserting that the "actual demographic structure of the slave population . . . is rarely known." This is true, but the work of other scholars can give us a better understanding of this structure.[16]

Walter Rodney was among those historians who long ago pointed up the preference for males over females in the slave trade. According to Rodney, "Slave buyers preferred their victims between the ages of 15 and 35, and preferably in the early twenties; the sex ratio being about two men to one woman." Indeed, the Royal African Company (1672–1752) instructed its buyers to purchase slaves fifteen to forty years old and to strive for a ratio that was two-

Table 2.1. Slave Populations of the French Antilles

Martinique		Guadeloupe		Guiana		Saint-Domingue	
1664	2,700	1671	4,300	1695	1,000	1681	2,000
1686	11,100	1700	6,700	1698	1,400	1739	117,400
1696	15,000	1710	9,700	1707	1,400	1754	172,000
1700	14,600	1715	13,300	1716	2,500	1764	206,000
1736	55,700	1720	17,200	1740	4,700	1777	240,000
1751	65,900	1753	40,400	1765	5,700	1779	249,100
1770	71,100	1772	78,000	1789	10,700	1789	452,000
1790	84,000	1816	81,700	1814	12,100	1791	480,000
1831	86,300	1831	97,300	1831	19,100		
1838	76,500	1838	93,300	1838	15,800		

Source: Philip D. Curtin, *The Atlantic Slave Trade: A Census* (Madison: University of Wisconsin Press, 1969), 78.

thirds male. Official inquiry into the operations of some slave vessels also revealed a preference for male slaves. Before the British banned the slave trade in 1807, the government sent Captain Parrey to Liverpool to take the dimensions of the infamous slave ship *Brooks,* as well as *Vénus, Kitty,* and others operating from the port. In his report to the British House of Commons, Parrey noted that the *Brooks* was built to accommodate 297 slaves but had recently embarked 351 adult males, 127 adult females (that is, a little over one-third), 90 boys, and 41 girls—a total of 609 slaves.[17]

More contemporary sources support a 2:1 ratio in the export trade from Africa irrespective of the carriers, which were mostly foreign vessels—Spanish, British, Dutch, and Danish—in the case of the French Antilles. According to Herbert S. Klein, who has examined the rates of participation of African women in the Atlantic slave trade using records from British, Dutch, and Danish shipping, "in all trades, between two-thirds and three-quarters of all slaves arriving in America were males. But this general trend obscures some interesting internal variations. In some periods and from some regions more women were sent than was the norm."[18]

Klein concluded that "African women did not enter the Atlantic slave trade in anything like the numbers of African men. At all ages, men outnumbered women on the slave ships bound for America from Africa." Over 60,000 slaves were shipped to the West Indies in the late seventeenth and early eighteenth centuries by the West India Company and free traders. Of this total, "females were only 38 per cent of the forced migrants. Even when slaves are examined by age group, the same disproportionate representation of males is apparent. Thus the adult ratio was 187 men for every 100 women, and the child ratio was 193 boys for every 100 girls."[19]

A smaller sample, obtained from Danish shipping records of the second half of the eighteenth century, corroborates this trend. Indeed, Klein adds, "In the two decades of recorded trading, the Danes shipped from their own Guinean forts and from areas on the Guinean coast to the west of them some 15,000 slaves, of whom only 36% were females. Just as in the case of the Dutch, this sexual imbalance appeared among both adults and children, with 186 men to 100 women and 145 boys to 100 girls."[20]

A last set of examples, drawn from British shipping, is worth considering. Between 1672 and 1713, the Royal African Company delivered about 100,000 slaves to the British colonies. "Of those delivered alive," Davies reports, "the majority were adult males. An analysis of 60,000 slaves delivered between 1673 and 1711 shows that 51 per cent were men and 35 per cent women; of the remainder 9 per cent were boys and 4 per cent were girls." Also, in the last decade of the eighteenth century, the British transported 83,000 slaves from West Africa to the Caribbean. Of these, 38 percent were female slaves.[21]

Other scholars have confirmed the bias toward male slaves, using British shipping data. Colin Palmer's statistics on the gender of 970 slaves imported into Spanish America in the period 1715–35 show that about two-thirds of the cargoes were males.[22] Barry Higman noted that in the last decade of the slave trade, sex ratios were about 150–180 males per 100 females.[23] After analyzing data on slave exports, Joseph Inikori too concluded that "the sex ratio of the people exported from the west coast of Africa in the eighteenth century was in the neighborhood of 60 per cent for men and 40 per cent for female slaves."[24] These figures are not out of range with the samples of age and sex distribution of slaves exported across the Atlantic given by Paul Lovejoy, who showed that on average males made up 65 percent of slave cargoes and women 35 percent. Lovejoy argued that there was a strong preference for women and children in the Islamic slave trade, which made males cheaper and an "attractive investment for slave owners." He adds, "The competition between domestic and foreign markets for females and children raised their prices to levels that were often twice that of males." In heavily slaved areas such as west central Africa, therefore, women and children made up a disproportionate number of the slaves.[25]

Curtin's data are much larger in scale than those of other scholars heretofore cited, and they cover all linguistic regions of the Caribbean. He indicated that Caribbean societies received a random sample of slaves, "who tended to be young people with a high ratio of male to female." However, the question remains whether specific data for French shipments to the French colonies tell a different story. French trading companies and individual merchants usually told ship captains where to trade and how many slaves to purchase. Normally, a merchant in the eighteenth century would instruct a captain to buy young, good, healthy slaves. In 1725 the Compagnie des Indes Occidentales instructed Captain Le Seur to take orders from one Mr. Derigoin, the company's director, at Ouidah in Dahomey (now Benin), who "is supposed to put together a cargo of blacks as well assorted as possible; the company does not order Captain Le Seur to take a certain quantity, but nonetheless estimates that he can take at least 400."[26]

Where does all of this leave us in terms of the demographic structure of the French Antillean slave population? David Geggus's analysis of two samples of slaves in Saint-Domingue suggests that female slaves usually made up more than one-third of slave cargoes. The first of Geggus's samples consists of 177,000 slaves shipped by the French between 1714 and 1792. The second sample is derived from almost four hundred plantation inventories consisting of more than 13,300 plantation slaves in the period 1721–97. Geggus put forward a sex ratio of 179 males to 100 females as average for the Atlantic trade, and supported the view that males constituted somewhere between 60 and close to 70 percent of captives in the Atlantic trade as a whole. This would mean that around 64 percent of slave cargoes were males and 36 percent were females, figures that are not significantly different from the 2:1 ratio of males to females advanced by other scholars. Geggus noted that sex ratios fell below this level for some branches of the French slave trade, including those to French Guiana and Guadeloupe, but gave no detail save to cite secondary sources that claim that the French exported equal numbers of men, women, and children in the seventeenth century.[27]

It is important to emphasize that, despite their preferences, slavers could not dictate patterns of supply in Africa, which depended to a large extent on political factors. It is well known that most of the Africans who entered the Atlantic slave trade were prisoners of war, taken in military raids. The frequency of wars was unpredictable, which explains, in part, why it usually took European ship captains several months to obtain a full cargo. It is likely that, in African warfare, at least as many women as men were captured and probably more women, as many males died in resisting capture or were killed. Philip Curtin has argued that in West Africa, lack of facilities to guard newly captured prisoners on a permanent basis, and means to exploit their labor gainfully in captive areas, would have meant that they "had little or no value at the point of capture." If we accept this argument, it seems logical that African women would be exported in similar numbers to African men, as far away as possible from the point of capture. But given the overwhelming dependency of African agricultural systems on women's labor, however, it may well be that more women were retained within African societies. As women were also valued for their reproductive capacity and used to expand kinship networks, there may have been less incentive to export them overseas. As John Thornton noted, "Many Africans retained females from the raids and sold off males, because the Atlantic trade often demanded more males than females." Indeed, in the second half of the nineteenth century, when slaves from Africa could no longer be exported legally, the slave trade within Africa increased markedly and focused heavily on women and children in areas of the western Sudan. In Senegal, for example, large numbers of female slaves from the French Soudan (now Mali) were integrated into Wolof households, where they became engaged in peanut production geared mostly to the export market. The foregoing suggests that the pattern of retaining female captives in Africa as much as possible, while exporting as many males as possible, was consistent but varied over time.[28]

If we accept that the records of non-French shippers—the majority of the suppliers, as we have noted—show a bias in favor of male slaves over female slaves, then the only other data that would make a difference would be French shipping data. But these have been found to be insufficient before 1711 and deficient in the late eighteenth century. French shipping data are based on inventories that ship captains prepared on their return to France. They listed the number of captives and their sex, but the sex of the slaves has somehow not been reflected in the historical literature. The French slave trade focused on particular areas in France, the most important of which was probably Nantes. As we have seen, Curtin's examination of these records reveals a similar pattern to those of other shipping records in terms of a sex ratio that favored male slaves. What deserves comment, therefore, is the actual situation in the colonies, where statistical data often indicate an equilibrium between the sexes or a larger number of female than male slaves, either on particular plantations or in the population as a whole.[29]

SEXUAL DIVISION AND THE PLANTATION

During the era of indentureship, as we have seen, French colonists often had equal numbers of male and female slaves, but this may have been due to circumstances and to miscegenation rather than to precise and consistent import patterns. Planters clearly valued women and were quick to recognize a bargain and to exploit women's sexuality, as the following case demonstrates. François Monel, an honorary councillor, surgeon, and planter from the district of Carbet in Martinique, started out with ten to twelve sick women slaves, whom he purchased from a ship captain for next to nothing, as the women were not expected to last beyond four days or so. Père Labat noted that the women recovered and produced "an infinite number of children, such that the three sugar plantations that [Monel] owned in addition to other estates, were all flourishing with the most beautiful creole slaves on the island." On one of these estates in 1664, Monel had five *engagés,* ten male slaves and ten female slaves, and was already well on his way to becoming a large planter.[30]

Slaveowners also appear to have acceded to the wishes of male slaves for female companionship, thereby providing more female slaves than might otherwise have been the case. Xavier Tanc, a magistrate in Guadeloupe during the nineteenth century, captured the dilemma of a male slave who, along with his owner, witnessed the arrival in Saint-François of a slave ship in 1828. Among the three hundred slaves to be auctioned was a woman he recognized as his wife. He implored his owner to purchase the woman since they "would both die if they did not have each other." As he did not wish to lose a reliable domestic slave who had been his property for two years, the slaveowner purchased the woman.[31] Whether the slave was using his ingenuity to play upon his owner's sensibilities, or merely experienced a stroke of good fortune in encountering a wife he likely thought he would never see again, is worth asking. He called the woman slave "Ima" and she called him "Lichi," but beyond that there appears to have been no attempt to verify his story. What is worth emphasizing, however, is the recognition by both slave and slaveowner of the need for women slaves.

By the eighteenth century, females slaves outnumbered male slaves on some plantations, but male slaves still constituted the majority of the slaves in most cases. There were further shifts in the nineteenth century, a period when the equilibrium in sex ratios that began in the late eighteenth century became a general phenomenon across the Caribbean. Thus while birth rates remained low, even negative, creole slaves changed the structure of the population such that there were more slave women relative to slave men, especially after the British abolished the slave trade in 1807. In other words, creolization evened out the sex ratios.

Some examples are worth highlighting. In 1767, on the plantation Roche-chouart in L'Anse-à-l'âne near Trois-Ilets, Martinique, adult women outnumbered adult men, but there were slightly more males on the estate than females. Of 162 slaves, there were 44 men, 55 women, 39 boys, and 24 girls. By the early nineteenth century, the slave population in Martinique had evened out in favor of women, however. There were 78,080 slaves in Martinique in 1835 consisting of 37,584 males and 40,496 females. Similarly, Guadeloupe's slave population of 96,322 in 1835 was composed of 46,168 males and 50,154 females.[32]

Specific examples from Guadeloupe reinforce the perception of change in the structure of the population. In 1786 there were 229 slaves on sugar plantations owned by one d'Arnouville in Petit Cul-de-Sac (now Petit-Bourg). Of these, 79 were men, 96 were women, and 54 were children. Even though the sex of the children is unknown, the fact that adult women constituted 42 percent of the slave population compared to 34 percent for adult males is significant.[33] A second and more representative sample of Guadeloupian slaves should suffice. Nicole Vanony-Frisch compiled an inventory of 8,820 slaves—about 10 percent of the slave population—from death registers, marriage contracts, and sales for the years 1770 to 1789. Vanony-Frisch was largely concerned about ethnic origins but included information on gender. She grouped the slaves according to eight types of commercial activities in which they were engaged, including sugar, coffee, and food production. In most categories women outnumbered men. In the thirty-nine sugar plantations in the sample, for instance, women represented 51 percent of the population and men 49 percent. On provision plantations, the figures for women and men were 54 percent and 46 percent respectively. The only notable exception was on coffee plantations, where the percentage of women was 46 and that of men, 54.[34]

Martinique and Guadeloupe experienced a greater degree of creolization than did French Guiana and Saint-Domingue, but the trend toward balanced sex ratios was no less striking in these colonies. On some plantations in French Guiana, males were dominant up to the late eighteenth century. By the early nineteenth century, however, the picture changed. Statistics from the sugar plantation Gabrielle can be taken as a guide, as this was a model estate that was considered to be representative of the general situation in the colony. On

Table 2.2. Slave Population on the Plantation Gabrielle, French Guiana

Year	Adult Males	Adult Females	Boys	Girls
1817	105	109	56	41
1829	103	121	127	36
1834	93	115	31	48
1841	78	100	39	36
1843	74	98	39	35
1847	72	101	36	31

Source: Anne-Marie Bruleaux et al., eds., *Deux Siècles d'esclavage en Guyane française, 1652–1848* (Paris: L'Harmattan, 1986), 123.

Table 2.3. Slave Population on the Hecquet Plantation, Saint-Domingue

Year	Adult Males	Adult Females	Boys	Girls
1769	36	30	18	23
1782	53	50	18	20

Source: François Girod, *Une Fortune coloniale sous l'Ancien Régime: La Famille Hecquet à Saint-Domingue, 1724–1796* (Paris: Annales litteraires de l'Université de Besançon, 1970), 101–103.

Gabrielle, as table 2.2 indicates, the slave population moved from equilibrium to a solid female majority in the nineteenth century.

As for Saint-Domingue, data from some plantations during the second half of the eighteenth century show an equilibrium in the slave population or a slight female majority. Inventories of the Hecquet Plantation taken in 1769 and 1782 show this to be the case. As table 2.3 indicates, the slave population moved from equilibrium in 1769 to a female majority by 1782. In the period between 1769 and 1782, fertility rates were low and there was constant replacement of adult slaves through purchase. By 1782, however, creolization was an important factor as 54 of the 103 adult slaves fell into that category. Writing to her brother, Jean-Baptiste Hecquet, in 1788, Victoire Hecquet, a relative of the proprietor, boasted that "we have more women than men and the slave population has never been as large." Hecquet also emphasized that there were more infants born on the plantation than ever—six per year.[35]

There are other notable examples of plantations in Saint-Domingue in the late eighteenth century where slave women were in the majority. One such example is the sugar plantation Bréda in the North Plain. Of 191 slaves on the estate in April 1784, there were 77 men, 82 women, 15 boys, and 17 girls. The deficiency in men may have been a concern, as the owners purchased 15 males and only 2 females in the second half of 1784. Inventories carried out by the British during the period when they occupied Saint-Domingue also showed that women outnumbered men after 1791, often by a significant mar-

Table 2.4. Slave Population on the Plantation Des Vases, Saint- Domingue

Year	Adult Males	Adult Females	Boys	Girls
1776	52	38	17	8
1783	47	33	19	14
1790	71	47	32	19
1798	49	49	34	25

Source: Gabriel Debien, "Comptes, profits, esclaves et travaux dans deux sucreries de Saint-Domingue, 1774–1778," *Notes d'histoire coloniale,* no. 6 (Oct. 1944): 18.

Table 2.5. Slave Population on the Labarre Plantation, Saint-Domingue

Year	Adult Males	Adult Females	Boys and Girls
1790	71	47	51
1796	44	50	57
1798	49	49	59

Source: David Patrick Geggus, *Slavery, War, and Revolution: The British Occupation of Saint-Domingue, 1793–1798* (London: Oxford University Press, 1982), 292.

gin. Debien has attributed this phenomenon to a significant loss of black men during the revolution of 1791, and the recruitment and conscription of others by the British. But he has argued that Jamaica, in the absence of a revolution, was also experiencing a trend toward a higher female slave population on the scale of Saint-Domingue. He therefore attributed the phenomenon to an increase in the infant birth rate, at least among plantation slaves.[36] In general, there was an equilibrium in the sex ratios among slaves in Saint-Domingue after 1791. In the case of the Vases Plantation, for example, women remained in the minority until at least 1790, but their numbers came into line with men by 1798, as table 2.4 indicates.

David Geggus drew conclusions very similar to Debien's about sex ratios in Saint-Domingue during the period of British occupation. Table 2.5 shows the demographic structure of the slave population on the Labarre Plantation. There women moved from a minority before 1790 to a majority by 1796, after which the sex ratios evened out.

Both Debien and Geggus cited the impact of the Saint-Domingue revolution, in which males suffered more casualties than females, as a possible cause of a balanced sex ratio. But this does not explain a similar balance in other parts of the Caribbean. Geggus concluded that "On the caféières the sexes were almost equally balanced (103:100) but on the sugar estates where the sex ratio was 93:100, women clearly outnumbered men."[37]

The sex ratios of the slave populations in the Caribbean evened out by the early nineteenth century, but the evidence shows that there was a trend toward female dominance well before that. Hilary Beckles has shown that the slave population of Barbados was predominantly female from the mid-eighteenth century.[38] Barbados was clearly an exception in the region, but there is no doubt that scholars have underestimated the presence of women in Caribbean slave populations as a whole. Aside from creolization, it may well be that mortality rates were higher among males than females and that women lived longer than men. Michael Craton found that slave women in the British Caribbean "lived at least five per cent longer than men on the average," leading to a "feminisation of the population."[39] It is probable that this was the case in the French Antilles as well. Thus, in the end, Curtin is correct in arguing that "the rate of slave imports is related to slave population, but only as one variable among many."[40]

The emphasis that one finds in the scholarly literature on the number of males in the slave populations of the Caribbean has led to skewed assumptions about their contribution in labor and other areas of plantation life. Statistics and gender misconceptions have therefore worked against women. Evidence of fewer women than men was taken to mean that women made a lesser contribution. But while male and female slaves played essential roles in the development of the sugar plantation economy in the French Antilles, it was women who carried the heaviest burden. Inadvertently or not, they were used to achieve balanced sex ratios. And whether their numbers were small or large, they were the backbone of the sugar plantation economy from which planters realized their greatest fortunes. Balanced sex ratios simply meant that more women were available for hard labor. And hard labor was the bane of the slave woman's existence.

3

Women and Labor
Slave Labor

RICHARD DUNN's assertion that slavery in the British Caribbean was "ruth-lessly exploitative from the outset" and "nakedly racial" is applicable to the French Caribbean as well.[1] Indeed, Père Du Tertre inadvertently gave cre-dence to this assertion in a statement invoking the notion of original sin and hinting at the harsh conditions under which slaves in the French Caribbean labored in the seventeenth century. Suggesting that slavery was perhaps di-vinely ordained, Du Tertre wrote, "If the work that God imposed on original man was a chastisement for the latter's rebellion; and if His vengeful justice has so penalized the children of this guilty father (who nonetheless, according to Job, is the natural father of these children) . . . , then one can say that Ne-groes have been given the most severe penalty for this revolt."[2]

Du Tertre was referring to the biblical curse of Canaan, one of Ham's four sons. (Noah in turn was the father of Ham.) Medieval Arab writers and Europeans of a later period invoked this curse as a way of explaining why the presumed descendants of Ham "had been blackened and degraded to the status of natural slaves as punishment for their ancestor's sin." As David Brion Davis has explained, Africans' black skin color came to symbolize sin, degradation, and evil. Color symbolism, linked as it was to this biblical curse, provided justification for enslavement.[3]

If Davis's argument is valid, then Du Tertre was drawing upon venerable ideas with religious sanction. Du Tertre was not alone, for even before his *His-toire général des Antilles* appeared, Père Pelleprat, a Jesuit priest, referred to slaves in the French Antilles as "designated creatures of Satan."[4] The act of branding the slaves once they arrived in the Caribbean also reveals a certain thinking about the permanency of the slavery of Africans. In reference to slaves imported into Saint-Domingue, Antoine Métral wrote, "A fiery torture awaits them at the gateway of servitude. With a hot iron on the chest of the slave, one imprints the first letter of the master's name, and that of the planta-tion, as much to recognize him if he runs away, as to indicate that his heart must only beat for slavery."[5]

Ideas about how slaves could redeem themselves from the inevitable fate of slavery were almost predictable. When Père Labat—"the epitome of racial bigotry," in the words of Gordon K. Lewis—observed that his slaves were not working with zeal and enthusiasm, he told them a tale about how he himself had once been black. Further, he explained, he served his master more diligently and with more goodwill than they, and it was by so doing that he then became white. Labat then had "the pleasure to hear them dispute the impossibility and improbability of such a metamorphosis."[6]

The Bible seems to have served as a convenient tool to justify the collective degradation of a people, so much so that even as the end of slavery approached, slaveowners in the Caribbean and the American South still echoed Du Tertre's utterances. In one way or other, they fostered the view that blacks were naturally suited to the role of hewers of wood and drawers of water. This view was articulated by Rose Price, owner of the Worthy Park Plantation in Jamaica, in a pamphlet he published in 1832. Aimed at members of the British House of Commons, where the abolition of British slavery was being debated, Price's pamphlet pronounced that blacks were "destined by Providence to labor in a state of slavery, of some sort or other, till the curse of Adam is removed from the face of the earth, and from the brow of man in God's appointed time." The anonymous author of a similar pamphlet declared that the slave trade was "a fortunate event for these miserable captives, as well as an advantageous bargain for their various purchasers. They are justly doomed as our own delinquents to transportation, either to exile, imprisonment or execution." Likewise, the prevailing view in the literature of the American South during the mid-nineteenth century was that had it not been for an "all-wise Creator" who "perfectly adapted [Africans] to the labor needs of the South, its lands would have remained 'a howling wilderness.'"[7]

On plantations in the French Caribbean, gender was not a consideration in the allocation of most tasks requiring hard labor, as women were required to do the same work as men for the most part. Du Tertre hinted at this phenomenon when he stated that the only difference between slave men and slave women was that, at times, women's work was somewhat lighter than men's.[8] What Du Tertre failed to consider was the fact that women were fewer in number than men overall for most of the slavery period and performed proportionately more hard labor than men as a consequence. Thus, the allocation of tasks obliterated gender and placed the burden of hard labor on women. They performed a variety of tasks but were mostly relegated to the fields, where they outnumbered men in the labor gangs into which slaves were divided for efficiency. However, some occupations, including midwifery, nursemaid, and housekeeping, were the preserve of women and were, as such, gender specific.

DIVISION OF LABOR

A somewhat awkward and imprecise hierarchy based on the occupations of the slaves was instituted on the plantations, and it catered to the psychological needs of both slaves and slaveowners. *Commandeurs* or slave drivers of the first gang, along with sugar boilers, specialist slaves, and some domestics, such as the housekeeper and the *hospitalière* (a health care provider), fell into the general category of "elite slaves" or "head people." Most other slaves were designated as *nègres* or *négresses de place*—field slaves. Within this hierarchical division, plantation owners allocated most of the specialized tasks, predominantly artisanal, to men. Thus, as in Africa, slave men maintained their traditional spheres of influence and only they were coopers, carpenters, masons, and blacksmiths. But slaveowners also allotted to men certain nonspecialized tasks, such as driver of the first gang, sugar boiler, messenger, and coach driver. Thus the occupational hierarchy which characterized the plantation society strongly favored males. This hierarchy had other consequences besides economic ones for it reinforced male dominance in Caribbean societies.

Divine ordination aside, was the black woman merely a victim of circumstances that she should have been made to labor so in a strange and hostile environment? For many years, Africanists have demonstrated that in Africa there was more demand for female slaves than for male slaves, that they consistently fetched higher prices, and that they were more valuable than male slaves, not just because of their reproductive capacity but because of the variety of tasks that they could perform. Indeed, Claude Meillassoux argued that in Africa, slave "women were valued above all as workers, mostly because female tasks were predominant in production." Robertson and Klein also noted that in sub-Saharan Africa, the dominant pattern "was for women slaves to do the same things that most free women did, which meant most of the agricultural and virtually all of the domestic work."[9] In the early stages of the development of Caribbean plantations, however, sugar planters had virtually no knowledge of African cultural patterns. They could not have automatically placed black women into the structural slots to which they were traditionally ascribed unless they followed the examples of others who used African slaves, or unless European societies operated along lines similar to African societies in allocating labor. There is no doubt that patriarchy, both European and African, played a role in the black woman's condition, but on the European side there were the added elements of chauvinism and racism. Different standards were applied to the black woman, for even in the worst days of indentureship, the white woman was still seen as somewhat fragile and unsuited for hard labor.

Attitudes toward labor were sometimes personified in satirical stereotypes that ridiculed some groups while making hard work the sole preserve of others. For example, a proverb popular in the seventeenth century held that the French colonies were "hell for Frenchmen and Paradise for their wives; on the other hand, they were hell for Native American women and Paradise for their husbands." The idea was that while Frenchmen worked themselves to death, their wives spent their time beautifying themselves; and while Native American women worked like slaves, their husbands strolled idly about or trimmed their beards.[10] In reality, neither the French nor other Europeans distinguished between Native American males and females; their numbers were virtually wiped out by a combination of brutal treatment and disease. As for Frenchmen, many went to an early grave after a life of hard drinking.

Paradoxically, the French found it convenient to articulate the view that whites could not perform hard labor in the tropics, and promoted African slavery over European indentureship. Governor Houël of Guadeloupe subscribed to this view, as evidenced by a letter he wrote to the king of France in 1647, in which he complained that the few *engagés* who arrived in Guadeloupe were insufficient and lacked the resistance needed for sugar cultivation. Furthermore, they were incapable of adapting to the climate and the food, "such was their predisposition." He hoped that the *engagés* would be supplemented or replaced by African slaves, whose labor he credited for the economic success of Barbados. And yet the classic stereotype of blacks as indolent liars and thieves was pervasive in Saint-Dominque by the eighteenth century.[11]

Governor Houël conceptualized the problem of labor in racial terms, for he implied that whites were incapable of performing hard labor in tropical climates. There is no scientific basis to support this view, and the heavy work that Europeans performed as *engagés*—clearing forests and establishing farms—should have been sufficient to dispel doubts about their physiological state. As we have seen, the bias toward African slave labor prevailed over white European indentured labor. As African slave labor displaced European indentured labor, sugar production became inextricably linked to slavery, with dire consequences for black women and men. From the outset, the sugar plantation was associated with hard, intensive labor and its success in Barbados left little doubt that African slave labor was the key. In 1698, after purchasing twelve slaves for 5,700 francs for the Fond Saint-Jacques Plantation in Martinique owned by his ecclesiastic order, proprietor Père Labat told his superior general that it was "absolutely necessary to have slaves unless we wish to discontinue the work of the sugar operations." He assured his order that while the slaves would be used in other branches of labor, sugar production would not be jeopardized, as sugar was needed to pay for the slaves and to purchase salted meats and other food supplies for them. The exemption from taxes on slaves and other possessions that Louis XIV granted the Jesuits in 1651, in addition to the likely credit they received in this initial transaction, must have been an encouraging beginning.[12]

Paradoxically, hard labor became synonymous with male labor, a primary reason being the preference expressed by Caribbean planters for male rather than female slaves. This preference fit their patriarchal views of work and society, where women were seen as the weaker sex. However, the reality of the plantation made a joke of this gender preference. On sugar plantations in the Caribbean, labor, it is said, was allocated based on the planter's needs and the slave's capacity to work.[13] In reality, need was the primary factor, and it was blind to sexual differentiation.

ORGANIZATION OF LABOR

In the French Caribbean, the law was virtually open ended as to how much labor a slaveowner could demand of a slave. The Code Noir of 1685 placed no limits on the slave's workday, but Article 6 forbade slaveowners from working slaves on Sundays and on such holidays as Ascension, Corpus Christi, All Saints' Day (Toussaint), Christmas, and New Year's Day. If they disobeyed this law slaveowners risked being fined as well as having the state confiscate the slaves they put to work illegally, along with the commodities they produced. Slaves were therefore at the disposal of their owners, except for a limited number of hours that were open to manipulation, so it is not surprising that slaveowners reduced holidays to a bare minimum and worked slaves as they pleased.[14] Pierre de Vassière believed that there ought to have been a law limiting the number of hours slaves could be worked, but that any such law would pose difficulty due to different crop cycles.[15] He drew upon the work of eighteenth-century observers of Saint-Domingue to show that the social condition of the slaves there had not changed much, if at all, over time. As early as 1702, one observer, Monsieur de Galliffet, noted that "the majority of planters . . . worked their slaves beyond human endurance, all day and most of the night."[16] Around the same period, another observer, a Monsieur Deslandes, wrote that "colonists deal with their slaves with the utmost severity; they work them beyond their human endurance and ignore proper feeding and education." Four decades later, in 1742, Monsieur Le Normand de Mézy, a planter and treasurer of Le Cap in the north of Saint-Domingue, wrote that "the condition of slaves in Saint-Domingue is one of working all day long except for a few hours break for lunch."[17]

Field slaves were at the bottom of the slave hierarchy, where women and men labored like beasts for hours on end. They were awakened as early as 5:00 A.M. by the blowing of a conch shell, repeated cracks of the *commandeur's* (slave driver's) whip, or by a bell mounted on a tree on large plantations of a

hundred slaves and more. In addition to the whip, the *commandeur* carried a
club shaped like a French *baguette,* which the slaves nicknamed *coco macaque.*
After prayers, which were obligatory but not always observed, roll call was
taken—a measure which permitted the slave driver to report sick and absent slaves to the *économe* (overseer), who was in charge of the day-to-day
operations of the plantation. It was left to the *économe* and the *gérant (géreur*
in creole)—a manager who ran the plantation in the absence of the *colon*
(owner)—to verify the number of absentees and to ensure the care of the sick,
a daily rate as high as 22 percent on the Lugé Plantation in Saint-Domingue
in the period 1778–91. On some plantations the *régisseur* took the place of the
économe; on others, the *économe* was assisted by a *sous-économe.* However,
the *gérant,* like the overseer in the British Caribbean, was the principal administrator.[18]

Slaves worked until around 8:00 A.M., at which time the *commandeur* directed the convoy of slaves leaving for breakfast, disciplining those who were
late. After a short break, they returned to the fields and worked until noon,
when they were given a two-hour break to eat and rest. Normally, an elderly
slave woman or a pregnant slave close to term cooked for the slave gang. During the lunch break, the slaves could take the food to their huts if nearby or
eat in the fields. Slaves often worked on different fields in the afternoons depending on labor needs. At around 2:00 P.M., they returned to the field once
more, this time to work until sunset and sometimes as late as 11:00 P.M., depending on the crop cycle. Before leaving, each slave gathered animal feed or
firewood. According to Jacques Cauna, "No one left with empty hands." After
the evening meal, prayers, and the taking of a head count, slaves were free to
return to their huts. The only exception to this routine was at harvest time,
when slaves were required to work at night. During this period, the workday
lasted for about eighteen hours, and the other six were often dedicated to
searching for food.[19]

At the end of the seventeenth century, Pére Labat estimated that a sugar
plantation with 120 slaves required 25 slaves (20 percent) to cut canes and another 16 (13 percent) to work in manufacturing sugar and distilling rum. But
sugar manufacturing was done not only by males but by females, who labored
in the fields during the day and the mill works at night. That being the case,
Labat's figures suggest that a little more than one-third of the slave force was
involved in field labor. About 12 percent of the slaves were artisans, while 15
percent were engaged in diverse occupations (mostly manual) such as cutting
wood, transporting merchandise, guarding animals, and caring for the sick.
Labat allotted 5 percent of the slaves to domestic chores. When elderly, infirm,
and sick slaves, as well as child slaves are taken into consideration—a total of
42 slaves (35 percent)—there can be little doubt that field slaves, who were
mainly women, were the backbone of the sugar economy.

Since technology was limited during this period, field slaves cleared and prepared the fields for cultivation using the basic hoe. They planted sugar cane cuttings, kept the fields free of weeds through regular weeding, and cut and transported sugar cane to the mill site, where they also worked in the manufacturing end of the sugar works. Women field slaves, in particular, distilled rum from molasses, a by-product of sugar. They also cultivated individual and collective garden plots, which provided food to sustain the slave force. Women marketed some of the produce grown on individual plots, thereby acquiring a personal source of income that gave them a measure of independence from the strict confines of the plantation.

Women made up the majority of slaves in the field gangs, which varied in number according to need. Though a single, primary gang was the choice of some planters, on most plantations slaves were divided into two gangs and occasionally three. The first gang or *grand atelier* (great gang) consisted of the strongest male and female slaves above fourteen years of age, who performed the most arduous tasks. On the Bréda Plantation in the north of Saint-Domingue, slaves entered this gang at seventeen years, which suggests that there was variation from plantation to plantation. Less robust slaves, newly arrived slaves who had to be acclimatized, pregnant slaves, and nursing mothers made up the second gang, whose importance varied according to the agricultural calendar, the health of the slaves, and the interest of the planters. The third slave gang was made up of children (where numbers warranted) between the ages of eight and thirteen years, who worked under the supervision of an elderly female slave performing what were considered to be small tasks.

Plantations depended primarily on the great gang for the heavy labor that made them economically viable. It is no wonder that this gang was always led by a stringent and exacting male slave driver who had a stake in the system and who was regarded by planters as the most precious slave on any estate. According to Debien, it was the slave driver of this gang who decided on the timing and execution of labor tasks and determined which slaves would be allocated to them. The slave driver had a sense of how long a task would take and could assess the strength of individual slaves. The work of the great gang was the most arduous and included clearing and preparing the soil. According to Maurice Satineau, this task required great care so that the canes could grow without obstruction. Runners not only had to be cut but dug out of the soil to prevent them, or other weeds, from attaching themselves to the canes and destroying them within a short time. Trees were normally cut to a meter above ground if they could not be removed altogether. These tasks, in addition to the removal of rocks and the digging of irrigation canals, were done only by first-gang male slaves, however.[20]

First-gang slaves had to plant and cut the canes as well as cultivate food crops. Canes were planted in squares a meter apart, or in rows. The seventeenth-century method that Père Labat described, of sugar cane planted in parallel rows, has gone through modifications, but Dale Tomich's version of the holing method is as good as any. "With a hoe and a stake," he explained, slaves

> formed a line across the field. A *commandeur* stood at each end of the line and stretched between them a cord that was knotted or marked at regular intervals. Each slave put his or her stake in the ground at the mark and proceeded to dig a hole two feet square and nine inches deep. After it was completed, three cane cuttings prepared in advance were placed in it. If the planter used fertilizer, a quantity of manure was applied; if not, the plant was re-covered with dirt, leaving a centimeter of the stem exposed. The slaves then moved ahead to dig the next hole. Each slave had to dig about 28 holes an hour, depending on soil conditions.[21]

Barry Higman's calculation of the work involved in holing in the British Caribbean is also relevant, as it speaks of the magnitude of slave women's labor contribution. Higman noted that the "number of holes dug in a day varied between 60 and 100, or even 120; depending on the dimensions of the holes and the stiffness of the soil." This means that "the slave digging an average of 80 holes moved between 640 and 1,500 cubic feet of earth per day."[22] Stated in different terms, "A field gang of thirty slaves, working with hoes, could hole or trench two acres in a day."[23]

Holing was a particularly demanding task across the Caribbean, where soil types varied widely. In areas where the land was clayey or stiff, as in Antigua, holing "imposed a heavy physical strain on the slaves, and it had the additional disadvantage that it prejudiced the planters against the use of cattle in manuring the field which was to be planted."[24] In Guadeloupe the soil was more variable than in Antigua, but some soils were clayey and compact. Even so, planters neglected to use manure, believing in the natural fertility of the soil. Though it was introduced during the era of indentureship and used in tobacco and indigo cultivation, the plow was phased out once sugar became dominant. Lavollée blamed its high price and unsuitable soils, but the availability and low cost of slave labor were the major variables.[25]

The tasks that slaves in the second gang performed were lighter and more varied than those of the first gang, but were demanding nonetheless. Weeding was a main occupation of this gang. Tomich highlighted the importance of weeding to cane cultivation in Martinique during slavery when he noted that it "had a great effect on how well the plants grew and how much sugar they yielded. Grasses that would choke off the plants if left unchecked had to be cleared. . . . Weeding usually continued until the cane was between 7 and 10 months old. The frequency of weeding depended upon the quality of the soil and the amount of rain. Nearly everywhere on the island, the cane had to be weeded from four to six times."[26]

Besides weeding, second-gang slaves also cultivated millet, corn, and other food crops, spread manure in the cane and coffee fields, transported ashes from the furnaces to the field, gathered weeds for animal feed, and bundled the *bagasse*—sugar cane residue used as firewood for the sugar mill furnaces. On some sugar plantations, weeding was the occupation of women in this gang.[27]

Slaves in the third gang picked weeds and gathered cane trash and *bagasse* from around the mill. Each child carried a basket, hence the term "basket children." The existence of a gang of child slaves depended not only on the number of child slaves on a plantation but also on their health and the socio-economic status of slaveowners and their overseers. According to Debien, the poorer the slaveowner, the greater the chances of a child slave gang.[28]

The work that women performed in the first gang, in particular, gave credence to the association between slaves and beasts of burden. In the mid-seventeenth century, Père Pelleprat wrote that the "French use neither oxen nor horses in cultivating the soil. They only use slaves from Africa or the distant shores of America."[29] Père Labat also observed that "slaves performed the work of horses, transporting merchandise from one place to the other."[30] Girod-Chantrans, a Swiss traveler who visited Saint-Domingue in the eighteenth century, captured the association between slaves and beasts of burden when he remarked that "there is no domestic animal from which as much work is required as slaves, and to which as little care is given."[31] Without distinction, male and female slaves—the "vile populace," as he saw them—"were destined to the hardest of labor and the most barbarous punishment for the least fault." He also noted that the slave driver used his whip "indiscriminately on animals and slaves."[32] Girod-Chantrans brought out the rigorous nature of the work performed by first-gang slaves and drew no distinction between males and females. The gang consisted of

> about a hundred men and women of different ages, all occupied in digging ditches in a cane-field, the majority of them naked or covered with rags. The sun shone down with full force on their heads. Sweat rolled from all parts of their bodies. Their limbs, weighed down by the heat, fatigued with the weight of their picks and by the resistance of the clayey soil baked hard enough to break their implements, strained themselves to overcome every obstacle. A mournful silence reigned. Exhaustion was stamped on every face, but the hour of rest had not yet come. The pitiless eye of the manager patrolled the gang as several foremen armed with long whips moved periodically between them, giving stinging blows to all who, worn out by fatigue, were compelled to take a rest, men or women, young or old, without distinction.[33]

The driver of the third gang was a woman who often served a dual purpose. She not only administered discipline to those in the gang but was able, according to Poyen de Sainte-Marie, to care for younger slaves. The plantation did not subject the leader of this gang to much scrutiny before awarding her the position, but Poyen de Sainte-Marie underlined its importance by stressing the tender care which he felt only women, the "gentler sex," could provide, and the education which they were uniquely positioned to impart to young slaves. In effect, these women socialized young slaves into slavery. To quote Poyen de Sainte-Marie:

> The primary task of the female driver of the child gang must be the preservation of the children's health. She must monitor them constantly and prevent them from eating harmful substances. She must teach them how to perform all their duties well and stimulate the quick-witted to make the effort to conform. She must also instruct them to obey orders without question and to resist bickering among themselves. As nothing accounts more for laziness among blacks than chigoe [chigger] infection, she must inspect, clean and remove chigoes from their feet daily. At a young age, children are very receptive. Thus, much depends on authority figures who mold them into either good or bad subjects. Those who execute their task well merit much from their masters. On the other hand, those who neglect their tasks and shatter the planters' confidence are guilty.[34]

The disproportionate number of black women in the field gangs was striking indeed. Numerous examples of this labor pattern are mentioned in the work of Gabriel Debien. Debien's demographic study of the Bréda Plantation in the North Plain of Saint-Domingue listed 210 slaves individually by ethnic group, age, sex, and occupation. It shows that of 89 adult males on April 1, 1789, 36 (40.4 percent) were field workers. But about 72 (87.8 percent) of the 82 adult female slaves were field workers. Also, 15 (21 percent) of the women field slaves were aged fifty and older, among them the one-armed, fifty-two-year-old Constance. Apart from the washerwoman, a servant, the fifty-one-year-old nurse, and the fifty-three-year-old child-slave guardian, all able-bodied women were field workers, including 15 creole women. By contrast, male slaves were heavily represented in the industrial side of the sugar operations as boilers; they also worked in the skilled trades and as valets and watchmen. An equal number of men and women were nonworkers. Whereas 4 of the 6 men not working were over fifty years old, however, the 6 women ranged in age from twenty-nine to thirty-eight. Given their age, it is possible that pregnancy may have been a factor. According to Debien, slaves at age fifty were considered old and were only allowed to remain in the great gang if they had a strong constitution.[35]

Two other poignant examples of the predominance of women in field labor can be taken from the Citronniers district of Léogane in Saint-Domingue. The first of these comes from the Plantation Beaulieu, where there were 141 slaves in 1768, of whom 87 were males and 54 females. But only 9 males (9.6 percent) worked in the fields, whereas 20 (37 percent) of the females were field workers.[36] In 1768 a similar labor division existed on the Galbaud du Fort Plantation, where female slaves slightly outnumbered male slaves but performed almost all the field work. Of the 54 males on the plantation, only 9 (16.6 percent) were in the fields. But 44 (75.8 percent) of the 58 females were field workers. Also, on the Flauriau Plantation in Saint-Domingue in the late eighteenth century, 60 (75 percent) of the 80 slaves working in the fields were women.[37]

A list of 218 slaves mostly from Martinique, Guadeloupe, and French Guiana who were granted freedom in 1847 reinforces Vanony-Frisch's findings. It contains mainly women field slaves. French grammar makes it possible to make this assertion as the slaves were listed by occupations in the masculine and feminine noun forms. Moreover, there are instances in which two and three generations of slave women are all confined to field work. For example, fifty-two-year-old Geneviève of Martinique was listed along with her three daughters, Marthe-Louise, thirty-two, Augustine, twenty-four, and Jeanne-Rose, eleven—all field workers. While the women worked in the fields, Auge, fifty-three, Genviève's husband, cracked the whip in his role as slave driver. Likewise, Célestre, forty, of Guadeloupe, was a field worker, while her husband, Pierre-Louis, fifty-eight, was a slave driver. Another Guadeloupean woman slave, Séverine, forty-six, was also a field worker while her husband, Pierre-Noël, fifty-one, was a sugar boiler.[38]

The association between slave women and field work is also brought out by the case of the forty-year-old field slave Félicie of Guadeloupe. She had eight children ranging in age from one to fifteen years. Her fifteen-year-old daughter, Célaine, also worked in the fields, as did her other daughters: Eugénie, fourteen, Angélina, eleven, and Marie-Gabrielle, nine. Her only son, Félix, nine, was a field slave as well, but the fields would have been the only place for him at that age. Félicie's other children, age five and under, were too young to work.

Many other such cases were common among women slaves from French Guiana, such as Mémée, thirty-eight, a field slave married to thirty-eight-year-old Wacoulé (Emder), a slave driver. But there were also women slaves like Marie-Rose the sixth, seventy-nine, who gave religious instruction to young slaves on the Gabrielle Plantation. Several older women collected *roukou,* a red grain used to make sauces. (In the French Antilles, *roukou* is still used to flavor the broth in which fish—preferably red snapper—is simmered, a dish people of the region call court bouillon.) At the same time, men pursued a variety of specialized tasks and engaged in knackery (hunting wild animals), a popular occupation in French Guiana, where wildlife abounded.[39] These examples show that the working lives of most slave women changed little over time. Vanony-Frisch's study of 8,820 slaves in Guadeloupe between 1770 and 1789 shows that of 735 slaves with listed occupations, women constituted only

176 or 24 percent. Even then, only 5 percent of the adults in this group (mostly mixed-race women) had a precise and specific occupation. Male slaves—Africans, creoles, and those of mixed race—dominated the specialized occupations.[40]

French scholars have acknowledged the numerical superiority of female over male slaves in the field gangs, but have generally accepted this labor division as the natural order of things. Like Michael Craton, who has found it "a curious society, as well as an inefficient agricultural economy, in which women for the most part were the laborers and men the specialist workers,"[41] and Hilary Beckles, who explains it by saying that West African women were "acculturised to agricultural tasks, more so than men, and might have been considered more adaptable, at least in the short run,"[42] they have attempted to put this issue into proper perspective. In the nineteenth century, André Lacharière expressed the opinion that in the French Antilles such a labor division "will become more serious and will have a negative effect on reproduction. For this reason, there is no item more important and worthy for the legislature to concentrate upon than on the increase by reproduction of the agricultural population whose maintenance is indispensable to the existence of the colonies."[43]

However self-serving it may be, Lacharière's comment strengthens the view that although slave women were primarily used as labor units, they were still expected to reproduce. Victor Schoelcher, the philanthropist who sought to dramatize the plight of the slaves in the French colonies during the nineteenth century as part of the antislavery struggle, believed that slave "women were perfectly suited to field work" and attributed the larger presence of women in the fields to the systematic promotion of young male slaves from fieldwork to artisanal and other types of specialized labor.[44] That is to say, since men possessed most of the skills that plantations required, they monopolized all the skilled labor tasks, leaving the heavy tasks which required no skills to women. As he explained,

> It is often the case in the field gangs that there are more women than men. This is how it can be explained. A plantation is, in itself, a small village. As it is usually established a considerable distance from major centers, it must provide all of its needs . . . masons and blacksmiths as well as animal watchmen. All the apprentices who are destined to replace them are now in the field gangs (the [slave] driver included) and this diminishes the male population available for field work.[45]

This explanation has become institutionalized. Indeed, Gabriel Debien noted that there were always roofs rent by the wind and broken walls to repair, roads to improve, bridges to build—work that male slaves could do. Planters aimed to get much of this work done after the canes had been cut, but the work often dragged on for many weeks due to interruptions by hurricanes and other problems.[46] In the last quarter of the eighteenth century, some of the male slaves on the Boucassin and Vases Plantations in Saint-Domingue loaded barrels of sugar onto vessels and performed corvée labor in public works. As elsewhere, males engaged in a host of artisanal tasks. Whereas the ablest and strongest men were promoted in time to acquire enviable positions, becoming sugar boilers and other specialists, women had few positions which would have exempted them from field labor. Debien and Beckles have argued, quite correctly, that at the same age there was no differential in production between males and females; it is just that women spent their lifetime in the fields. According to Debien, women "were better adapted than men to continuous work in the fields, perhaps because work outside the plantation and cane-cutting—a task reserved for men—were considered to be the most demanding. As much as possible, it was seen as desirable for women to stay on the plantations. . . . They were never conscripted for forced labor for the state. It may also be that women were easier to subjugate or were less subject to illness."[47]

Debien is suggesting that gender restricted women's mobility and the occupations to which they were assigned. This is more plausible than his assertion that men did more strenuous work; they did not. It also underestimates the value of women's labor to state that cane cutting was a male occupation, for it was not. Nor was corvée labor, which included public works projects such as construction and road building, restricted to male slaves only. A list of dead slaves from the sugar plantation Noël in Remire in French Guiana includes the slave woman Doué. She gave birth prematurely to a stillborn boy and died on August 28, 1690, after returning from doing corvée labor during which she contracted a fever, a common occurrence among corvée gangs.[48]

The gendered division of labor means that women were put into structural slots that had no bearing on their abilities. Thus women were not permitted to move into roles traditionally performed by males. Their social condition was full of irony in that slaveowners disregarded the sex of slaves, ignored gender conventions at will, and treated them as labor units and not as individuals. Male slaves had opportunities to learn trades. It would have been counterproductive for planters to hire artisans to compete with slave labor. The experience of indentureship in the seventeenth century demonstrated this. Moreover, many of the Africans who came to the Caribbean as slaves were qualified artisans. Planters therefore encouraged a system of apprenticeship. Clive Thomas suggested that apprenticeship was vital to the success of the plantations when he argued that "To run factories efficiently and supervise cultivation, a strata of skilled and trained workers in field and factory had to be provided."[49] On the plantations, skills were indeed passed down through an apprenticeship system which gave young male slaves opportunities to acquire skills. To be sure, the allocation of tasks excluded slave women from most of the elite occupations, as a result of which they "suffered far more than male slaves from inevitable restriction to their ascribed occupations. Confined to the lower ranks, their opportunities of social mobility were severely limited."[50]

CANE CUTTING

Cane cutting, a task requiring no special skills, was performed by women and men in the first gang using a bill—a flat curved tool—or a cutlass. Père Labat's reason (however flawed) for assigning only twenty-five slaves to cut canes on the Fond Saint-Jacques Plantation was that, since it "was the lightest of tasks, women do just as much of it as men." This may well have been his reason for assigning mostly women to this work.[51] Cane cutting was, however, long and laborious and required constant bending. Care had to be taken to avoid being cut by the sharp cane leaves, an effort made more difficult by the fact that slaves were poorly clothed.

Slaves cut canes constantly from January to about July each year—the harvest period when labor needs were at their maximum. After July they did so five to six days per month, but there were variations in this schedule across plantations. The pressure on slave women was probably substantial during the harvest, as the sugar mill operated around the clock and had to be continuously fed with canes. As Dunn explained, "Harvesting, milling, and boiling required close synchronization. The cane, once cut, had to be crushed within a few hours before its sugar content deteriorated. The cane juice, once extracted, had to be boiled within a few hours before it fermented."[52]

The importance of timing is also brought out by Labat, who mentioned the custom of starting the cane-cutting on Saturdays so that there would be enough canes to begin the grinding process just after midnight on Sundays, when the Sunday break period for slaves ended. As canes were normally harvested everywhere at the same time, planters could not rely on one another for supplementary labor. And the canes had to be cut irrespective of illness among the slaves and the inevitable hurricanes. Harvest was also the period when the labor of the slaves in the first gang was heavily drawn upon to supplement the labor in the mills.[53]

MILL FEEDING

Sugar manufacturing involves the transformation of juice extracted from the sugar cane into crystallized sugar through a process of heating. As it was, a number of first-gang slaves, male and female, worked at the mill site. Some stoked the furnace and skimmed the boiling cane juice in the evaporating pans. Dale Tomich noted that these "were two of the most physically exhausting jobs on the plantation, and females were exempt from them." Cognizant of the intense heat and prolonged stench associated with sugar boiling, Tomich stressed the stamina that these tasks required, noting that "only the most robust slaves were given this job."[54]

Much has also been made of the role of the sugar boiler, who, in Dunn's words, was "the most valued laborer on the plantation staff" in the British Caribbean. This is because he turned raw cane juice into sugar by means of a long, tedious, and complicated process that required sound judgment and an acute sense of timing. Simply put, the planter's profit margin depended on the quality of the sugar the plantation manufactured, which means that the economic fate of the estate lay in the hands of a slave—the boiler. In the French Antilles, the head boiler was usually a white male, in which case the position was mostly nominal. The plantation relied on slave sugar boilers, who made every effort to safeguard the intricacies of their craft from whites, preferring instead to pass their skills on to other slaves. Whether white or black, head boilers were assisted by subordinate boilers, slaves who were all regarded as "kings of the slave gangs, receiving a larger portion of rations than field slaves, including beef or salt fish and *guildive* (local rum) daily." It is no wonder that the position was so highly sought after.[55]

The prestige of the sugar boiler and the exacting nature of the work of other male slaves at the mill notwithstanding, women's labor in the field and in sugar manufacturing was just as crucial as the labor that males performed; it was also more sustained and hazardous. An appreciation of women's contribution can be gained from considering their work at the sugar mill, whose technological shortcomings could have dire consequences. Women worked mostly with mills powered by animal traction, but some mills were powered by water and wind. All three varieties were a rudimentary form of technology that remained in place throughout the slavery period in the French Antilles, although not in Jamaica, where steam power was used in the eighteenth century. These were three-roller vertical mills designed to crush the canes placed between the revolving rollers, but they were inefficient and costly to operate.[56]

The slaves who fed canes into the sugar mills were women who worked on four- to six-hour shifts in addition to doing fieldwork. Père Labat has left a detailed description of mill feeding which reveals a great deal about women's labor. On many estates during his time, at least four women worked at the mill, but most often the nature of the work required five. The women were particularly taxed when the canes from the fields arrived at the mill so rapidly that there was hardly time to clean the equipment—a necessary measure which ensured the smooth running of the mechanism. When working with water-driven mills, which ground the canes much faster than wind- or animal-driven mills, or when the huts in which they stored *bagasse* were far from the mill, women also had to work harder.

After bundles of canes were brought to the mill by animal-drawn carts, one woman carried them inside. If time permitted, she arranged them into piles to the left of the principal mill-feeder, who positioned them on top of the mill table for feeding. If she was pressed for time, she simply dumped the bundle and went out to fetch others. Among other things, the first mill-feeder had to decide how much cane could safely be fed into the rollers. When the work piled up and she was in a hurry, she cut the two cords which held the bundles of sugarcane together with a bill and pushed the canes between the first two rollers.

The mill-feeder took greater risks when working with water-driven mills. The high speed of the mills meant that she seldom had the time to untie the bundles, and fed one tied bundle after another. Labat believed that this practice should have been discouraged, as "such great quantities of cane put enormous stress on the mill, forcing the rollers to expand in which case they extracted less juice."[57] However, Labat also recommended that mills be constantly and steadily fed. In no case should canes fed into the mill emerge at the outer end without others being fed in.

A second mill-feeder, positioned at the opposite end of the mill facing the first mill-feeder, received the crushed sugarcane. She folded it and fed it back between the first and third rollers so that the maximum juice could be extracted. One and sometimes two other women assembled the *bagasse* that was extracted from the rollers. They bundled and transported it to a large shed, where it was stored, dried, and used as firewood for the copper kettles in the boiling house. Small pieces which could not be bundled were gathered in wicker baskets and dumped near the mill as animal feed, especially for horses, cows, and pigs. When the storage huts were too far from the mill, the women were often too pressed to bundle the *bagasse* and resorted to dumping it as animal feed in order to rush back to the mill to retrieve more residue. This deprived the operations of valuable firewood which lit quickly.[58]

Mill-feeding was a vital part of the manufacturing process, but the toll it took on slave women has been virtually ignored. Gabriel Debien acknowledged that mill-feeding was dangerous work usually done by slave women, but that "for better food rations, one could attract as many volunteers as necessary to do difficult jobs where accidents were frequent." This does not explain why mill-feeding was exclusively female. Mill-feeders were given about the same rations as sugar boilers, but the dangers involved would hardly have made the extra pickings attractive. Planters considered mill-feeding women's work and work that dishonored male slaves. In fact, Labat used it as a form of punishment. He assigned the second woman mill-feeder's work to male slaves whom he deemed slack or lazy. Feeding crushed sugarcane into the mill was supposedly a task given to the weakest woman slave at the mill. This position did not require strenuous effort, but it involved hazards nevertheless.[59]

Fraught with danger, the grinding process was a continuous operation during the harvest period, when labor was particularly intensive and slaves were taxed to the limit. Apart from miscarriages and other misfortunes which women alone experienced, female slaves suffered numerous accidents at the mill site that often resulted in infirmity and death. The danger of being crushed by the rollers was ever present, for as soon as canes or fingers touched the edge of the rollers they were drawn rapidly into the machinery. Accidents were frequent at night when mill-feeders were fatigued from laboring in the cane fields all day. Graphic though it may be, Père Labat's description of the accidents that resulted in the maiming and death of mill-feeders is a stark and dreadful reminder of the perils that slave women at work faced long ago, and is worth citing in full. To quote Labat:

> They [accidents] are certainly frequent among female slaves . . . particularly at night, when, exhausted by hard labor during the daytime and full of slumber, they fall asleep while passing the canes. Dragged towards the machinery which they follow involuntarily still clutching the canes in their hands, they thus become caught up in it and crushed before they can be rescued. This is particularly the case when the mill is water-driven for the movement is so rapid that it is physically impossible to stop it in time to save the lives of those whose fingers are already drawn in. On such occasions, the quickest remedy is to promptly sever the arm with a bill (which is why it makes sense to always keep one without the curved tip at the head of the table, sharp and ready to use if needed). It is better to cut off the arm than to see a person passing through the rollers of a mill. This precaution has been very useful to us at Fond S[aint] Jacques where one of our women slaves was drawn into the mill. Fortunately for her, . . . a male slave was able to stop the mill on time to give us the opportunity to sever half of the mangled arm, and thus save the rest of her body.
>
> A woman slave belonging to the Jesuits was not as fortunate. In attempting to pass something to the woman on the other side of the mill, her shirt sleeves became caught in the cogs, and her arm, followed by the rest of her body was drawn into the machinery in an instant, before she could be helped. Only the head does not pass; it separates from the neck and falls on the side where the body entered.[60]

Planters did not focus on these accidents, no doubt because slaves were considered dispensable, but it is highly probable that they occurred in all the French Caribbean colonies. In 1699 a woman slave owned by a Monsieur Gressier of Trois Rivières, Guadeloupe, suffered an accident similar to the ones that Labat described. One of her hands became caught in the machinery. She attempted to free it with her other hand, but both became entangled.

Hearing her cries for help, the sugar boiler on duty rushed to her assistance, trying to extricate her arms from the rollers. At the same time, another male slave wedged a piece of iron between the moving cogs of the mill to stop it. But the force of the water-driven mill cracked a cog, forcing out the piece of iron, which then lodged between the spinning rollers. The pieces of shrapnel which this explosion created were so forcefully ejected that they punctured the stomach of the slave who installed the iron wedge, in addition to fracturing his head. Meanwhile, backed by the increased force of the water, the rollers drew the sugar boiler in along with the woman mill-feeder, killing them both.[61]

Writing in 1845, Jean-Baptiste Rouvellat de Cussac mentioned that a woman slave had a hand crushed by the mill, a common occurrence. In another incident on a plantation near Fort-Royal, Martinique, a twelve-year-old girl was crushed by the rollers, her head falling on top of the mill table. In this instance the accident was blamed on the *économe,* who normally supervised night work.[62] These cases indicate that working conditions around the mill remained hazardous. Also, while Rouvellat de Cussac and others might have highlighted such cases to enhance the struggle for abolition, which they favored, the use of young girls as mill-feeders suggests that there was little regard for females, whatever their age. Also, young girls may have been pressed into service of this kind without consideration to age, depending on the need of the plantation. It is possible that some mill-feeders lost fingers rather than their lives. Several advertisements of slaves in prison described women, but not men, as having missing digits. In 1788 the black slave woman Lucille, aged thirty to thirty-five, an inmate of the Pointe-à-Pitre prison in Guadeloupe, had a missing finger on her left hand. It could hardly be chance that the black slave woman Marie-Anne, aged forty-five, a maroon detained in the Pointe-à-Pitre prison in 1788, had three missing fingers on her right hand and two on her left hand. Théresse, aged twenty-two, another black woman detained in the Pointe-à-Pitre prison in 1788, had four missing fingers on her left hand. All of the women with missing digits were field slaves from whose ranks mill-feeders were drawn.[63]

Père Labat had important advice for those who had the good fortune of stopping the machinery when a limb became entangled in the rollers. The drums should be moved backwards, the rollers loosened, and the limb removed to prevent additional compression from taking place. But he also believed that slave women could avoid accidents at the mill by adopting preventative measures. They should avoid standing on racks or other objects to gain a height advantage in performing their duties, particularly the second mill-feeder, who handled *bagasse.* Also, since slumber was the principal cause of accidents, planters must ensure that the women smoked and sang as they worked. How this was to be achieved is not clear. Normally, the sugar boiler acted as a supervisor, but he was not necessarily in sight of the women. Planters put the emphasis on preventing women from slumbering, but the problem was fatigue caused by overwork and unsafe working conditions. Indeed, during the harvest in Saint-Domingue, observers in the 1780s heard the constant grinding of the sugar mills, day and night. This was also the case in other areas such as Jamaica, where women suffered similar accidents.[64]

Although she cites no evidence, Arlette Gautier may well be right in attributing the high incidence of infirmity among women to mill-feeding, which remained, according to the iconography of the region, a woman's preserve until the end of slavery.[65] Records from the Bréda Plantation in Saint-Domingue show a larger number of elderly women than men, but also a larger proportion of infirm women than men. There were also more women (mainly field slaves) than men who were considered old and worn-out though they had not yet reached age sixty. Of eighty-nine adult males in 1784, nine were infirm; of eighty-two adult women, fifteen were infirm. What is significant is that the Bréda Plantation may have been better than most in its treatment of slaves. For many years the overseer, Bayon de Libertat, patron of Toussaint-Louverture, a slave on the plantation who was to become a principal leader in the Saint-Domingue revolution, had a reputation for being fairer than others in working slaves.[66]

Women swept the sugar works and washed and cleaned the vertical rollers with a broom and water. Père Labat indicated that the mill tables also had to be properly washed. Women washed the muslin used in the filtering process as well. These tasks appear simple enough, but the actions of planters hint at the importance they attached to the cleaning of the sugar works. In 1846 the slaves Jeanne, Louise, Cadet, Céeré, Joseph, and Adélaïde—children of the field slave Jenny—were given fifteen strokes each, as Lehimas, manager of a sugar plantation in the district of Prêcheur, Martinique, was displeased with the cleaning job they had done.[67]

RUM DISTILLATION

The distillation of local rum was important work performed by slave women in the French Antilles. In fact, the Rochechouart Plantation in Martinique had two women distillers.[68] This strong rum, which the slaves called *tafia* or *guldive,* was made at the *vinaigrerie* (vinegar factory), a place which Labat correctly acknowledged should have been more appropriately called the *distilatoire* (distillery). Local usage of *vinaigrerie* had been so ingrained, however, that it remained in vogue. The fact is that women made rum, not vinegar. The label *vinaigrerie* may well have devalued, in the minds of many, the skills required to make this economic activity a success.

The reasons why planters preferred women distillers are cynical if not patronizing, however. They assumed that women were less apt to drink than men. Even so, they had no confidence in women's ability to abstain. Thus they selected slave women considered loyal, and carefully monitored their behavior in an attempt to prevent them from yielding to the temptation of overindulgence. To guard against this possibility and to deter them from stealing, Labat occasionally gave women distillers a jar of *tafia*. It would be interesting to find out whether this form of bribery was successful in light of the fact that there was a local market for *tafia*.[69]

The sale of *tafia* accounted for an important part of a planter's revenue.[70] Besides being shipped abroad, it was sold in the colonies. In late seventeenth-century Martinique, it fetched six *sols* per jar, and more in areas not engaged in sugar production. When wines and liquor from France were scarce, *tafia* fetched higher prices as well. With 120 (the entire slave force) slaves working steadily for forty-five days per year, Labat calculated that the Fond Saint-Jacques Plantation produced sixty barrels of *tafia*, of which at least fifty-four could be sold. It is no wonder that the distillery was off limits to unauthorized slaves.[71]

Women's labor in the distillery enabled planters to defray their costs and shirk their responsibilities to slaves. Indeed, some masters gave slaves a quantity of *tafia* per week in place of flour and meat—a clear violation of the Code Noir. Labat observed that such slaves were sometimes forced "to roam about on Sundays trying to trade their liquor for flour and other essentials. This they use as a pretext for arriving very late and tired for work on Mondays. Those who drink their supplies are forced to steal from their masters at the risk of being killed or imprisoned."[72]

On January 1, 1717, a decree prohibited planters in Martinique from giving slaves *tafia* in place of food. Later laws, such as that passed in Saint-Domingue on June 20, 1772, prohibited slaves from selling wine or *tafia*. Citing low price, easy access, and potential health risks, administrators in Saint-Domingue banned its sale in taverns and on plantations except in barrels or other large quantities, which slaves could not afford. A similar ruling in 1785 suggests that slaves still marketed *tafia*, which may indicate that slaveowners continued to distribute it to them as a substitute for food, or that they had a thriving business with stock obtained from plantation stores.[73]

Besides distilling *tafia*, women did a number of odd jobs around the mill and distillery that sometimes involved heavy lifting. Women transported cane syrup and scum from the mill to the woman distiller. Women also changed the hot copper kettles and lifted and loaded merchandise into small boats. We may never know for sure what physical, social, and psychological impact these occupations had on slave women, and how they dealt with them. Many women survived to old age, but most did not. The combination of factors that determined survival would have varied from plantation to plantation and would have included biological, social, and environmental variables. The temptation to speculate in the absence of concrete data is strong, but the act of survival in and by itself was an important dimension of resistance in slave society.

HOUSEHOLD PRODUCTION AND MARKETING

The workday left field slaves little time for themselves, but slave women in particular used their break periods and Sundays to cultivate kitchen gardens on plots of land allotted by their owners. They also engaged in small-scale independent production and petty trade. There were two types of slave plots. One was a small plot of land around the slave huts, which were called *polinks* in the British Caribbean; the other was a common plot at the extremities of the main plantation fields. Slaves cultivated crops such as peas, peppers, manioc, and sweet potatoes on both plots, but crops such as millet and yams appear to have been reserved for the common plot, whose produce slaveowners used as weekly rations for the entire slave force.

By engaging in food production, women inadvertently subsidized their owners and prevented the slave system from collapsing. Under Article 22 of the Code Noir, slaveowners were obliged to provide specific quantities of food that the French referred to as the *ordinaire*. Slaves over ten years of age were to be given two and a half measures of manioc flour or three cassavas weighing at least two and a half pounds each, or the equivalent in other food. Slaveowners also had to provide two pounds of salted beef or three pounds of salted fish, or the equivalent. Child slaves under ten years were to receive half of the weekly rations allotted to adult slaves. However, slaveowners reneged on their obligations to feed slaves, as evidenced by the numerous ordinances drafted by administrators and local councils in the French colonies beginning in the period before the Code Noir and continuing to the end of slavery. The ordinances usually required slaveowners to cultivate specific quantities of provisions to ensure the proper feeding of slaves, but they were all to no avail. As Labat noted, "slaves who received what the King's Ordinance authorized were lucky." In 1696 he boasted about providing extra food rations to slaves in order to ensure that they could support hard labor, "which I do not wish to see slacken, even among the female slaves." Some planters resorted to giving slaves Saturdays off in place of food rations, hence the term *samedi nègre*. Others gave Sundays as a rest day. Still others offered quantities of *tafia*, though these actions contravened Article 24 of the Code Noir. The result was that many slaves went hungry and consequently turned to stealing to survive, and were sometimes killed in the act. Many other slaves simply took to the woods. In a circular of 1818, the lieutenant governor of Guadeloupe complained about the practice of giving Sundays in place of food and attempted, at this late stage, to prohibit it through legislation, but without success.[74]

Some slaves cultivated while others hired themselves out on Saturdays in return for food, produce, or cash. According to Debien, the tendency was for women to cultivate their gardens and for men to seek paid employment.[75] Du Tertre indicated that colonists generally preferred the hired-out system to borrowing slaves from their neighbors, and they gave hired slaves tobacco as wages. Other slaves were fed and given ten *livres* of tobacco for a day's work. Planters regarded the granting of Saturdays or Sundays as a privilege, and they withdrew it from individual slaves or the whole plantation gang at will, particularly when there was a failure to meet production quotas or when slaves turned to *marronnage* and committed acts of theft and other crimes and did not divulge who the guilty parties were. In the 1840s Rouvellat de Cussac wrote, "I know a slave woman who was deprived of Saturdays in very similar circumstances. She would no doubt have died of hunger had a male slave from a neighboring plantation not shared manioc flour and root crops with her."[76]

Dale Tomich has argued that slaves "felt that they had a right to such 'free' time and resisted any encroachment upon it."[77] But it is clear from the foregoing that the allocation of "free" time was at the whim of slaveowners. To be sure, slaveowners had the power to enforce their wishes, but the slaves' capacity to resist placed limits on the use of that power. Indeed, although their labor was exploited by the plantation, slave women used household production and marketing skills acquired in Africa to accumulate resources that they then used to improve their condition and even combat slavery. As marketeers, women bucked the system as much as possible. A pass had to be obtained from the slaveowner or the manager on Saturday evenings. In a circular dated July 30, 1818, the lieutenant governor of Guadeloupe made it clear that all slaves were required to obtain passes signed and detailed by their owners in order to sell items such as charcoal and manioc flour outside their districts. With pass in hand, slaves could leave early Sunday morning to return at sunset. On many plantations, however, slaves left without passes. Also, "there was a traffic in false passes where dates were adjusted according to circumstances." The manner in which these passes were obtained could reveal much about slave resistance, but this area remains to be researched.[78]

At the markets women sold herbs and other produce from their gardens, such as cucumbers, melons, manioc, and sweet potatoes. They also sold eggs and chickens. In Saint-Domingue, slave women sold chickens to ship captains, who longed for fresh meat, at four times the usual price. In return they received fabric, liquor, and other items, some of which they used to barter with the proprietors of restaurants for necessities.[79] Markets were usually held close to churches on Sundays after mass. This has led Debien to question whether the slave women marketeers first attended mass and then turned to marketing. This would seem an unlikely prospect, unless other women set up the stalls. Also, from very early on—as early as 1669—there were complaints about slaves holding Sunday markets and staying away from church. Markets were forbidden during church services. Moreau de Saint-Méry noted that slaves held markets in the savanna near the church at Limonade, Saint-Domingue, on Sundays and holidays. The location of the church facilitated the transportation of their produce. It seems likely that markets were strategically located and timed to maximize sales from the emerging congregation. The unregulated sale of produce was seen as an unmanageable hawking—an inadmissible disorder which administrators viewed as negligence on the part of planters. But in Martinique, where society had come to depend on the produce from slave gardens by the 1830s, authorities did not crack down on marketing activities. Indeed, in the 1840s, Rouvellat de Cussac bought fruits and vegetables at a Saturday market from a woman slave in Fort-Royal. Thus throughout slavery in the Caribbean and other parts of the Americas (such as South Carolina, as Robert Olwell has demonstrated), the market scene was dominated by women.[80]

Marketing provided an escape hatch of sorts for slave women, although Morrissey aptly observes that slave men profited more than women from the household economy in that they achieved "social dominance."[81] To the end, the life circumstances of field slave women remained quite dreadful. Apart from hard labor in dangerous conditions, poor nutrition, and inadequate health care, these women suffered economic and other forms of exploitation, more so than other slaves. As a whole, women received no special consideration because of their sex; in fact, they suffered more. Domestic slave women fared somewhat better, but their condition was often precarious, as the next chapter shows.

4

Women and Labor
Domestic Labor

THERE HAS BEEN a strong tendency among many observers of slavery in the French Antilles to emphasize, even exaggerate, the number of domestic slaves in plantation households, to view the labor they performed as easy and often inconsequential, and to conclude that their condition was infinitely superior to that of field slaves. A critical examination of the condition of domestic slaves reveals a more complex picture, however. Indeed, the number of domestics varied both within and between colonies depending on the residence patterns of slaveholders and on their individual economic standing. This makes it difficult to make sweeping generalizations. There were also variations in the allocation and execution of domestic tasks that had a direct and sometimes adverse impact on the lifestyles of domestic slaves. While domestic slaves usually fared better than field slaves in that they performed lighter tasks, received various privileges such as better food and clothing and accommodation in or near the plantation Great House, and had easier access to manumission, they were still slaves and remained subject to the whims and caprices of their owners.

When Moreau de Saint-Méry wrote that "In Saint-Domingue everything takes on an air of opulence," he was referring to the number of slaves in the domestic service of Europeans and the manner in which the slaves catered to their owners. According to de Saint-Méry, a multitude of slaves awaited orders or a signal from a single man, who reveled in the grandeur that such a scene produced. As he further commented, it was part of the dignity of a rich man to have four times the number of domestics that was necessary.[1]

De Saint-Méry may as well have been articulating the view of domestic slavery in any of the Caribbean colonies. Indeed, William Dickson, who lived in Barbados from 1772 to 1785, and held the post of secretary to the governor, referred to domestics as useless and numerous.[2] About the same period, the absentee sugar planter Stanislas Foäche of Saint-Domingue was unsparing. He wrote, "It is unfortunate that domestics are not very busy. The less busy they are, the more vicious they are." He therefore recommended to his *gérant*, Paris, that domestics on the Foäche plantation be made to cultivate small kitchen gardens in order to acquire revenue to purchase their own clothing and to sustain themselves, and as a way to impress upon them the value of such labor. Only when they had to live solely on the produce of such gardens "that required weeding, watering and helping field slaves" would domestics appreciate the value of work, Foäche believed. As if to suggest that they were a parasitic lot, he insisted that "Their well-being should be the result of the fruits of their labor."[3] Even so, Foäche placed domestics with particular strengths in positions which best suited the needs of the plantation.

Interestingly, whites held a negative view of domestic slaves in antebellum South Carolina, as Norrece Jones has pointed out. In the Old South their labor was scarcely appreciated, according to Elizabeth Fox-Genovese, and their owners treated them with a mixture of cruelty and kindness. But Pierre de Vassière, a keen observer of Saint-Domingue society during the eighteenth century, regarded domestics, especially those who cleaned and served, as a fortunate lot.[4] Granier de Cassagnac, who visited the Caribbean during the 1840s and took a pro-slavery stance in his work, amplified de Vassière's view when he declared that every creole white woman in the French colonies was a "grande dame" who was

> habitually surrounded by an incredible staff of servants. In general, each individual has an assigned domestic: father, mother, every young girl and boy all have servants. Add to this a cook, two washerwomen, two or three seamstresses, two or three women who run errands, a half dozen spoiled young black males who treat their masters like slaves, and one gets an idea of the domestic personnel of a West Indian plantation. These servants do as they please and are lazy and greedy. They are well-groomed in stylish embroidered clothing from Paris adorned by jewellery. Indeed, a creole woman who steps out forms a virtual convoy that consists of a squadron of servants who never leave her side either night or day, and without whom she never ventures out.[5]

Curiously, the *Gazette de la Martinique* reproduced an article that first appeared in the Barbados newspaper *Mercury* in the early nineteenth century in which similar views were expressed. The opening sentence of the article set the tone: "Some creole dames have the very bad habit of having their servants in tow when they step out to visit their acquaintances."[6] Whether Granier de Cassagnac had access to this or other such articles must be left to speculation. But it is possible that his idyllic view of the condition of domestic slaves was an attempt to deflect criticism of the slave system, coming as it did at a time when the debate over the abolition of slavery in the French colonies was approaching its zenith. But the question of whether domestics were tripping over one another in plantation households, and living a life of relative comfort and ease while doing as little work as possible, is pertinent. Who were these domestics? How numerous were they? What did their labor entail?

Both male and female slaves were domestics, but in most cases, as we shall see, there was a division of labor within their ranks. That being the case, Vanony-Frisch is still correct in asserting that the domestic workforce was more feminine than masculine, and that there was a preference for mixed-race household workers, especially females. This position runs counter to Gabriel Debien's claim that domestic staffs were mostly male and black. It should also be emphasized that, for the most part, slaveowners preferred to engage creole slaves as domestics. Indeed, Moreau de Saint-Méry observed that they were preferred in all areas of domesticity, and that their prices were at least 25 percent higher than those of African-born slaves. To be sure, mixed-race creole slave women were prominent in this occupation. As later chapters reveal, they often had conjugal relations with their owners and acquired manumission, both formal and informal, as a result.[7]

There may well have been a general tendency among slaveowners to have more domestics than they needed, as Moreau de Saint-Méry's comments suggested. However, slaveowners who resided in the colonies were the ones who usually engaged in this lifestyle. Thus the perceived abundance of domestics in Saint-Domingue, to which Gabriel Debien also subscribed, is all the more intriguing, given the high level of absenteeism among planters in that colony. There can hardly be a doubt that, apart from colonists, administrators such as *gérants* and *économes* profited from the economic success of Saint-Domingue —the richest colony in the Caribbean in the eighteenth century—to live as lavishly as they could, at least in good times. But the likelihood is that only slaveowners with adequate resources indulged in excesses. In reality, most slaveowners appear to have had a modest number of domestics. Of the 141 slaves on the sugar plantation Beaulieu in Saint-Domingue in 1768, only 5—3 males and 2 females—or 3.5 percent were domestics. Similarly, in 1768, 4 of the 112 slaves (3.5 percent) on the sugar plantation Galbaud du Fort in Saint-Domingue were domestics. With a total of 169 slaves in 1790—of which 110 were between the ages of fifteen and sixty years—the sugar plantation Vases in Saint-Domingue had only a male cook and 2 or 3 servants, according to Debien. Interestingly, David Geggus's study of 197 absentee plantations in Saint-Domingue during the revolutionary period 1796–97, when the colony was occupied by the British, gave a crude estimate of about 1 percent of the slaves working as domestics on sugar plantations.[8]

Statistics from some plantations in Martinique appear to be in line with those of the plantations Beaulieu and Galbaud du Fort in Saint-Domingue, but the data are too thin to be conclusive. Besides, the variations were likely as marked in Martinique as in the rest of the French Antilles. Four of the 120 (3.3 percent) slaves on the Fond Saint-Jacques Plantation (owned by Père Labat's ecclesiastic order in Martinique) were domestics, but this was not the norm. On the L'Anse-à-l'âne sugar plantation in Trois-Ilets in Martinique, the 10 domestics—6 males and 4 females—constituted about 9.3 percent of the adult slave force of 108 in 1746. As Debien noted, this was a very small percentage compared to estates in Saint-Domingue, where the domestic contingent was proportionately much larger.[9]

The view from Guadeloupe, where most of the sugar planters resided on their estates and where the tendency toward having numerous domestics was, according to Vanony-Frisch, perhaps more pronounced than in the rest of the Caribbean, was still somewhat similar to that of Martinique. On the estates of some of the rich sugar planters, domestics accounted for as much as 15 percent of the slave force in the period 1770–89, but this was the exception rather than the norm, Vanony-Frisch stated. Vanony-Frisch also gave the example of a sugar planter from Petit Cul-de-Sac (now Petit-Bourg) who had 229 slaves in 1786, 14 of whom worked in the Great House. This means that the female servant-seamstress, the valet, the male cook, the butler, the midwife, and the 9 servants represented about 6 percent of the slave force. Had the pen-keeper been added, domestics would still have accounted for less than 7 percent of the slaves. Vanony-Frisch did not indicate whether the planter had a family and, if so, what the size of the household was. However, the presence of a seamstress, who usually catered primarily to the sewing needs of the women in a planter's family, suggests that he did.[10]

There is no doubt that in all of the French colonies, there were always slaveowners who viewed a sizable contingent of domestics as an appropriate manner in which to display their wealth and status, but these would have been the minority. What delight they must have taken in doing so! Although he provides no details in reference to the eighteenth-century sugar estates Saintard, near Arcahaye, Caradeux in Cul-de-Sac, and Motmans in Léogane in Saint-Domingue, Debien indicated that their owners prided themselves on having a multitude of domestics. "It is after a visit to one of these establishments that travelers described with astonishment, half filled with wonder and half with shock, the bevy of valets, cooks, and a variety of female servants," Debien wrote. As he pointed out, however, "this was out of the ordinary."[11]

Other examples of extravagant lifestyles are just as striking, if not more so. In 1782 Monseigneur L. F. Lemercier de Mainsoncelle, equerry and former major of the battalion in Abymes, Guadeloupe, along with his wife, Françoise Coquille, had eighteen slaves in their lavish and luxurious dwelling in the town of Morne-à-l'eau. After selling his sugar plantation in Abymes to his brother-in-law, Coquille Dugommier, for 450,000 *livres* in 1779, Lemercier de Mainsoncelle became an urbanite. In addition to the domestics, he could boast a cuckoo clock from Paris, a gilt-edged mirror, silverware, porcelain, crystal, and objects made of marble and ivory. It would be interesting to know what the domestics in the Lemercier de Mainsoncelle household did, aside from the usual household chores. Since there were young slaves among the eighteen, it is possible that some were apprentices. A second example from

Guadeloupe is that of Sieur J. Vatable, a militia major and merchant in Basse-Terre, who in 1785 had thirteen slaves, among them a laundress, two male cooks, a female servant, and two washerwomen. In this household, domestics therefore accounted for almost 50 percent of the slaves.[12]

One conclusion that can be drawn from the statistics and examples cited above is that the number of domestics is large only if viewed against the small number of whites in plantation and private households, and not so much in relation to the total number of slaves in a unit—the plantation being the best and most relevant example. What needs to be emphasized as well is that there were proportionately more domestics in urban areas than rural areas where the plantations were located. Failure to take this factor into account has led some scholars to a skewed vision of large numbers of domestics everywhere across the slave system.

A good picture of the level of domesticity in urban areas can be obtained from an official list that identified the occupations of 218 slaves in Martinique, Guadeloupe, French Guiana, and Bourbon (Réunion) who received their freedom in 1847, under the provisions of a royal ordinance issued on April 29, 1836. The list showed that most of the slaves in the urban areas were domestic slaves, while those in rural areas were largely field slaves, artisans, and slave drivers. Of the 10 urban slaves in Martinique, 4 (40 percent) were domestics, 5 were manual laborers, and 1 was a field hand. None of the 26 rural slaves were domestics. Likewise, all 5 adults among the 11 urban slaves in Guadeloupe were domestics—seamstresses—the remaining 7 slaves being children of the adults. As in Martinique, there were no domestics among the 30 rural slaves in the Guadeloupe listing. French Guiana had the largest contingent—119 slaves, of which 40 were urban and 79 were rural. Of the 32 adult urban slaves, 17 were domestic slaves, mostly washerwomen and seamstresses. Only 2 were field hands. The domestic representation among the 79 rural slaves was small—5 in all—a housekeeper, a servant, a watchman, and 2 nursemaids. Thus urban slavery in the French colonies constitutes a rich potential area of research that deserves serious consideration.[13]

The looseness of the category "domestic" also deserves comment, for it bloated the ranks of slaves who were attached to the plantation Great House in one way or other and thus came to be called domestics. Had Labat included the animal watchman and the nurse among the domestic slaves on the Fond Saint-Jacques Plantation in Martinique mentioned above, the number of domestics would have increased from four to six, and the percentage from 3.3 to 5. All things considered, the number of domestics in plantation households depended on the ability and inclination of slaveholders to assign slaves to do domestic chores. It bears reiterating that the percentage varied within and between colonies.

Domestic labor entailed a multiplicity of functions that were mostly but not exclusively assigned by gender. They sometimes began when slaves were as young as seven or eight years of age. Thus males were valets, butlers, barbers, wigmakers, tailors, watchmen, gardeners, fishermen, canoemen, coach drivers, hunters, and, most surprisingly—if considered in the context of African societies, where the kitchen was and remains a woman's domain—cooks. As for slave women, they served as midwives, nurses, *hospitalières*, housekeepers, and seamstresses—their most important functions. In addition, they were cooks, servants, and washerwomen. Most often, generations of slave women in domestic service worked in the same household, performed multiple domestic tasks, which varied over time. Undoubtedly, the prospect of being shifted from one domestic position to another or to the field gangs was very real, and amounted to a lack of security on the part of domestic slaves. Indeed, rarely did a slave retain the same position for life. However, Arlette Gautier's assertion is valid that slave women were assigned domestic tasks that relegated them to the maintenance of the household, while slave men were allocated the more public functions that brought them into direct contact with the world outside of the plantation. From within the confines of the plantation, nevertheless, the domestic slave woman executed her functions with ingenuity, resourcefulness, and sometimes even revolutionary fervor. Within this context, her role as midwife, nurse, *hospitalière*, housekeeper, and cook can be explored.[14]

SLAVE WOMEN IN HEALTH CARE POSITIONS

Slave women who delivered health care on the plantations have come under more scrutiny than other domestic slaves, perhaps because of the relationship between their occupations and issues of life and death in slave society. Those involved in health care were mainly midwives, nurses, and *hospitalières*, but it was often the case that slaveowners assigned a single, capable slave woman to provide the entire range of health care. In general, however, the role of black females in the health care arena has been minimized in the literature on slavery, and their functions have usually been ill defined, if at all. Of the health care practitioners, midwives attracted the most attention from slaveowners and were both praised and condemned in practicing their craft. As the work of midwives was seen as crucial to the growth of the slave population, suspicion fell upon them whenever infant mortality was high—a constant throughout slavery. Slaveowners believed that a good midwife could ensure more live births and that a hostile one was a danger to the expansion of the slave force. Thus, the occupation of midwifery left slave women open to charges of infanticide, which planters in the eighteenth century believed they committed as a means of resisting slavery.

These issues are explored at greater length in the next chapter, but it is important to mention here that the planters' theory of sabotage was fueled by low birth rates among slave women. Indeed, high mortality and low fertility rates were characteristic of the French slave plantations. The death rate among newly arrived slaves was 50 percent and about 5 to 6 percent among acclimatized slaves in the eighteenth century, while the birth rate was less than 3 percent. Mortality was so high on the Cottineau Plantation in Saint-Domingue that the entire slave force had to be replaced between 1765 and 1778. The plantation La Souche in Sainte-Anne, Guadeloupe had a death rate of 38 percent between 1783 and 1787, when the slave population dropped from 308 to 118. The planters attributed some of these deaths to poison, and this made them all the more suspicious about the activities of midwives. Planters believed that women who aborted made a conscious choice not to reproduce; and when infants died within a few days of their birth, planters suspected their mothers, or the midwives, had killed them. So planters appeared convinced that the key to live births rested with the midwife. Thus midwives and mothers were punished when infants died at birth.[15]

The possibility of delivering stillborn infants or infants who would perish within days of birth must have placed great stress on midwives, who were also accused of inducing the condition of lockjaw (tetanus) in infants in order to deprive planters of new slaves. During the late eighteenth century, midwives on the Flauriau Plantation who were suspected of such actions were forced to wear rope collars. This happened to the midwife Arada, whose rope collar contained seventy knots, each knot representing a child she had allegedly killed. In 1786 a Monsieur Desuré, the attorney for two Saint-Domingue plantations owned by Madame Dumoranay, a widow, ordered that the midwife on one of the plantations where infant mortality was high should be got rid of "for the greater good," although no firm evidence was presented against the midwife. French observers like Thibault de Chanvallon (who visited Martinique in 1751) believed that neonatal tetanus was caused by infection of the umbilical cord and was responsible for 80–90 percent of child mortality in the French Caribbean during the seventeenth and eighteenth centuries. Also plausible is Marrietta Morrissey's undocumented assertion that the "use of rusty or dirty instruments or muddied stones to cut the cord also contributed to infection." In the eighteenth century, however, planters in the French colonies subscribed to the theory of infanticide. It is highly improbable that arbitrary killing was the primary cause of infant mortality. Were it so, there would be greater variation in the death rate. This means that some midwives may have been falsely accused of infanticide. Given the interrelationship between the health care professions, *hospitalières* and nurses were almost as vulnerable as midwives, however.[16]

The distinction between doctor (*hospitalière*), the primary caregiver among the slaves, and the nurse (*infirmière*), her assistant, is often blurred in the literature on slavery in the French Antilles due to the synonymous use of the terms. For the most part, these occupations are not differentiated. In a discussion of slave labor on the Hecquet-Duval Plantation in Saint-Domingue in the 1760s, for example, François Girod used the terms *infirmière* and *hospitalière* indiscriminately. So did Geneviève Leti in her 1998 study of Martinique in the years 1802–48. However, Gabriel Debien differentiated between the occupations. He argued that while the *hospitalière* was a domestic slave of note, the *infirmière* was a mere aide, since nurses were the ones who kept the hospital and its surroundings clean and prepared baths for sick slaves, whose linen they also washed. He noted that on many plantations, nurses cared for orphans and newly weaned infants while their mothers worked in the fields. But some plantations had nurses and not *hospitalières*, which means that nurses likely did more than cleaning, washing, and child care.[17]

Like Debien, Arlette Gautier used the terms *infirmière* and *hospitalière* independently, but the lack of precision in the data upon which she drew resulted in a common treatment of both. Gautier cited no date, but noted that in Jacmel, Saint-Domingue, there were *hospitalières* on only two of the plantations that had a population of more than 97 slaves.[18] In her eighteenth-century inventory of Nippes, a community in Saint-Domingue, she also found that nurses and *hospitalières* were rare. All told, there were only nine of them among 1,857 slaves, 730 of whom were women. Rarer still were slave surgeons, two of whom turned up in her inventory of Nippes, in spite of a general regulation that prohibited slaves from acquiring drugs—a lethal weapon in their struggle against slavery.[19] Gautier concluded that only on large plantations were there infirmaries. In Nippes, five plantations, each of which had more than 80 active slaves, had three infirmaries among them; seventeen other plantations, each with a workforce of 25–79 active slaves, had only four. Likewise, in Vanony-Frisch's sample of 8,820 slaves in Guadeloupe (10 percent of the slave population) in the period 1770–89, 306 slaves executed paramedical functions, but only 9 of them were women.[20] Taken together, these statistics suggest that nurses and *hospitalières* were few and far between, and that their presence was tied to plantation size. It is instructive that in the period 1781–91, Cadush-Barré, a large, well-run sugar plantation in Saint-Domingue owned by Barré de Saint-Venant, had twenty-two cane fields, 202 slaves, and two *hospitalières*—Antique, a thirty-one-year-old creole who suffered from asthma, and Jeanne, a mixed-race slave woman.[21] Thus it appears likely that only planters with adequate financial resources slotted slaves into health-related domestic positions, unless the well-being of the slaves took precedence over profit margins—an unlikely prospect. Whether out of curiosity, intrigue, or recognition of their invaluable skills, *hospitalières* (more so than nurses) attracted the attention of observers and slaveowners alike but have still remained rather obscure. Who were these slave women?

Barbara Bush has defined *hospitalières* as "traditional folk healers" who "were typically midwives and provided postnatal care for mothers and infants."[22] Like Richard Sheridan, she has linked them to African medicinal practices that have been passed down from generation to generation from precolonial times. With regard to these practices, Sheridan gave, among other examples, that of the women of the Mano ethnic grouping in Liberia, who "commonly combined the functions of midwife, gynecologist, pediatrician, general practitioner, as well as surgeon . . . when girls were circumcised."[23] The role that *hospitalières* played in the French Antilles can also be viewed in this broad context, given the multiplicity of the tasks they performed. Indeed, they engaged in paramedical functions that would almost certainly classify them as nurse practitioners and more today. Geneviève Leti suggested something similar when she noted that the *hospitalière* was "a privileged doctor's assistant."[24] To be sure, the *hospitalière* worked closely with plantation doctors and surgeons on estates where they were present, and on her own when they were not. On the Cadush-Barré sugar plantation in Saint-Domingue, where there was a *hospitalière* among the domestic staff in the period 1781–91, the surgeon's quarters were located next to the hospital, which points to a close working relationship. The *hospitalières* were usually mature, carefully chosen slave women who had authority and whose position was coveted by other slaves. They often began their working lives in the fields and were given positions considered prestigious as a measure of compensation. Besides caring for the sick, they were expected to administer the hospital as well as monitor and regulate the activities within it, including the comings and goings of patients.[25]

The work of Père Labat and Rouvellat de Cussac can be used to illuminate the multifaceted duties of the *hospitalière*. At the end of the seventeenth century, Labat gave the position to "a well-behaved and intelligent slave woman" who looked after the slaves diligently, made the hospital beds, fetched food for the sick, kept the hospital clean, and permitted entry only to those authorized by the surgeon. In the 1840s, Rouvellat de Cussac noted that in addition to a daily visit by a doctor, there was "a slave woman called a *hospitalière* who has the function of mid-wife and nurse; she prepares medication, and executes the orders of the doctor." Much earlier, in the 1770s, however, Stanislas Foäche suggested that, in her spare time, the midwife could assist the *hospitalière*. Health personnel therefore varied from estate to estate.[26]

Stanislas Foäche, perhaps more so than any other slaveowner, provided keen insights into the working life of a *hospitalière,* while drawing attention to her indispensability and to the centrality of her workplace. She had to know the various methods employed in setting fractures, Foäche wrote in 1775. She was expected to keep a supply of used household linen to dress wounds, as well as a supply of sheets, shirts, blouses, and blankets for the seriously ill. Foäche also indicated that slaves usually required preliminary treatment and refreshing teas while waiting to see the surgeon prior to hospital admittance. This could only have been work done by the *hospitalière*. His declaration that "there is no time to waste with illness" indicates that the *hospitalière* had to be quick and efficient.[27]

It is worth emphasizing that she was knowledgeable about both European and African remedies, whereas European doctors lacked expertise about African medical practices. In this respect she had an advantage over them. European doctors and surgeons in the French colonies were part of the marine corps until very late in the slavery period, which means that they were tied to the French state. As in the rest of the Caribbean, few inspired confidence. In the late eighteenth and early nineteenth century, when legal reforms in France made the medical profession more open, civilian doctors, some from the Caribbean, began to practice in Martinique with credentials from a wide array of French institutions. There were also marine and civilian pharmacists who prepared and sold their own drugs to doctors (though not to slaves). Medicine also began to be imported from France, including quinine tablets.[28]

The remedies that the *hospitalières* distributed on the Vases sugar estate in Saint-Domingue in the late eighteenth century included European medication such as castor oil, wine-flavored balsam, and, after 1750, a notorious powder concocted by a French doctor, Aixois Aillaud, to which some attributed miraculous healing powers, but in the view of others it served only to enrich the pharmacists.[29] In addition to these, syrups, herbal teas, and herbal remedies formed part of the *hospitalières'* pharmacopoeia. Given the quickness with which plantation owners tended to assign blame, however, the pressure that a *hospitalière* must have come under to preserve the lives of slaves against the backdrop of high mortality rates may well have been intense, at least at times. In any case, the value Foäche placed on a good *hospitalière* is evident from the following comments:

> A good *hospitalière* is a precious subject. She must be intelligent enough to distinguish between the onset, developing and advanced stages of fevers, and be able to communicate her findings to the surgeon who is unable to constantly monitor the sick. She must know how to dress wounds and use bandages in a multi-purpose way. She must be strong enough to resist the indiscreet demands of the sick and prevent their relatives and friends from bringing them substances that may do them harm. If she performs her duty enthusiastically, treat her as well as you do the slave driver of the first gang. Next to him, she is the most valuable slave on the plantation. If the plantation can manage it, give her a young, intelligent slave woman to assist and be trained by her. This is essential as the loss of a *hospitalière* can be devastating.[30]

The setting in which the *hospitalière* worked on the plantation is revealing about her undertakings and the influence she wielded. During slavery, most hospitals were really sickhouses or infirmaries. On the Lugé sugar plantation in Saint-Domingue in the eighteenth century, a hospital was set up in a large hut away from the slave quarters. On the Cottineau Plantation in Saint-Domingue, the *hospitalière* attended patients in a private room with a chimney and a bathtub made of stone that was normally reserved for her use. There were also two adjoining rooms with camp beds for male and female patients, separated by a barrier. Another room consisted of canvas beds and beds made of sticks and straw mattresses for slaves with serious illnesses. Slaves, male and female, with venereal diseases, were confined to two smaller rooms with camp beds.[31]

The *hospitalière*, along with the *économe*, ensured that the meals that sick slaves ate were properly prepared and distributed. Foäche recommended rice, millet flour, and bread for the average sick slave, and meat and wine for slaves who were rendered weak by hard work. However, he warned of the potential for abuse and believed that careful surveillance was fundamental in avoiding it. He noted that slaves, especially those with weak constitutions, sometimes presented themselves at the hospital under the pretext of being ill, but advised his overseer to turn a blind eye to this abuse unless it became a frequent occurrence. Foäche apparently considered it acceptable for slaves to take two or three days of rest in this manner. It was no doubt left to the *hospitalière* to monitor their condition and to ensure their fitness. As Foäche noted, "Slaves must leave the hospital not only sane but in a state that can support light work."[32]

The *hospitalière* was responsible for enforcing security measures at the Foäche Plantation hospital. This could only have been an onerous task. According to Foäche's instructions, the hospital had to be constructed with surrounding walls and iron bars on all entrances and exits to prevent unwanted intrusion. In Foäche's words, "one cannot do enough to make sure that the entrance to the hospital is off limits to all slaves; this is necessary in all cases." To ensure maximum security, the only exit door had to be the exterior door of the *hospitalière*'s room. In this way, she could be held responsible for breaches of security. As the sole custodian of the hospital keys, which she was expected to carry in her pockets at all times, she was instructed to keep patients locked up as a means of ensuring that their wounds would heal, and that they would refrain from smoking and drinking *tafia*. Foäche estimated that out of around thirty patients, there would always be around twenty or so who had only cuts on the legs and feet, but who had to be restrained in order to heal.[33]

Aside from her caregiving and surveillance duties within the hospital, Foäche also expected the *hospitalière* to accompany the surgeon on surprise visits to the slave quarters, a tactic he believed would uncover the presence of venereal diseases among the slaves, who were apparently inclined to conceal the condition. He placed great emphasis on curbing venereal diseases, as "the wellbeing of the present and future generations depends on it." Slaves who came forward were to be treated with indulgence; those who knowingly spread it were to be severely punished in public.[34] Given the nature of work she performed and the magnitude of her role, it is little wonder that some scholars have questioned the effectiveness of the *hospitalière*. Indeed, Marcel Reible viewed them as doing more harm than good. In the late eighteenth century, according to him, slaves on the Lugé sugar plantation in Saint-Domingue "were abandoned to the negligence and incompetence, more so than care, of two or three *hospitalières* performing the functions of *infirmiers*." Interestingly, the owner, Pasquet de Lugé, had no desire to engage a surgeon. Thus it seems reasonable to assume that he either did not wish to spend money on the health of the slaves or that the care they received from the *hospitalières* was adequate in his judgment. After Lugé's death, a surgeon, Mondor, was hired, but he apparently considered the 1,500 *livres* per year he was paid for his services insufficient, and gave up the position within months. With more than a hint of skepticism, Reible argued that during his short stay, Mondor cured 26 slaves of skin ulcers. After his departure, the hospital admittance rate went back to 5 percent of the slave population, which stood at 345 in the period 1788–91. On the other hand, Félix Patron, an apologist for slavery, used the fact that *hospitalières* staffed some plantation hospitals to chide the French abolitionist Victor Schoelcher, who characterized slaveowners as "veritable monsters" who had no consideration for slaves. What must not be lost sight of in any examination of the *hospitalière*'s role is the way in which she interpreted her own condition. She was, after all, a fairly independent slave who must have been conscious of the plantation's dependence on her, and of her own potential for inflicting damaging blows to the slave system. In this respect, she likely faced the same dilemmas as plantation cooks.[35]

The consumption and entertainment habits of Caribbean slaveowners ensured cooks a central place within the domestic configuration, and a position from which to strike at the slave system, as chapter 8 demonstrates. The French placed a high premium on cooks. Virtually every visitor to the Caribbean was astonished by the elaborate meals that planters served and the eating and drinking that went on for hours on end. It is no wonder that the estimated value of cooks was higher than that of most other slaves, the median price in Guadeloupe being 2,600 *livres* in the period 1770–89. But on May 27, 1783, M. L. Delagrange, a slaveowner from Guadeloupe, sold the slave cook Céladon for a record 8,000 *livres*. Another male cook, Gilles, owned by the merchant and militiaman E. Druault of Guadeloupe, was valued at 4,500 *livres* in 1785.[36] The age of several female cooks may mean that they either retained their positions for a good deal of time or that they were appointed as cooks late in life. In 1784 Bernadine, a creole black woman, 66, was the cook of Monsieur Botreau Roussel of Guadeloupe. Another example from Guadeloupe is that of Constance, a mixed-race slave, 63, who cooked for Monsieur Gagneron. In a will probated in 1783, Gagneron granted her freedom as recompense for "good and loyal service."[37]

Cooks aside, most domestics who fell into the servant category on plantations and in private dwellings in urban centers were women. Most worked as washerwomen, seamstresses, and housekeepers. Washerwomen and laundresses had the lowest status in this group, which may explain why flight was more pronounced among washerwomen than other domestics. According to Vanony-Frisch, only colonists who could afford it had washerwomen. She further stated that washerwomen were more often a symbol of pride rather than a necessity, particularly for the wives of colonists. Given the social elevation of white females to a position of prestige in the Caribbean, and the aversion to manual labor that accompanied it, however, it would be difficult to imagine a planter household without a washerwoman. Besides, washing may not necessarily have been a full-time occupation. Indeed, French sources indicate that on small plantations the *gérant* arbitrarily selected slave women from the fields and imposed the position of washerwomen upon them. This would mean that washing was seen as not requiring any special skills and did not therefore merit apprenticeship. Nevertheless, washing certainly took stamina, all the more so since washerwomen were not provided with soap or other cleaning agents, and may have had to travel a distance from the plantation to wash clothing. However, French sources indicate that washerwomen used ropes, oranges, lemons, and limes for soap, and that laundresses used the flowers of orange, lime, and frangipani trees when pressing to give the clothes a fresh and pleasant scent.[38]

Slaveowners did not appreciate the work that washerwomen (who were usually black) did. The sugar planter Stanislas Foäche spoke about them in a very derogatory manner, and rated their performance as being very poor. Also, in a letter he wrote to his mother in France in the late eighteenth century, Regnault de Beaumont, a young apprentice sugar boiler on the Motmans estate, spoke about how washerwomen adopted the haughty posture of the colonists and sabotaged the laundry of the *économe* as a way of degrading him. Regnault de Beaumont painted washerwomen as spiteful and calculating, as women who would willfully damage the clothing of lesser plantation officials if forced to work. On Motmans, washerwomen rent new clothing belonging to the *sous-économe* into two or three pieces but were careful not to do the same to the head *économes,* who had power. However low they may have been in status, this account shows that washerwomen assessed the power relationship within the white plantation hierarchy and selected the most vulnerable targets. It also points up the relationship between work and resistance; while not refusing to do the washing, they were able to use it defiantly.[39]

In the late eighteenth century, slave women in Petit-Trou, a parish in the

south of Saint-Domingue, washed clothing in the Petit-Trou River. "It is surprising to find that this was the only use of the river for the town, and that it
does not provide water needed by the inhabitants for other uses," Moreau de
Saint-Méry wrote with some astonishment. In the 1770s this area boasted very
fertile soil and was the site of several sugar and indigo plantations.[40]

Père Labat considered it advantageous to have a river running next to a
plantation, so that water could be diverted to operate the sugar mill and to
satisfy the other needs of the plantation, including those of the slaves, "who
never tire of washing themselves." So crucial was a water supply to Foäche
that in 1774–79 work was carried out on a canal he requested built on his estate to facilitate operations at the mill. However, slave women on plantations
that were not close to rivers and other surface water had to draw upon alternative sources. This often required travel over long distances, an aspect of
women's work still common to Africa that has hardly been mentioned in the
literature on slavery. Women in Saint-Domingue, Moreau de Saint-Méry reported, were always in search of water, which was sometimes stored after rains
or drawn from wells. At Le Cap in the north of the island, where most sugar
plantations flourished, there were very productive wells, but many were as
deep as ninety feet. He suggested that the slaves were undaunted by the challenge of drawing water from such a depth, as they "are principally the most
knowledgeable about well water since they find it tedious to procure other
sources." While washing for their owners may have been their principal task,
washerwomen likely did not neglect their own personal needs, for as Moreau
de Saint-Méry observed, "cleanliness was one of the characteristics of the
blacks, and, in particular, the women." Neatness of appearance among slave
women did not go unnoticed in slave society either, but the extent to which
the plantation seamstress had a hand in this is still unknown.[41]

Sewing was a very popular occupation among slave women in the French
Antilles (especially Martinique) by the nineteenth century, as evidenced by
the significant number of seamstresses who made a bid for freedom under an
1832 law. For this reason it is curious that both Gautier and Vanony-Frisch
found relatively few seamstresses among domestics in Guadeloupe, except in
wealthy households. Apparently, the presence of seamstresses in plantation
households was usually a sign of prestige. There were seamstresses on only six
of the plantations in the district of Nippes in Saint-Domingue, but Gautier
gave no details as to the specific time period and the total number of plantations. Of the more than 8,000 plantation slaves in Vanony-Frisch's sample of
Guadeloupe in the period 1770–89, only 12 were seamstresses, while 3 were
apprentices, their median value being 2,500 *livres*. It is also noteworthy that 10
of the 15 were mixed-race females.[42]

If the number of seamstresses in plantation households was very small,
it is tempting to conclude that their work entailed sewing for slaveowners

and their families—usually the women in the family—and not for the slaves. Was this the case? Vanony-Frisch has stated that sewing for the slaveowner's family, including the sewing of wedding dresses, was the major preoccupation of seamstresses in Guadeloupe. Debien's work points in a similar direction when he describes the efforts some rich planters in the French Antilles made to ensure that accomplished seamstresses were a part of their domestic staff. Debien noted that in such households, planters and their creole wives, who took pride in their homes, sent their linen maid and seamstress to France, under the watchful eye of a ship captain or returning friend, to apprentice for several years. Upon their return, they made, repaired, and altered the dresses of the planters' wives, and made clothing for the slaves from cloth distributed by planters on Christmas Eve. They also altered ready-made clothes given to slaves by their owners.[43]

While the primary occupation of seamstresses was sewing for the slaveowners' household, it is possible that the extent to which they sewed for the slave gangs has been underestimated. Most planters distributed issues of clothing once or twice a year, but the question is whether this distribution was enough to keep a seamstress occupied year-round. Indeed, in 1778 Foäche instructed his overseer, Paris, to keep the seamstress occupied sewing the yearly issue of clothing for the slaves, and to encourage female domestics to sew. Foäche normally gave seamstresses the cloth in bulk, as it was easy to purchase. To avoid abuse, he recommended that Paris record the amount of cloth issued because some, considered "mischievous subjects," might sell some of it to buy liquor. In the mid-eighteenth century, Véronique, a twenty-eight-year-old mixed-race slave, sewed for the slave gangs on the L'Anse-à-l'âne plantation. She altered skirts, blouses, and ready-made pants for them and also patched clothing.[44]

There were also slaveowners who put young women to work as apprentices in anticipation of exploiting their labor as seamstresses, among other occupations. In a letter to his mother dated August 6, 1786, Regnault de Beaumont, who arrived in Saint-Domingue in 1774 to seek work as a refiner and make a fortune, commented that he had bought young slaves both as domestics and as investment. To alleviate the economic hardships he faced, he told his mother that he bought a boy and girl (ten to eleven years of age), whom he made into a valet and an apprentice seamstress. Of the girl he wrote, "She shows great promise of becoming a first class seamstress, but she possesses every imaginable fault, among them stealing and a tendency towards *marronnage*." De Beaumont found the going tough in Saint-Domingue, as salaries were low and irregularly paid and night work was frequent. He was reduced to wearing his father's old clothing after the latter, a planter in Léogane, died. The fact that he purchased the slaves in spite of what he regarded as exorbitant prices—2,500–2,700 *livres*—suggests that he considered the investment economically sound. Certainly, as slavery was coming to a close, a considerable number of women slaves between the ages of seventeen and twenty-four were seamstresses, including several of 218 slaves freed by a royal ordinance in 1847.[45]

Women slaveowners often made hucksters out of female slaves, who retailed items such as fruits and vegetables and who can be considered domestic slaves. In 1779 Anna, a trusted twenty-one-year-old domestic slave from Guadeloupe, sold fruits and vegetables with the knowledge of her owner, Gillet, a merchant in Basse-Terre to whom she gave an accounting.[46] In the 1840s another such slaveowner in Saint-Pierre, Martinique, bought bulk goods and sent one of her women slaves to towns and villages to market them. According to Rouvellat de Cussac, "This old woman had several such women slaves engaged in a profitable enterprise." The severity of the punishment administered to slave women who did not live up to their owners' expectations may mean that the revenue that retail operations generated was important to them. Referring to the slaveowner above, de Cussac observed that it was "hell for the slave who buys too dear or credits goods" as her "old mistress would whip her with the *rigoise*"—a thick thong of cowhide.[47]

For some slaveowners, the challenge was to find a slave woman who could manage the household, regulate its spending, and supervise the domestic staff. This was apparently no easy undertaking for in the minds of slaveowners the possibility of discord was very real. For that reason, Père Labat advised colonists to avoid engaging white domestics as much as possible. Apart from "the higher cost and constraints involved in having them at the dinner table," Labat wrote, "they often become entangled in schemes with black women that result in great disorders, and at times, the death of one party or the other."[48] Similarly, in a letter of February 1758, Lory de la Bernardière advised Primeteau, the *gérant* on the Cottineau estate in Saint-Domingue, to refrain from showing favoritism to women slaves in the plantation household. The reason he gave was that "A slave woman who lives off the Great House has her relatives, friends and others, some of whom do little or no work, while others are overburdened." As he continued, "Such a situation leads to vexation, quarrels and vengeance, and can result in the total collapse of a plantation. This constitutes a good lesson, *monsieur,* if you know how to profit from it."[49] This stern lesson, couched in discretion, was apparently designed to alert Primeteau to the dire consequences of becoming involved in conjugal relations with domestics. But it inadvertently revealed that women used their positions in the Great House to help other women and ensure the continuity of personnel and personal relationships. In 1784, for example, Marie-Christine, a forty-one-year-old mixed-race pregnant servant, had ten children with her in a Great House in Guadeloupe, among them Reine, twenty-four, also a mixed-race servant. On the same plantation, Babée, a forty-year-old mixed-race servant said to be incurably ill, had two children in the Great House with her, including Calixte, a nineteen-year-old mixed-race servant, whose value was estimated at 3,400 *livres.* As Vanony-Frisch pointed out, these cases were not at all exceptional.[50]

The advice that Primeteau received deserves further consideration, for it illustrates both the ways in which slaves could resist slavery and the realization on the part of the planter class that all they accumulated could be wiped out in no time. In essence, the advice was an admission that the planters' control over the slaves was tenuous and limited. That being the case, a good housekeeper was a slave woman not worth tampering with at all.

Foäche sought a housekeeper who could be called "manager," a slave woman he envisioned as "a very interesting subject whom the plantation lacks." He suggested to his *gérant* that a recent acquisition, a *griffe*—the female offspring of a black and mixed-race person—would probably be the ideal choice. As he noted, "She is young and appears to be intelligent, but she no doubt has faults that are drawbacks." Whatever her "faults" may have been, this slave woman appears to have been well-positioned for the job, given Foäche's conviction that an outsider, rather than one of the plantation slaves, would be preferable as a housekeeper.[51]

At times, slaveowners pampered housekeepers and other domestics, but the effects of such treatment are difficult to evaluate, given the mobility and uncertainty that characterized the everyday existence of domestic slaves. The contradiction inherent in their social condition is thus all too revealing. To entice domestics as he took up his appointment as *gérant* on the Foäche estate in 1775, Paris was expected to buy and distribute two issues of fabric and clothing for each domestic, including serviettes, white shirts, and blue and white undergarments from Rouen, France, as well as shirts and bonnets for all the breast-feeding children on the plantation. The *hospitalière* and prospective housekeeper came in for special treatment, Paris having been instructed to buy them Indian petticoats. These issues were over and above the blouse that the plantation gave to each female domestic once a year.[52]

Besides receiving special issues of clothing, some domestics had the possibility of earning cash. Among them were those who used their positions and their wit to their advantage. A possible example is the domestic slave on Foäche's estate who kept a chicken coop. He does not indicate whether any of the revenues it provided accrued to her. But the fact that he enthusiastically endorsed her in this position, and was aware that neighboring plantations had made tempting offers for her chickens and eggs, suggests that this "intelligent and refined" slave woman may have had access to a source of cash. The plantation profited from her efforts because her stock provided food for the Great House, so Foäche would have been naturally concerned about the prospects and impact of outside sales. With social control clearly in mind, a cynical Foäche wrote, "She is no doubt in fear of losing her position. This fear can be used to keep her in check." Social control aside, Foäche's strategy points up, once again, the vulnerability of domestic slaves.[53]

Seamstresses were probably better situated to earn money than most other domestic slaves because there was a need for clothing, among the slave population in particular, that they were uniquely positioned to fill. In Caribbean slave societies appearance was important, in spite of the collective degradation to which slavery reduced its subjects. Moreau de Saint-Méry's patronizing description of enslaved black women in Saint-Domingue, whose appearance was apparently so glamorous that it astounded whites, may be seen in this light, the inherent exaggeration notwithstanding. This appearance depended upon attractive clothing made from a variety of imported fabrics such as *Brin* and *Ginga* and material from areas such as Bretagne and Flanders. As Moreau de Saint-Méry remarked, "One finds the extent of the spending done by a female slave woman hard to fathom." De Saint-Méry claimed that these women placed great importance on obtaining cloth to make skirts. But he seemed certain that the metamorphosis that occurred between wearing rags in the fields during the week, and sporting fine clothing at church or at local markets on Sundays, was far more pronounced among female slaves than male slaves. Whatever the purchasing power of female slaves, their dependence on seamstresses must have been constant.[54]

On the L'Anse-à-l'âne estate in Martinique around the mid-eighteenth century, the mixed-race seamstress Véronique altered and patched the clothing of field slaves. She must have been rewarded for her efforts, as she was able to redeem herself and three of her children from slavery for five thousand *livres* in 1761, when she was thirty-five years old. By 1763 Jeanne, a twenty-year-old mixed-race master seamstress, was officially working in the Great House, though it is uncertain how long she had been there. Jeanne had two mixed-race children, born in 1761 and 1762. Did she too follow Véronique's path?[55]

The case of the domestic slave Marie, a coquettish black seamstress born on the La Barre sugar plantation in Saint-Domingue, who in 1786 had the means to purchase garments worth 67 *livres* 10 *sols,* and a hat which cost 57 *livres* 15 *sols,* is even more telling than that of Véronique and Jeanne. In 1788 Marie bought shoes twice, another hat, ribbons, handkerchiefs, and four *aunes* of Polish fabric for a further 8 *livres,* 5 *sols.*[56] More purchases followed in 1789. These included substantial quantities of fabric, including Indian cloth, two handkerchiefs, three pairs of shoes and an umbrella. To outfit her black daughter, Marie bought cloth from Bretagne, France, in 1790. How did Marie acquire her funds? Debien provided a not so subtle hint when he stated that men greatly appreciated gifts of hats, handkerchiefs to cover the head, and, most of all, large buttons for overcoats, as they came from afar. Indeed, fashionable buttons were very much in vogue in the 1790s. They adorned an overcoat worn by Toussaint-Louverture and the clothing of fashion-conscious men, as Ann Geracimos has indicated.[57] But it was also an open secret that slaves employed the services of seamstresses. To quote Debien, "The means were discreet, but well known on all plantations. In the course of several years, a seamstress could be assured of a small nest egg."[58]

Domestics attached to the Great House had opportunities to develop personal relations with members of the slaveowning class, but how well they were served by these ties is a relevant question. The work that guardians and wet nurses performed brought them into particularly close contact with their owners' children. Letters written by Madame des Rouaudières, a white creole of Saint-Domingue, to her daughter, Paschalite, who was born and raised in the colony but left to attend boarding school in France, hint at the nature of some of these relationships. In correspondence dated November 25, 1775, Madame des Rouaudières wrote, "I am forever obliged to tell you about the young black female slave who cared for you from the time you were weaned until you left for France. Do you remember her? You were as closely attached to her as she was to you. She inquires about you specifically every time I receive a letter from you. She is a good subject. I no longer own her, but she remains a domestic here."[59] One would expect Paschalite to remember the woman who, by all indications, raised her, and she probably did, so it is odd that her mother should ask such a question. Other correspondence reveals that the slave woman in question, Marie-Jeanne, nurtured the relationship over a period of years by sending small gifts to Paschalite and her four children in France in packages sent by Madame des Rouaudières. In 1777 Marie-Jeanne sent jewels made from local shells, "and many compliments in her language [creole]." The following year, her gift consisted of a necklace and "a thousand compliments." In a creole message that accompanied the gift of 1778, Marie-Jeanne expressed the desire to see Paschalite before she died—an eventuality that would make her unhappy. Two calabashes, one containing a small gold chain adorned by a garnet wrapped in cotton, constituted Marie-Jeanne's gift to Paschalite's daughter, Caroline, in 1785. In a thoughtful act that demonstrated continuity, Marie-Jeanne sent Paschalite's daughter gifts she had given Paschalite as a child—rings made of tortoise shells.[60]

It would be instructive to know what Paschalite thought of her former guardian. In 1775 her mother, Madame des Rouaudières, expressed anger at losing ownership of Marie-Jeanne, along with the firm belief that her daughter was grateful for the care that this slave woman gave her as a child. She vouched for her daughter's desire to reward her, though in what manner she did not say. What is most telling is that eleven years later, in 1886, Marie-Jeanne was still a slave, still serving the Rouaudières family, most probably as a hired-out servant owned by someone else, a common aspect of domestic life during slavery.[61]

Marie-Jeanne's story shows that women in domestic service had to be prepared to do multiple tasks. The uncertainty that accompanied such a life requires emphasis. On Foäche's estate, the midwife was expected to contribute to other spheres of domestic labor. This contribution was not always in the line of health care. Foäche instructed his *gérant* to have the cook or midwife on the Jean-Rabel estate learn how to make bread. Also, the nurse on the estate was once a cook and baker and "like all intelligent people, she has succeeded in all the positions she has held. Fortunately, she is not old."[62]

There were many drawbacks to being a domestic. One was that the hours of work were indeterminate for those in the Great House. Unlike field slaves, who could be virtually sure of having Sundays and holidays off when the Code Noir was respected, domestic slaves had only a half-day off periodically. Another, and perhaps the most serious drawback was instability, which affected male and female slaves alike. Of the thirty-two slaves (seventeen males and fifteen females) who worked in the Great House on the L'Anse-à-l'âne plantation between 1746 and 1778, few served out their lives there. Only the male slave Gomme, considered "a good cook," died in the household in 1761 at the age of forty-three years. Domestics who were not sold away from the household were usually given other jobs, but those who were sent to the fields suffered the worst demotion of all. Indeed, the threat of being sent to the fields was a psychological weapon that slaveowners used to keep domestics in line. In 1792, in the midst of the Saint-Domingue revolution, Dumas, a member of the Assembly in Le Cap, in the north of the island, was convinced that he had witnessed a revolutionary spirit in his domestics, and threatened to send them all to the fields and replace them with whites. He blamed domestics for eavesdropping on the conversation of whites, and for intently following their every move.[63]

Relegation to fieldwork was not uncommon for male and female slaves, as the following examples from the L'Anse-à-l'âne Plantation demonstrate. Joseph, a domestic in 1746, was demoted to fieldwork in 1749. The assistant cook, Scipion, suffered a similar fate in 1752 at the age of thirty-four years. In 1753, however, he was sent to the sugar works. Whereas men could move from domestic work to occupy positions in the manufacturing sector and other areas outside of field labor, however, slave women had no such chance. For them, the fields were usually the only place of refuge. At fifteen years of age, Agathe became a domestic in the Great House. At eighteen she was demoted to the fields, where she remained until 1763, when she returned to the Great House. By 1767, at the age of thirty-eight, however, she was sent back to the fields, where she remained for life. It is noteworthy that the situation in the British Caribbean was similar in terms of gender. On the Rose Hall estate in Jamaica in 1832, for example, "All the women said to be of 'bad' or 'indolent' disposition were placed in the field gangs, but males with such reputations were employed in much more independent occupations."[64]

Instability was a fact of life even for the most prized domestic slaves, as they were more likely to be sold when plantations changed hands and when slaveowners left the colonies to return to France. In some cases, according to Debien, "dethroned" domestics were so traumatized by such changes that they were led to become maroons. Since domestics (mixed-race males and females in particular) had higher estimated values than field slaves, and usually sold for more irrespective of the differential between estimated value and actual sale price, they were an attractive investment. The median price of slaves in Guadeloupe in the period 1770–89 was 1,400 *livres*. This figure is similar to the average price of 1,200 *livres* that slaves in the French Antilles paid to redeem themselves from slavery in 1847. Measured against these figures, the estimated value of domestic slaves stand out. In 1753, on the L'Anse-à-l'âne plantation in Martinique, the mixed-race seamstress Véronique Quianquionne was valued at 3,000 *livres,* the servant Charlotte at 3,000 *livres,* and the seamstress Rosette at 2,200 *livres.* At 3,300 *livres,* the *hospitalière* on the Hecquet-Duval plantation in Saint-Domingue was among the slave women with the highest estimated value in 1782. In Nippes the housekeeper, female cook, and seamstress had higher estimated values than other female slaves in the period 1721–60. Of the seamstresses, it is worth noting that a quadroon with many white racial features had the highest estimated value of all.[65]

Length and quality of service, intimacy with whites, and good character did not protect slaves from being sold. Noël-mulâtre, a domestic slave, and his wife, Victoire, a well-esteemed slave who moved up from the fields to become a midwife at the age of thirty-six, remained in their positions on the L'Anse-à-l'âne Plantation for many years, but were sold, along with the youngest of their eight children, in 1769, when the estate fell into difficulty.[66] When Barré de Saint-Venant left Saint-Domingue in 1789 to return to France, he instructed his *gérant,* Dujardin de Beaumetz, to rent or sell the domestics, who had numbered twelve in 1781, when he bought the sugar plantation Cadush-Barré.[67] In other words, the domestics were not to be at the disposition of the *gérant.* As for the field slaves, it was left to Dujardin de Beaumetz to work them as he pleased. Jean Fouchard has documented several cases where colonists advertised a full complement of domestic slaves for sale before leaving Saint-Domingue to return to France. In 1786 a Monsieur Mornet advertised six black women for sale. One had three children, but members of this slave family could be sold either separately or collectively. If the children were minors (under fourteen years of age) they could not legally be separated from their parents under Article 47 of the Code Noir,[68] but slaveowners disregarded the laws. At a liquidation held in Saint-Domingue in the late eighteenth century, nine carpenters and nine field slaves were listed among the sale contents. But so were fifteen domestics, mostly female, including Marie-Louise and her two children. In November 1784, the heirs of the estate of a Monsieur Soller, held a public auction in Croix des Bouquets, Saint-Domingue, and sold several domestics. Aside from a "battalion" of young females, a live-in concubine and domestic along with her mixed-race son, and a twenty-four or twenty-six-year-old washerwoman named Marie, there were three other female domestics and two young valets in the auction.[69]

Normally berated for poor performance, washerwomen were miraculously embellished with talents once advertised for sale. In April 1791, months before the outbreak of the Saint-Domingue revolution, Hudicourt, a military official who was about to leave for France with his wife and three children, put up for sale a wig maker, a baker, a postilion, a cart maker, a valet, a mixed-race seamstress along with her six-month-old son, and a "good" washerwoman. In 1792 a newspaper in Saint-Domingue advertised several female domestics for sale, including a black woman who was "a good cook and washerwoman" and who could also sew and iron. Advertised for sale in 1803, a mixed-race eighteen-year-old slave woman from Martinique could not only wash but iron and sew as well. That same year, M. J. Papin of Martinique advertised a mixed-race slave woman, Félicité, as a "very good washerwoman" with ironing, housekeeping, and cooking skills to boot. As Félicité was in prison at the time (due to *marronnage,* no doubt), Papin was willing to accept any reasonable offer to guarantee a quick sale. In 1806 in Martinique, the owner of a mixed-race slave woman advertised her as a "good washerwoman, seamstress and laundress." In spite of these qualities, however, he was willing to trade her and her infant mixed-race son for a slave cooper if he could not secure a sale.[70]

A field slave who was sold could expect to do fieldwork ad infinitum, which meant no change in work status. But the same could not be said for domestic slaves. Thus, if domesticity was mostly female, it seems certain that female domestics were subject to a greater degree of instability than were male domestics. A newspaper advertisement from Martinique in 1804 is instructive in this regard. An entire plantation with fields planted in coffee and ground provisions was advertised for sale that year, along with only one slave—a female.[71]

Some female domestics had to remain single as a result of their ties to their owners' household. The Jesuit priest Mangin, who lived in Martinique in the seventeenth century, also noted that some French slaveowners refused to consent to the marriage of their female slaves so as not to be deprived of their services, especially child care at night.[72]

Domestic slaves were trapped by slavery, regardless of the occupational categories and class distinctions that elevated them above field slaves. Nothing more clearly illustrates this point than Pére Labat's statement that domestics in the Great House were not under the command of the slave driver, unless the slaveowner called upon him to give them a whipping when they were judged to merit it.[73] A domestic slave in such a situation no doubt fell to the level of the field slave, and the psychological impact that the blows imposed, while left to the historian's imagination, could only have been devastating. What is certain is that the division between the two types of labor—domestic and field—served to legitimize the former, making it respectable in relation to the latter. In terms of gender relations, the consequences of the division of labor may have been equally severe. While slave women did most of the house and field work, men for the most part did the whipping. This situation had important social implications, in that it pitted black men against black women, though both were exploited under slavery. However, this common exploitation provided the basis for complementary forms of resistance to slavery.

5

Marriage, Family Life, Reproduction, and Assault

AN EXAMINATION OF the lives of slave women in areas such as marriage, reproduction, family, and assault requires us to enter the intimate recesses of the slave woman's world. From any vantage point, such an examination is a daunting task, for it was a world that remained largely concealed from the view of slaveowners and contemporary observers, who nevertheless trespassed and wrote about it, quite often with an air of authority and self-assurance, and a good deal of ethnocentricism. Extrapolation from various accounts shows that in the areas of life mentioned above, the burden of slavery fell disproportionately upon slave women. However, the strength and resilience of slave women, their capacity to endure, and their will to survive in spite of the crushing blows that slavery delivered are the qualities that enabled them to carry on from one generation to another. Throughout the generations, from the earliest days of slavery, whites viewed conjugal relations between slaves as a curiosity more than anything else. The state provided the legal framework for slave marriages, but the institution of slavery itself was antithetical to the promotion and development of strong family units on a broad scale. In the 1840s, the French abolitionist Victor Schoelcher suggested something similar when he argued that marriage was incompatible with slavery, a degrading institution.[1] The Catholic orders, which owned slaves, recognized this fact but stopped short of advocating the abolition of slavery, opting instead for ridiculing the blacks while promoting their salvation.

MARRIAGE

With regard to conjugal relations, the most persistent and resounding complaint among contemporary observers and church officials in the French Antilles was that slaves refused to engage in legal marriages, that is, marriages conducted by a priest either in the Catholic Church or on a plantation. In the late seventeenth century, Père Du Tertre related the story of a young Guadeloupean slave woman, La Pucelle des Isles (Virgin of the Islands), who refused to yield to her owner's wish that she marry a male slave he had handpicked for her. Her owner continued to ignore her wishes and brought her to church one Sunday for a prearranged wedding with the prospective mate. On this occasion, the woman remained resolute and as quietly defiant as ever. Rather than protesting at the outset, she waited until the priest asked whether she was willing to marry the man before her, and then responded with an emphasis that shocked those who were present. "No, my Father," she is said to have responded, "I do not wish to marry this or any other man. I am miserable enough as it is without having to bring children into this world to be more miserable."[2] In the nineteenth century, the abbot Castelli reported similar sentiments among slaves in the French colonies, who told him that they were already in a state of destitution which they had no desire to exacerbate by marrying. For them, procreation would only serve to aggravate their pain, as their offspring would share the ordeal of bondage. While state and church made provisions for the marriage of slaves, they appeared oblivious to the socio-psychological impact of slavery itself, and to the fact that the slaves had minds of their own.[3]

By her actions, La Pucelle des Isles offers insights into the slaves' own thinking about marriage. Similar insights can be gained from other slaves. In a letter of May 23, 1840, the abbot Dugoujon stated that he would never forget the response given the previous morning by a male slave from the plantation Amé-Noël in Guadeloupe to his owner, the abbot Lamarche. The abbot had asked him whether he envisioned marriage, a means of setting a good example for the rest of the slave gang. "Father," he responded, "such as thing is not really possible. How could it be? The person I want to marry does not belong to my master." The slave in question was among those of good character and was selected to express his views to Dugoujon. Thus it seemed certain that Lamarche was privy to the slave's thinking on marriage and questioned him in the presence of Dugoujon to highlight the inhumanity of slavery. Also, not long after the exchange, Lamarche told Dugoujon that he would use the slave's response to refute arguments promoted by those who favored incremental rather than outright abolition of slavery. Even if the slave's performance were a staged event, there were certainly other slaves of like mind and spirit. What should be emphasized is the inherent constraints imposed by slavery—the common thread in this story and that of La Pucelle des Isles.[4]

Under a regulation of 1664, the French colonial administration made it contingent upon slaveowners to baptize newly arrived slaves, and to attend to their marriage in due course as well as to the baptism of their children. Noncompliance with this law drew a fine of 150 *livres* of tobacco for a first offense, 300 *livres* for a second, and sale of the slaves to more religiously inclined slaveowners for a third offense.[5] Reflected in the first several articles of the Code Noir, which appeared a little more then twenty years later, this regulation is evidence that French colonists placed a certain importance on religious conformity and marriage. The regulations governing marriage were very stringent in tone but were likely ignored by slaveowners, not only because of their general disregard for the law but because colonial policy was often contradictory. What mattered most was not so much respect for the rules governing slave marriages or the fact that the slaves were reluctant to marry; the primary concern of French administrators was the prevention of sex and marriage between blacks and whites. This issue consumed the colonial administration from beginning to end. As a result, meaningful reform that would truly have promoted marriage among slaves came almost at the end of slavery—too late to make a difference. In Martinique, the Conseil Superieur introduced a decree on May 18, 1683, under which the publication of three banns on three separate holidays or Sundays was required before a marriage could take place. Among many other particulars, officiating priests had to check the residence and background of prospective couples, and ensure that permission, where required, was granted. The presence of four witnesses was mandatory at marriage ceremonies. These and other formalities were subsumed under the Code Noir and applied to slaves and free people alike. Indeed, in an 1807 letter to the parish priest of Saint-Pierre, Martinique, François-Augustin Trepsac, the apostolic prefect, insisted that three banns must be published before all marriages unless the parties concerned obtained authorization from the head of the Catholic Church. But he also highlighted the need to keep baptismal registers for slaves, which indicates that the identity of the slave woman's child was at issue, and underlying that the issue of interracial sexual relations.[6]

Under slavery it would have been up to slaveowners to ensure that the regulation requiring the publication of banns was carried out. If they were vigilant in this regard, it would be possible to argue that they had more than a passing interest in wanting their slaves to marry. What did the publication of banns mean to the slaves? Did the slaves attend the churches where the banns were announced? Did they have access to the media in which they were published? Antoine Gisler cited a case in which a Jesuit priest was expelled from Saint-Domingue by his order for using chimes and chants—reserved for whites—at the marriage celebration of slaves. This may seem an insignificant matter given that whites considered blacks to be subordinate, but if the blacks did not accept this vision of themselves as lesser beings, then legal marriages may not have been that attractive to them.[7]

In accordance with Article 10 of the Code Noir, slaves could marry legally without the consent of their parents, but Article 11 prohibited priests from marrying them without their owners' consent. Article 35 forbade slaveowners from marrying slaves against their will, but only the state had the power to prevent them from doing so, and it usually did not. Thus the customary rights of family members were superseded by the authority of slaveholders, making slaves, in effect, minors. Also, the African concept of marriage—a socially recognized union between socially recognized males and females such that children born of the union are socially recognized as offspring of the union—was not considered legitimate.[8] However, Patterson, Bush, Beckles, Morrissey, Gautier, and other scholars have been consistent in their view that slaves in the Americas adopted a variety of African forms of conjugal unions and family organization that co-existed. For example, Patterson has categorized these into "stable unions," "unstable unions," "multiple associations," "stable monogamous and legal marriages," and the like.[9]

There were many attempts to modify the regulations on slave marriages after 1685. Some of these sought to prohibit marriages between slaves and free people, particularly between male slaveowners and their female charges, but abuse of slave women was common, as we shall see. In any case, baptism of slave children and the penance of black women became prominent issues with regard to qualifications for manumission. Also, registration of slave marriages (along with births and deaths) became objects of scrutiny, especially in the nineteenth century. In 1805, for example, correspondence between colonial officials and priests in Martinique indicate that the keeping of slave registers had become an issue, if only to verify the status of the newborn infants of slave women.[10] In 1839 the Minister of Marine and Colonies reminded colonial governors to abide by the decree of August 4, 1833, under which slave marriages had to be registered. "Pending the drafting of another decree," he wrote, "I am asking that [slave] marriages be declared and registered." However, marriages between slaves remained legal and continued to generate as much controversy as ever.[11]

In 1845 French authorities drafted thirty-four decrees governing slave marriages and family issues aimed at ameliorating slavery. After some refinement, these decrees formed the basis of a royal ordinance of 1847, a follow-up, according to King Louis-Philippe, of previous royal ordinances of August 1833 and June 11, 1839, which called for the taking of censuses among slaves. Under the 1847 ordinance, parental consent was necessary before male slaves under twenty-one years of age and female slaves under eighteen years could marry. However, eighteen-year-old male slaves and fifteen-year-old female slaves could marry with the permission of the colonial administration or an apostolic prefect. Marriage banns had to be posted on the front door of the church or chapel in the districts where the slaves lived, and read aloud during Sunday prayers at least eight days prior to the marriage. A marriage had to be registered within eight days, and only the death of one spouse could dissolve it. Once married, a male slave could exercise authority over his wife, and limited paternity rights over his children, so long as they did not clash with the legal rights of the slaveholder or those stipulated in Article 4 of the Mackau Law of July 18, 1845, concerning child welfare. Much like the Code Noir, the 1847 law prohibited the breakup of the slave family as long as the children were minors—under fourteen years of age. But it went beyond the Code Noir in terms of age specificity for marriage. Efforts to encourage slaves to marry were of crucial importance in the new law, for it provided the Minister of Marine and Colonies with a subsidy that was to be given to governors in the French colonies for that purpose. Thus in the era of amelioration of slavery, the new law overrode regulations in the Code Noir and undercut the power of slaveholders. Coming as it did a year before the end of slavery, it was too late to be truly effective.[12]

Throughout slavery in the French Antilles, there were few legal marriages among slaves. With few exceptions, African marriages, patterns of residence, and the interpersonal relationships that the slaves practiced on a wide scale were condemned, often in racialistic tones. Most of the Europeans in the French colonies were generally critical of African customs, but African forms of marriage were particularly deprecated. For example, Moreau de Saint-Méry declared that Africans were accustomed to polygamous marriages and were not furiously jealous. He noted that there were several Africans in polygamous unions "living in harmony." But it seems obvious that he did not consider such marriages legitimate for in the same breath he wrote that "marriage is rare among them. Indeed, the most pious masters are basically obliged to abandon the practice of promoting marriage among them—a scandalous state of affairs." De Saint-Méry blamed African cultural mores, which he regarded as "primitive," and the disproportionate number of black women compared to black men, all compounded by the hot climate.[13]

André Lacharière sounded a similar note when he wrote that "polygamy reigns in the colonies . . . where unions among slaves are tenuous." He indicated that male slaves had several women and were never too tired to visit one of them, irrespective of hurdles such as hills, rivers, and precipices that they had to surmount, and the fatigue that they suffered as a result. "It is," he wrote, "a fatigued body that goes to work the next morning."[14] Like others, the abbot Castelli employed the word "rare" in reference to marriage among African slaves, adding that as a result, "there are no family ties among them."[15] Writing from Guadeloupe in May 1840, the abbot Dugoujon remarked that "slaves respond just as enthusiastically as freed slaves to religious instruction. However, few take the first communion, and virtually none dreams of marriage. Their reluctance to engage in legitimate marriages is the sole obstacle that stands between them and holy communion."[16]

Dugoujon cited official documents that alluded to the fact that legalized marriages among slaves were indeed rare and that slaveowners were either indifferent or opposed to them. Marriage was said to be repugnant to slaves in Martinique, among whom concubinage was natural and illegitimacy carried no shame. In French Guiana, the situation was apparently identical. Indeed, the French newspaper *L'Abolitionniste français* highlighted the fact that in 1841 there were only twenty marriages out of a slave population of 75,225 in

Table 5.1. Legal Marriages among Slaves in Moule, Guadeloupe

Year	No. of Marriages
1834	1
1840	4
1844	3
1847	31

Source: Raymond Boutin, "Les Esclaves du Moule au XIXe siècle (naissances, mariages et décès)," *Bulletin de la Société d'histoire de la Guadeloupe,* nos. 75–78 (1988): 23–24.

Martinique. The corresponding figures for Guadeloupe and French Guiana were fifty-seven marriages out of a slave population of 93,558, and forty-three marriages out of a slave population of 14,883. Evidently, the fact that slave-owners and slaves are said to have contributed to weddings made no difference at all.[17]

Recent studies support the general picture of few legal marriages among slaves. In a study of Moule (Guadeloupe) between 1845 and 1848, Jacques Adélaïde-Merlande found that in 1845 and 1846, few such marriages took place. The findings on Moule—a district that contained the largest number of slaves in Guadeloupe on the eve of emancipation—are significant, as they may well be representative of the colony as a whole. There were 7,012 slaves in the district in 1830, 8,018 in 1840, and 7,733 in 1847. Raymond Boutin's study of Moule between 1830 and 1847, when slaves represented 80 percent of the total population, corroborates Adélaïde's findings in terms of the low level of legal marriages among slaves, as table 5.1 shows. The number of marriages in 1847 stands out statistically in relation to the previous years, but may have been a result of the new regulations that were introduced in 1847.[18]

Among the reasons Boutin gave to explain the statistics are the following: the inability of parents to enforce their authority; the fact that the slave husband was powerless in the face of the slaveowner and other plantation personnel such as the *gérant, économe,* and slave driver; the difficulty of marrying outside of the plantation; the opposition of slaveowners; and the failure of planters to register slave marriages with local authorities. In spite of a lack of data for some periods, Boutin found that in 1847, about 64.5 percent of slave marriages in Moule were not registered on time, with an average delay of just over four months.[19] This is consistent with the example that Adélaïde-Merlande gave of the marriage of the slaves Simon and Celeste of Moule. This marriage "took place on July 3, 1847, [but] was not registered until November 26, 1847." Adélaïde-Merlande even found cases where registration took place after the death of the husband.[20]

Of the reasons given for the lack of enthusiasm for legal marriages among slaves, the limited choice that slaves could exercise in selecting their partners deserves special consideration. In this context, a French administrator's report of a slave woman's maxim of 1842, "My body is yours, but my heart is still mine," needs no elaboration. Dugoujon indicated that being forced to accept their owners' choice and limit their affections to the plantation on which they lived were an issue for slaves. Du Tertre noted that a slave couple belonging to different owners could marry if one owner agreed to accommodate the other by selling either the male or female slave, thereby joining the slave couple under a single owner. Du Tertre went on to point out that this arrangement had its limitations and did not always work because slaveowners, particularly those with several female slaves wishing to marry, were reluctant to part with them. In this respect, it may well be that the slaves were encouraged to choose from among their counterparts on the same estate rather than going farther afield. Citing a ministerial letter of July 25, 1708, addressed to the Compte de Choideul, which revealed that it was difficult for slaves of different plantations to marry and that consequently there were plantations where no marriages could take place, Lucien Peytraud took a hard stance against white colonists for not instilling "morality" in their slaves.[21]

In Moule, Guadeloupe, marriages took place mostly among slaves on the same plantation. "Of the 54 marriages recorded between 1845 and May 1848," Adélaïde-Merlande wrote, "only two took place among slaves who did not belong to the same owner." In 1847 twenty-nine of the thirty-one slave couples were the property of the same owners. It seems certain that slaveowners expected slaves to choose mates from within the confines of the plantation. This ensured their continued domination over the slaves and explains why they were so lax in registering slave marriages. Boutin suggested that the casual attitude of slaveowners may have resulted from their desire to circumvent the law that prohibited the breakup of slave families, since the only witness to marriages among slaves of the same owner was usually a priest. He would not represent an obstacle to the sale of the slaves, as would other witnesses who had a stake in the matter in cases where a slave couple belonged to two different owners.[22]

By and large, legal marriage may have been a last resort for slaves. As Adélaïde-Merlande noted, the slaves who married were usually advanced in age. Although the average age of marriage was 47.7 years for males and 43.4 years for females, slaves in their seventies and eighties also married. Thus, marriage often "took place at the end of one's life, or when one of the partners was almost at death's door. Marriage was the final goal of family life, rather than the beginning." Similarly, Patterson notes that in the nineteenth century, when legal marriages became possible in Jamaica, old couples sometimes married under pressure from the missionaries.[23]

Bernard David's study of the district of Carbet, Martinique, in the period 1810–48 yielded results very similar to those from Moule. During this thirty-eight-year period, there were only 46 legal marriages among the slaves, that is, about 1.2 marriages per year on average. In 1807 there were 2,881 slaves in Carbet; in 1821 there were 2,772. Curiously, there were 3,574 baptisms among creole slaves, and 437 among African slaves during the same period. These statistics suggest that while the rate of legal marriage among slaves in Carbet was negligible, the level of conjugal relations was not. However, it is possible that the rate of legal marriages among slaves in urban centers was greater than in rural areas like Moule and Carbet. In the city of Cayenne, French Guiana, this appears to have been the case. From January 1, 1828, to December 31, 1835—a period of eight years—there were 160 legal marriages in Cayenne and the surrounding areas, or about 20 marriages per year. A statistical study of French Guiana found that "marriage was seen as crucial to civilizing blacks."[24]

The emphasis on legal marriages in the historical literature of the French Antilles must not be allowed to overshadow the fact that the slaves valued kinship and in many cases constructed family units—European- or African-centered—under the toughest of conditions. There are many families on a list of 218 slaves who acquired their freedom in the French colonies in 1847. Most of these families were headed by women, some of whom had as many as eight children, but there were also two-parent families. For example, the *commandeur* Auge of Martinique, aged 53, was married to Geneviève, a 52-year-old field slave. Their three daughters, Marthe-Louise, 32, Augustine, 24, and Jeanne-Rose, 11, as well as their three grandchildren, aged 1-4 (borne by Augustine), all appeared on the same list. Another *commandeur,* 47-year-old Hildevert the second, and his 51-year-old wife, Véronique-Amaranthe of French Guiana, appeared on the list along with their four children, aged 4-11 years. The listings from French Guiana contain more married couples than those from either Martinique or Guadeloupe, an interesting phenomenon. Often *commandeurs,* who did the whipping, were married to field slave women. These could not have been easy unions, especially when such a couple had female children who worked in the fields, and who, like their mother, had to be subjected to corporal punishment.[25]

Other French sources point to a significant number of married couples on some plantations, among them the sugar estate La Rochefouchard-Bayers in L'Anse-à-l'âne, Martinique, which had 134 slaves in 1749 and 141 in 1778. During this period of almost thirty years, there were 52 conjugal families on the plantation. According to Debien, "This is a far cry from Saint-Domingue where one is at pains to point to one or two marriages per plantation, the difference being the more ardent practice of christianity in Martinique."[26]

An indication of the importance of kinship and family ties can also be drawn from an observation Du Tertre made in the seventeenth century about Nègre Dominique, a male slave owned by the Dominican order to which he was attached. For more than two years after the death of his wife, Nègre

Dominique took their son and daughter to the grave site where she was buried and wept in their presence for a good half hour, the children often imitating him. Du Tertre's observations can help us to get at the inner reaches of the world the slaves inhabited. He suggested that, as mothers, slave women cared for their children as best they could. They never forsook their children. Du Tertre described in detail how they tied their children on their backs using cloth called *"pannes"* [*sic*], much as women in Africa do today. "In this position," he noted, "the child could sleep as it would on a good bed, however much it is agitated by the field work activities of its mother." He also observed that upon returning from a day's work in the fields, slave parents collected their children from neighbors "and do not eat until they can account for them."[27] Likewise, Père Labat wrote about a male slave in Guadeloupe whose wife and children surrounded him and served him with the kind of "respect and reverence that domestics give to their masters." In relating this story, Labat was really more curious about African customs, appearing fascinated by the observation that an African husband seldom ate with his wife, however much he was fond of her. Labat also observed that after the husband had eaten, his children usually brought him his pipe, at which point he gave them permission to eat. On holidays they also brought him presents.[28]

As Nègre Dominique and the male slave that Labat described were owned by Catholic orders, both he and Du Tertre may have wished to show that the African slave was not beyond redemption. Whatever the clerics' motives, it is possible to argue that, although African kinship was radically assaulted by slavery, strong family ties still persisted. In some cases these were demonstrated in very dramatic fashion. Such was the case of Barthélemy, a slave owned by the Jesuits who, in March 1706, was found guilty of murdering the slave Colin. The latter allegedly paid nightly visits to Barthélemy's wife, Catherine, with whom he had a relationship of some long standing. However, the Conseil Supérieur of Martinique let Barthélemy go free and sentenced Catherine to thirty lashes. In addition, she was chained with an inscription bearing the words "adulterous and shameless slave woman." As for compensation, the Council awarded Bègue, Colin's owner, only 600 *livres,* which the Jesuits were required to pay. This compensation was less than half the cost of a prime male slave and was likely a token payment. Surely, it must have been seen as a victory for the Jesuits in the name of Christianity; but what of Catherine? Religious authorities, as we have seen, harped upon the roaming of black men, but they undoubtedly held black women to different standards.[29]

With regard to conjugal relations, caste and class mattered to the slaves as well. Among creole slaves in particular, the family backgrounds of prospective couples were examined to ensure a match of equal ranking. Certainly, as Labat noted, the daughter of a slave driver or laborer would not want to marry the son of a field slave.[30] Labat did not identify the ethnic origins of the slaves to whom he referred, but among the Wolof of Senegal in the nineteenth century, for example, it was difficult, if not impossible, to transcend caste boundaries in a strongly hierarchical society.[31]

REPRODUCTION

Since the slaves practiced many forms of conjugal relations, it would be reasonable to expect a child slave population over and above the rate of replacement. Certainly, "the proportion of adults on the plantations should have yielded a large and regular birth rate," as Debien stated.[32] This was not the case. Indeed, slaves in the French Caribbean, as elsewhere in the region save for Barbados, did not reproduce themselves. As in the rest of the region, the offspring of slaves in the French Caribbean were legally slaves and belonged to the slave woman's owner. If a male slave married a free woman, the offspring followed the status of the mother and were free, irrespective of the status of the father, according to Articles 12 and 13 of the Code Noir. Thus, whereas male slaves could produce free offspring, female slaves could not.

The data on natality are very fragmented, but scholars agree that there was a negligible birthrate among slave women that was compounded by a very high mortality rate, both among infants and adults. Interestingly, plantation births came from a small number of very fertile slave women. Gabriel Debien believed that these women were both African and creole, but Vanony-Frisch's survey of slaves in Guadeloupe in the period 1770–89 shows that fertility was lower among African women than among creole and mixed-race women. Mixed-race women had twice as many children as African women.[33] It also appears that childbearing was somewhat age specific in that women mostly bore children in their twenties and thirties. Indeed, although information on the age of slave mothers was not precise, Adélaïde-Merlande found that few slave women in Moule, Guadeloupe, had children before they reached the age of twenty. As he noted, "It was especially between the ages of 21 to 22 years and 32 to 34 years that women bore children."[34] These revelations mystified planters, colonial administrators, and observers, all of whom speculated about the causes and reverted to prescriptions that they believed would remedy the situation.

Writing from Fort Royal, Martinique, in 1764, Governor de Fénelon expressed astonishment that the slave population had not replenished itself since the outset of colonization, forcing the French colonies to depend on the Atlantic slave trade. Contemporary observers also commented on low birthrates. Both Girod-Chantrans and Félix Patron noted that there were few children on the plantations. General Joseph Romalet du Caillaud was more sweeping and emphatic in commenting that black slaves were the only people in the Americas who did not reproduce. Modern scholarship has confirmed this phenomenon.[35]

There were 172 slaves on the plantation La Rochefoucauld-Bayers in L'Anse-à-l'âne, Martinique, in 1764 when Governor de Fénelon wrote his report. Although Debien considered them to have been more fertile than usual, it is difficult to say whether the level of fertility he observed was representative of Martinique. Fifty-four married couples on the estate had a total of 211 children, an average of slightly less than 4 children per family. But of these, twelve families had 1 child each while one family had 9, another 10, and yet another, 16 children. While it is possible that not all of them had the same mother, these statistics seem to support Debien's claim that fertility was restricted to a limited number of slave women.[36]

Vanony-Frisch's data on Guadeloupe in the late eighteenth century point in a similar direction, in that there were a significant number of slave women without children. For example, 63 percent of African women in their fertile years had no children. A further breakdown of the figures reveals that 58 percent of creole women, 51 percent of black women, and 50 percent of mixed-race women had no children either. According to Vanony-Frisch, these statistics may well be on the high side, but at the very least they suggest that almost 50 percent of slave women had no living children. Another phenomenon worth highlighting is that many of those with children had only one or two with a gap of three to four years between them. This was particularly the case among African women. Large families were almost exclusively the preserve of creole and mixed-race slave women. For instance, data from the sugar plantation Valras in Sainte-Anne, Guadeloupe, show that in 1783, the black creole slave Rose, aged thirty, had seven children, the eldest of whom, the boy Silver, aged twelve years, was mixed race. When a slave woman had only one mixed-race child among her children, as was the case with Rose, that child was almost always her first. Vanony-Frisch has left it up to readers to speculate about why this was so, but a distinct possibility is rape. A second example of natality among mixed-race slave women on the Valras Plantation is worth citing. In 1788, thirty-five-year-old Scolastique, a domestic, was the mother of eleven living children. "Given her age," Vanony-Frisch noted, "there is nothing to suggest that she would stop at that," especially since she was freed from hard labor and promised unofficial liberty as long as she continued to provide "good service" and raise her children.[37]

Statistics from plantations in Saint-Domingue strengthen the case for low fertility among the slaves. On the Bréda Plantation in the late eighteenth century, 39 children, 12 of them under the age of two years, represented one-fifth of the slave population. This representation, according to Debien, was very small "to guarantee the future."[38] Indeed, the average birth rate on Saint-

Table 5.2. Births on the La Barre Plantation, Saint-Domingue, 1786–1790

Year	No. of Births
1786	2
1787	6
1788	5
1789	3
1790	1

Source: Gabriel Debien, *Les Esclaves aux Antilles françaises, XVIIe–XVIIIe siècle* (Basse-Terre: Société d'histoire de la Guadeloupe, 1974), 348.

Domingue plantations that have been studied in detail was less than 3 percent of the total slave population. On Galbaud du Fort, where there was an average slave population of 120 between 1741 and 1772, there were only about two births per year. After 1772, when the slave force increased to between 150 and 190, there were still only two to three births per year, and only rarely three.[39] The record of the La Barre Plantation in Vases, Saint-Domingue, where the average slave population was 150 between the years 1786 and 1789, and through purchase, 169 in 1790, was similar in that the birth rate was negligible, as table 5.2 shows.

While a low birth rate need not necessarily be accompanied by a high mortality rate, in the French Antilles, as in the rest of the Caribbean, this was the case. According to Debien, "more than half of the slaves died before the end of their acclimatization period. He estimated that the annual death rate among slaves in a year without epidemics such as diphtheria, dysentery, and gastric flu was 5–6 percent (about the same as the Jamaican rate), and 5 percent among whites. As epidemics were frequent in the French Antilles, during which death rates went as high as 10–15 percent, Debien concluded that the 5–6 percent rate may have been the minimum. He used an example from the sugar plantation Galbaud du Fort, Saint-Domingue, where the death rate was often 10 percent and higher between the years 1765 and 1786. In French Guiana, where slaves were not as numerous, mortality was also high. In 1817 there were 314 slaves on the Gabrielle sugar plantation; by 1847 the figure was 240, a decline of 24 percent. It is possible that some slaves acquired their liberty, but mortality on this estate was high, according to Bruleaux et al.[40] In Guadeloupe as a whole, as table 5.3 shows, deaths outnumbered births during the period 1845–47.

If the death rate among slaves was 5–6 percent, it is possible that the infant death rate was even higher. More reliable statistics became available after 1839 with the registration of births, marriages, and deaths among slaves, but the data remained fragmented. Thus, rather than offering statistics, Vanony-Frisch stated that the level of infant mortality wiped out any gains that an

Table 5.3. Births and Deaths among Slaves in Guadeloupe, 1845–1847

Year	Births	Deaths
1845	3,934	4,104
1846	3,604	3,922
1847	3,758	4,395

Source: Jacques Adélaïde-Merlande, "Demography and Names of Slaves of Le Moule, 1845 to May 1848," *Bulletin de la Société d'histoire de la Guadeloupe* 22, no. 2 (1974): 68.

already negligible birthrate could have made. Also, the workload decimated the adult slave population, particularly the men, such that the slave trade remained the only means of increasing the slave population. Boutin came to similar conclusions about mortality in Moule, where deaths exceeded births among the slaves. Infant mortality was high. In the years 1840, 1844, and 1847 the infant death rate went from 36 percent to 65 percent. However, Boutin believed that these figures were on the low side because deaths were often unregistered.[41]

Concern over high mortality led to an investigation of the sugar plantation de Hautmont in Marigot, Martinique, in the period 1807–22, during which the slave population fell to as low as 96 slaves. Defensive in tone, the administrative report that came out of the investigation showed that the death rate among adult slaves ranged from a low of 4 percent in some years to a high of 15 percent in others. It was careful to point out that in 1817, when 16 of 111 slaves died—the largest proportion over the fifteen-year period of the study—climate was a factor, as the plantation was hit by a severe windstorm. What is revealing is the recommendation that the slaves should be given increased rations, as they were apparently unable to cultivate sufficient food on the plantation itself. In this case, mortality was tied to deprivation; but as in former times, it was slave women and children who became the primary focus of attention.[42]

After a close study of the mortality phenomenon in 1764, Governor de Fénelon found overwork and underfeeding of slaves, the mistreatment of slave women—who were worked arduously up to the last minute before delivery—and illness among infant slaves, male and female, to be the principal causes. Of these causes he wrote, "It is impossible to suggest that one or the other would not impact on mother and child." De Fénelon thus regarded the condition of the slave woman as the central problem, and blamed greedy planters for exploiting her excessively and not educating her (as if they needed to) on how to nurture her children. "Their mothers carry them to the field on their shoulders, and leave them there all day long to the ardor of a burning sun," de Fénelon declared in a manner that lacked the acuity of Père Du Tertre. It is true that some slave women took their children to the fields. But they did so

in Africa as well, so the tropical climate was not really the problem. By highlighting the fact that the religious orders took comparatively good care of
slave women and their children, such that they were in a position to sell rather
than to purchase slaves, de Fénelon was suggesting that proper treatment of
slaves was the key. He gave the examples of Martiniquan plantations owned
by Monsieur Acquare of Basse-Pointe and the Jacobins, where slaves were no
longer being purchased but were being sold instead. The governor clearly felt
that he had a stake in the matter. He acknowledged that he took no action to
rectify the situation, even though the 1764 study convinced him of the need to
draft a law. However, he was cognizant of the fact that such a law would likely
not be observed. In the end, he considered the best solution to be the crea-
tion of slave clinics to be monitored by good surgeons in each district and to
which slaveowners would be obliged to send newborn slave infants. De Fénelon promised to consult Intendant de la Rivière on the matter, but the idea
of slave clinics never came to fruition. This is not surprising for de Fénelon
must have known that planters would never have agreed to any proposal that
would have removed slaves, potential capital and workers, from their direct
control. In focusing on child mortality, however, he pinpointed a problem that
remained a source of controversy for some time.[43]

General Joseph Romalet believed that the problem among the slaves was
not that they failed to procreate sufficiently but that the infants died. He also
believed that exhaustion compounded by the hot climate caused germs to
develop. In essence, Romalet was saying that the slaves no longer had the
resistance required to reproduce and were susceptible to diseases. On the
other hand, Boutin attributed the low birth rate to unsteady conjugal relations among slaves, fatigue due to overwork, lack of consideration on the part
of slave women for their children, and a will to limit reproduction. Most of all,
he blamed poor hygiene among slave women and, like many others, singled
out venereal diseases as a probable cause of low birth rates and even sterility.[44]

What was the response of slaveowners to low birth rates? They deplored
the low fertility of slave women, but economic calculations took precedence
over the lives of slaves, who were first and foremost dispensable labor units,
according to Debien. Slaveowners assumed that slave women were practicing
voluntary sterility and abortions. This assumption led to what Debien referred to as a "campaign of repression" during the last quarter of the eighteenth century. Debien indicated that there was no increase in the number of
abortions during this period, but offered no reason for the planters' actions.
It seems logical to assume, however, that the prospect of the abolition of the
Atlantic slave trade, which seemed inevitable by late in the century, was likely
a factor.[45]

Slaveowners adopted a two-pronged strategy aimed at raising the birthrate: they offered incentives to slave women to encourage them to reproduce

more, and punished those suspected of abortions and those whose children died at birth.

Planters in the French Caribbean fine-tuned the system of incentives that was also practiced in the British Caribbean, where slave women received money and other gifts as inducements to reproduce. In 1786, for example, planters in Barbados were encouraged to pay five shillings at the birth of every woman's first child, a practice which was common to Jamaica and the Leeward Islands from the end of the eighteenth century. In 1794, eight women who gave birth each received a dollar on the Worthy Park estate in Jamaica. Other inducements to fertility included a Jamaican slave law of 1787 under which females with six children were exempted from field labor. A similar practice was adopted by planters on Grenada in 1797.[46]

On the Foäche Plantation in Saint-Domingue in the late eighteenth century, a female slave who had four children was to be given a free day each week to work on her own account. When the last of the four children reached the age of fifteen, she was to be exempted from work altogether and given twice the amount of land normally allotted to slaves for kitchen gardens, but she was not permitted to leave the estate. Records from the Flauriau Plantation in Saint-Domingue show a strikingly similar system at work. Here a 1765 memorandum recommended that women with two children be given an extra day besides Sunday. For three children, she was to be granted two extra days; for four children, her husband was to be granted an extra day. If she had five children, she was allowed three extra days, and if she had six, she was to be permanently freed from plantation labor. But that was not all. For eight children, her husband was granted two extra days besides Sundays. And when two of the children reached working age and were able to replace their parents, the father was freed from plantation labor and allowed to do as he pleased with his time.[47] In this respect, males had a stake in this system and had nothing to lose: the more children they fathered, the greater their chances of liberty. They still lacked paternity rights, but this would not likely have mattered since these rights were never granted. However, women had some control over their fertility, which, by all indications, they consciously exercised. There are examples of slave women who had eight or more children, though not many.

On most plantations pregnant women and nursing mothers were exempt from certain tasks. On Flauriau, for example, they were exempt from night work at the mills, from field labor when it was raining, and from work before sunrise or after sunset. A month of rest after giving birth was recommended. Jacques Cauna gave the example of Honorée, forty-two, who was declared free on account of having seven children. But Bibianne, forty-nine, a mother of eight children, was still working as a nurse.[48] It may well be that some women were favored over others; it may also be that the need for certain skills forced planters to fall back on women who would normally be released from regular duties.

Correspondence between overseers and absentee plantation owners living in France attests to the pressure put on slave women to reproduce. Nowhere is this more evident than in the instructions that Stanislas Foäche of Saint-Domingue gave to his *gérant,* Paris, in 1775. These instructions reveal how precarious the position of midwifery was and how the fate of a midwife, and that of an expectant mother, hung in the balance depending on the outcome of a delivery. In stark terms, they demonstrate the barbarity to which women who could not produce a live infant were subjected. Foäche advised his overseer to put pregnant women in the hands of midwives when they were approaching their terms. For a live birth, Foäche ordered that the midwife be given fifteen *livres* and the mother cloth. If the child died at birth, however, both women were to be whipped, and the mother was to be placed in iron collars until she became pregnant again. In addition, "all female slaves who were expecting must, if they wished to avoid punishment, declare it to the midwife who must then report to the surgeon to have it registered."[49] Faced with the same predicament, other absentee planters with estates in Saint-Domingue issued similar instructions to their overseers. One, Chaurand, a shipowner and slave trader from Nantes, encouraged his *gérant,* Hamon de Vaujoyeux, to promise slave women fabric as an inducement. Yet another, Count d'Agoult, who owned a sugar plantation at Camp-de-Louise and a coffee plantation in Plaisance in the north of Saint-Domingue, wrote to his *gérant,* Feytant, in 1790 expressing astonishment at the low birth rate on the Plaisance estate, given that most of the slave women there were young and within their fertile years. After questioning whether this "inconvenience" was a result of libertinage or forced labor among the female slaves, he recommended a monetary reward for all slave women who gave birth on his estate. In addition, fabric to make blouses, skirts, and drawers was to be distributed to all if there was a particularly noteworthy crop of births. No expense should be spared in redoubling the care of pregnant women, d'Agoult stated. He indicated that he would rather have a contented lot of slaves than more revenue. "When the plantation is fully replenished," he ended, "I will certainly not be contented with this [stance]."[50]

It would be difficult to determine what psychological impact the pressure to produce live births had on slave women. But the observations of Monsieur Dazille—a French medical doctor who treated slaves in Saint-Domingue and published studies dealing with their illnesses—are instructive. More informed than most, Dazille sought to show that the phenomenon of low fertility went beyond slave women's resistance. Black women had the capacity to reproduce, but lack of health care, inexperienced midwives, inadequate nutrition, poor sanitation, and ill health were the central problems. In other words, one could not expect live, healthy births from overworked, undernourished, and unhealthy slave women.

As if to underscore this position, Dazille gave a detailed, clinical account of the pregnancy and delivery of a diminutive woman with a physical impediment. A slave on the plantation Desglereaux in the district of Morin in Saint-Domingue, Suzon was about three feet tall and afflicted with a growth on her breastbone that reached almost to her chin. "This deformity," according to Dazille, "did not prevent her from becoming pregnant in 1779 by a young slave, 5 feet, 6 inches tall." Her pregnancy became very difficult from the fifth month due to the size of the fetus, which put pressure on her diaphragm, resulting in difficult breathing. As an initial bloodletting relieved her for only fifteen days, Dazille performed eight other such surgical procedures on her during the last four months of her pregnancy. Although her pelvic cavity conformed to type, he prepared for a caesarian birth, mindful of the "excessive" size of her abdomen and the accidents that she had had during her pregnancy. After Suzon's water broke, however, Dazille was amazed and delighted to find that her contractions were slow and moderate, and that the infant's head engaged the pelvic basin in a manner consistent with normal deliveries. Thus the position of the child in the womb was of crucial importance in this case. But her labor lasted for thirty-eight hours, the longest Dazille had seen in the colonies. Paradoxically, it was, Dazille contended, the constant bloodletting that diminished Suzon's muscular force and permitted her to deliver a "voluminous" baby boy, "so disproportionate to his mother." In suggesting that a woman in a weakened physical state was in a good position to deliver a well-developed child, it is possible that Dazille was exaggerating in order to justify his medical techniques. In any case, he praised Suzon for her courage and stamina in delivering a robust child, whom she then nourished and raised, but he clearly felt that there was a correlation between the availability of medical expertise and live births, as the following case demonstrates.[51]

In 1788 Dazille was called to a plantation owned by Madame de Bellevue in Limonade, Saint-Domingue, to deliver two slave women. On this occasion, he was a substitute for Dr. Balay, the surgeon responsible for delivery on the plantation, so he was not familiar with the medical history of the slave women. Upon arrival he discovered that the women were not at all close to term. In fact, the more advanced of the two was only about five months pregnant. But her mother, who served as midwife on the plantation, was apparently persuaded that her daughter was further along in her pregnancy and that she possessed the will to accelerate or slow down its progress. Angry that her daughter seemed to be malingering, she slapped her in the face and, using her knee, administered several kicks to the stomach, all the while repeating that it was a little devil that was keeping her from experiencing birth pains.[52]

Dazille characterized the midwife's treatment of her daughter as outrageous, but noted that such actions had not yet caused any mishaps. Therefore, all he was required to do was to calm tempers.

It seems certain that the midwife was attempting to induce birth rather than to harm her daughter and her unborn child. That she did so at a time well before her daughter was due may well have been a reflection of the pressure midwives felt to produce live births. More knowledge about the reproductive history of this slave would be helpful in analyzing the midwife's action. For example, it would be useful to know if she had a history of miscarriages or faked pregnancies. Dazille noted that doctors were not generally consulted in cases of pregnancy and childbirth, or for postnatal care, but that their services were particularly needed in the countryside, as slave midwives had a tendency to act precipitously.[53] Because the majority of slave children were delivered by slave midwives, their level of knowledge could hardly have been as low as Dazille insinuated, however. Debien noted that in cases of difficult pregnancies, the plantation sometimes sent slave women to a surgeon to be delivered, though at considerable cost; this was the case in 1781, when a Saint-Domingue plantation paid 18 *livres* for one such delivery. For the most part, however, skillful slave midwives were summoned from far and wide and rewarded for their expertise. On September 23, 1787, for instance, the Bréda Plantation in Saint-Domingue paid the midwife Bêche 198 *livres* for "non-natural" deliveries.[54] Debien did not indicate whether Bêche was a slave. It was not unusual for slaves to earn cash by working outside the confines of the plantation. Whether she was or not, it would be interesting to know whether midwives like her came under the same pressure as others, and how failure on their part was regarded and dealt with by slaveowners.

What is certain is that the harsh measures that planters adopted in an effort to increase birthrates did not have the desired effects, because of the harsh practices of slaveowners and the health-related problems that Dazille identified. Indeed, neonatal tetanus—the infamous *mal à mâchoir* (lockjaw)— was frequent, but ignorance persisted with regard to its causes, so it was easy and convenient to blame slave women. Pierre de Vassière compared lockjaw to the use of poison by slaves. This comparison is striking for in both cases slave women could not always prove their innocence.[55]

Romalet, like some in the British Caribbean, believed that tetanus resulted from inhaling smoke emanating from the fires that the slaves lit to keep themselves warm at night and from exposure to the cool morning and evening air. He did not side with the planters in blaming slave women, but advocated more humane working conditions that would enable them to provide better care for their infants.[56] Dazille went much further. He did not rule out atmospheric changes in temperatures as a probable cause of tetanus, which he called "the most violent and destructive convulsive illness." In fact, he believed that the slaves' constant exposure to dwellings that were defectively constructed caused them not to perspire, a condition that led to tetanus. He too recommended that before and after pregnancy, slave women be kept at a room temperature of 31–33 degrees Celsius. But his work in treating illnesses among slaves at the state hospital in Saint-Domingue led him to conclude that material conditions lay at the heart of many of the diseases, including tetanus, that afflicted the slaves. As slaves went barefoot in performing their daily tasks, they were particularly susceptible to cuts that resulted in tetanus. Indeed, Dazille observed that there were usually several seriously wounded slaves in all the plantation hospitals. He found that tetanus was less frequent on plantations where the needs of the slaves were well met. It was also less frequent among white children, whose clothing and person were continually surveyed, than among black children. He wrote that during his visit to French Guiana from December 1763 to May 1765, he did not encounter a single case of child tetanus on account of the low population of blacks there.[57]

In highlighting the relationship between material conditions and tetanus, Dazille focused almost entirely on slave women. In their hands lay its prevention and cure; in their hands lay the key to live births. He recommended that slave women be given light work in the late stages of pregnancy and be sent to the delivery room at the first sign of birth pains. He regarded weekly examinations of pregnant slave women by surgeons and doctors as indispensable in detecting illnesses, especially venereal diseases. Too often slave children were born of hungry mothers, and they were usually so ill from the outset that they were too weak to suck their mothers' milk. Unable to swallow properly (a sure sign of lockjaw), they died within the first days of life, he contended.

He recommended that, in addition to the mother's milk, which is slightly acid in the first days after delivery but usually sufficient, the child should be given a half teaspoonful of palma-christie oil. This was especially necessary when the child had grippe. With these precautions, tetanus could be avoided in children, Dazille pronounced. However, children who contracted tetanus could be given a dose of "Laudonum de Sydenham" (laudanum) before the muscle spasms began. Another medication that Dazille administered daily to slave women and children in cases of lockjaw was a dose of two grains of mercury, which Dazille evidently found to be efficacious.[58]

There is no doubt that Dazille knew a great deal about the medical condition of slaves in the French colonies, but the explanations of the causes of tetanus that he and others gave reveal the ignorance surrounding the disease at the time. Clearly, his observations about child mortality suggest that Morrissey is correct in pointing out that neonatal tetanus accounted for most deaths among newborn infants.[59] Although Dazille drew a connection between cuts and tetanus, he ignored the probability that the instruments midwives used to sever the umbilical cord were contaminated and caused tetanus, as is still the case in modern Haiti, according to Kiple.[60] Also, apart from his medical prescriptions, most of his findings and recommendations were a matter of prudence and common sense. No slaveowner could expect to work a slave woman close to term as vigorously as one who was not pregnant without taking risks. A malnourished slave woman afflicted with disease could hardly be expected to produce healthy offspring. But slaveowners were reluctant to spend money for health care for slaves. This Dazille did not point out. Thus, although his contribution is valuable from the point of view of medicine, it falls short in that it sought to identify and treat symptoms without attacking the root causes of poor health among the slaves.

SEXUAL ABUSE

Slave women also had limited means at their disposal to combat sexual abuse and to keep their families intact. Not all relations between slave women and males in authority can or should be construed as sexual abuse, but whether single or married, slave women were assaulted by males of all ethnicities in the French Antilles. We have no personal testimonies such as that presented by Thomas Thistlewood, a young English overseer in Jamaica in the mid-eighteenth century, who sexually exploited a host of slave women and recorded his daily activities (partly in Latin) in a journal. However, the significant number of mixed-race children who, along with their mixed-race mothers, acquired freedom in the French Antilles the 1830s and 1840s (see chapter 9) suggest sexual abuse. There were also slave women whose owners allowed them to work away from the plantations in establishments such as taverns in the port city of Saint-Pierre, Martinique, where prostitution was rife.[61]

Between 1771 and 1778, Lory de la Bernardière, the white nephew of the owner of the Cottineau Plantation in Saint-Domingue, sexually exploited slave women. As his mother noted, "He is given to amusement and a life of debauchery. He has fostered a harem of black women who control him and run the plantation." Note the criticism of black women in the correspondence of de la Bernardière's mother, in spite of the fact that her son had power over the slave women and lived the life of a villain and demi-criminal and brought hardship to the plantation. Thus women were blamed for their own victimization.[62]

Slave women were particularly vulnerable to abuse by slave drivers because of the nature of their work and the power wielded by these "official tyrants," as Debien called them. Some slaveowners consulted slave drivers when purchasing new slaves, even taking them aboard slave ships to participate in the selection process. It is therefore possible that this was a factor in their relations with women. The September 11, 1792, issue of the newspaper *Journal Politique de Saint-Domingue* carried the story of Jean-Baptiste, fifty-nine, who, as Debien noted, had worked as a slave driver on the Foäche sugar estate in Jean-Rabel, where he sexually exploited slave women irrespective of their conjugal ties. The newspaper revealed that Jean-Baptiste had fathered more than 60 children on the estate. He was commended for keeping order on an estate of more than 500 slaves often frequented by bandits. For his services, Jean-Baptiste was given his freedom. Was Jean-Baptiste an isolated case, or was he living up to the reputation of *commandeurs* as the *coq des ateliers*—rooster of the slave gangs—mentioned in a document cited by Debien.[63]

Slaveowners treated the exploits of slave drivers rather lightly out of concern for a breakdown of authority on the plantation. This explains why slave drivers were never disciplined in front of the slave gang. The instructions that Foäche left to his *gérant* in the 1770s are instructive in this regard. Slave drivers were to be handled with great caution. Time would take care of any negligence resulting from their passionate distractions, Foäche believed. However, he was to be relieved of duties if he seduced the wives of other slaves—an unpardonable offense which merited a severe whipping in the presence of the plantation gang to prevent greater breaches. Debien noted that this order was never followed for, as he pointed out, Jean-Baptiste could not have had sixty children with his wife or with unattached slave maidens. It is not known if Jean-Baptiste had a household on the plantation.[64]

While the defensive mechanisms that slave women employed in fighting off sexual abuse may elude the historian, their response to physical abuse can be more easily charted. Fortunately, court records and other accounts reveal that slave women fought back when able, and sought redress by whatever means were necessary, including litigation. These responses, which are taken up in the next two chapters, may help to deepen our understanding of how they combated sexual abuse.

6

Discipline and Physical Abuse
Slave Women and the Law

IN ADDITION TO the low fertility rates and high infant mortality they experienced, slave women were subjected to severe physical punishment by slaveowners, male and female, other plantation personnel, and by slave drivers. Slaveowners and others in authority punished female slaves as harshly as they did male slaves, but slave women, being more directly in the line of confrontation with the slave system than men due to their subordinate position within the slave occupational hierarchy, were apt to be punished more frequently and, quite often, with more venom. Although there was "equality under the drivers' whip," as Beckles put it, gender played a role in punishment.[1] Indeed, with few exceptions, those who administered punishment were males, black and white, and they may have perceived slave women as easier to discipline than men. Also, slave women, not men, were the object of jealous rages.

Quite often, the punishment to which slave women, like men, were subjected amounted to sheer cruelty, as evidenced by the many dossiers in the French archives under the heading *Sévices contre les esclaves* (cruelty against slaves). But such treatment went unchecked and unpunished for most of the slavery period, in spite of the so-called "protective" clauses in the Code Noir and the innumerable amendments that were introduced after its promulgation. Thanks to slave women who initiated legal proceedings based on changes in the law in the 1830s and 1840s in particular, French authorities were forced to investigate cases of brutality against slaves that might otherwise have been ignored. Although the amendments to the law curtailed the disciplinary powers of slaveowners and gave more authority to colonial bureaucrats to rein them in, they neither nullified nor contravened the laws found in the Code Noir.

WHIPPING

Whipping was the most common form of discipline and physical abuse, and labor disputes were the most contentious issue between the slaves and the slave system that led to its use. Indeed, it is rare to find a French source on slavery that does not mention whipping. In the seventeenth century, Père Du Tertre quoted a proverb, albeit racist, that captures the relationship between whipping and blacks, as it was likely perceived at the time: "To look at a Native American askance is to beat him; to beat him is to kill him; to beat a black is to nourish him."[2]

From Du Tertre's time onward, this conception prevailed. So although flogging was common in Europe, it took on racial overtones in the Caribbean and became a panacea in dealing with slaves. At the outset of the *Black Jacobins,* for example, C.L.R. James used whipping to depict the relationship between slaves and slaveowners—the whip being the symbol of oppression. He wrote, "The stranger in San Domingo was awakened by the cracks of the whip, the stifled cries, and the heavy groans of the Negroes who saw the sun rise only to curse it for its renewal of their labours and their pains." In reference to Saint-Domingue as well, Jean Fouchard indicated that "For the least infraction, the slave was whipped to satisfy the sadistic pleasure of the [slave] driver." In a letter of April 1769, Bernardin de Saint-Pierre, a visitor, noted that slaves were frequently attached by the hands and feet to ladders and whipped until their skin was rent. "I have seen," he wrote, "male and female slaves whipped daily for breaking a bit of earthenware or forgetting to close a door." An observer and author of a historical work on Saint-Domingue also remarked that in the French Antilles, one spoke not in terms of "whipping" the slave but in terms of "trimming" the slave—a reference to mutilation. Similarly, France, a police superintendent in the French colonies in the 1840s, stated that whipping was tantamount to torture, "always excessive and barbarous, . . . with the potential of maiming the victim by assaulting his private parts or even killing him, if not instantly, as has already been the case, in due course, as is often the case."[3]

In the eighteenth century, reports of slaves receiving fifty, a hundred, and even two hundred lashes surfaced. Some of these reports may well have been exaggerated, or may have failed to mention that whipping was sometimes administered in installments and not all at once. There is no doubt, however, that the disciplinary powers of slaveowners were real and excessive, and were backed by a Code Noir that was mostly gender neutral and set no limits on whipping. Breaches of the Code Noir were really breaches of a code of conduct, but they were treated as criminal offenses for the most part. Under Article 42 of the Code Noir, slaveowners were allowed to chain slaves and administer discretionary whippings with branches, cords, and cowhides, but they were forbidden to torture or mutilate them—actions for which the state could prosecute them and confiscate their slaves. However, mutilation and death were permitted in cases of *marronnage* and physical assault on whites that drew blood, but not assaults against people of color.[4]

Following complaints about the unlimited whipping of slaves, the Conseil Supérieur of Cayenne, French Guiana, limited the number of lashes a slave could receive in that colony to twenty-five in 1777.[5] The council's action was backed by a royal injunction, which suggests that this limit became standard throughout the French Antilles, but there was variation in the region. In Martinique a local ordinance of December 25, 1783, set the legal maximum number of strokes at twenty-nine, but fifty strokes were allowed for a short time after 1783.[6] However, a royal ordinance of October 15, 1786, reinforced the 1783 ordinance and made it applicable to all the French colonies.[7] Even though the legal limit remained twenty-nine strokes for some time prior to 1845, however, administrative correspondence suggests that colonial officials were uneasy with a fixed number, reasoning, quite correctly, that much harm could be done to slaves by a whipping that stayed within the official guidelines. In 1842, for example, the Procureur Général of French Guiana wrote to the governor of the colony to say that the vast majority of magistrates were in favor of a law under which a certain number of lashes would constitute "barbarous and inhumane punishment even when such punishment did not result in illness or incapacity to work." The magistrates also believed that the determining factor should be the consequences of the whipping rather than the actual number of lashes. The Procureur Général indicated that magistrates were in need of clear guidelines on this issue, but it remained unresolved.[8]

By 1840 the Minister of Marine and Colonies in Paris considered proposals to abolish corporal punishment for female slaves, and to limit the number of strokes male slaves could receive to fifteen. Also, as a means of curbing their excesses, slaveowners would be required to record, within twenty-four hours of a disciplinary action, the offenses slaves committed, their age, sex, and occupation, as well as the punishment administered to them. Members of the Conseil des Délégues des Colonies, who commented on the proposals, raised concerns about how illiterate slaveowners in colonies such as French Guiana, where they were numerous, would follow the law. They expressed alarm at the prospect of the Minister imposing stiff fines and other penalties on slaveowners for the slightest infractions in record keeping in the French colonies, where slavery was "mild." However, the proposals were adopted. Magistrates could pay surveillance visits to plantations to verify slave conditions under a law enacted on January 5, 1840. And a law enacted on September 16, 1841, limited prison terms of slaves to fifteen consecutive days on the plantation. Beyond that, power was transferred to the justice of the peace, who normally set prison terms in public jails and work terms on state farms.[9]

In 1845 these and other measures that sought to protect slaves (at least nominally) while safeguarding the rights of slaveowners were incorporated into what became known as the Mackau Law. Promulgated on July 18, the law limited the use of chains and the number of hours slaves could work, and authorized magistrates and colonial officials, including the Procureur Général, to pay surveillance visits to plantations to ascertain whether slaveowners were abiding by the regulations. The Mackau Law was sweeping in scope, but its effectiveness was another matter altogether.

THE CODE NOIR AND THE TREATMENT OF SLAVES IN LAW AND CUSTOM

In view of the changes in slave law down to the 1840s, it would be legitimate to ask what legal options were open to slaves who wished to redress their grievances. Their most difficult problem was lack of direct access to the courts. Article 44 of the Code Noir declared that slaves were chattel—the property of their owners. In theory, all that they possessed also belonged to their owners. And their offspring were slaves in perpetuity, the property of the slave woman's owner. As chattel, slaves could not testify in criminal or civil matters, according to Articles 30 and 31 of the Code Noir. If they were ever required to testify (which they sometimes were), their testimony was to be used solely in aiding judges to evaluate their cases; however, the evidence they presented could also be disregarded. But Article 26 left an opening for slaves to lodge complaints of cruel treatment and deprivation against their owners with the Procureur Général, their legal guardian and chief representative of the Crown in the colonies, who had broad investigative powers and access to state funds. The existence of such provisions led Elsa Goveia to argue that, although the slaves in the French Antilles were private property, they did not cease to be a matter of public concern and that public interference in the management of slaves was taken for granted, at least until the expansion of slavery and the "development of a feeling of white solidarity." However, one should not infer, as did Goveia, that slavery was more humane in the French colonies, for it was not. As Louis Sala-Molins has pointed out, slaves could complain, but their testimony was considered worthless. Besides, both slaveowners and the colonial administration were secure in the knowledge that Articles 30 and 31 would be scrupulously respected, while Article 26 was regarded as a mere "legislative distraction," elevating the slave to the status of "subject" that was denied in the rest of the Code Noir. Another problem was that outcomes depended on the integrity of judicial officials and administrations, some of whom were slaveowners and had a vested interest in slavery. Not surprisingly, judicial rulings were uneven, spotty, and biased in favor of slaveowners. As a result, violations of the laws were rampant, although periodically some slaveowners were fined, banished from the colonies, deprived of owning slaves, and, less often, imprisoned.[10]

Slaveowners regularly committed atrocities against their slaves. Pierre de Vassière cited a letter written by Gallifet in 1699 in which he mentioned the case of a colonist who shot a slave in Léogane, Saint-Domingue, and was fined

100 *livres* after eight months of investigation by a judge and the Procureur du Roi, a subordinate of the Procureur Général. Another colonist spurred an eleven-year-old slave girl to death and was fined 600 *livres*. The outcome of these cases caused de Vassière to conclude that judges were unwilling to go beyond imposing fines in response to slaveowners' violations.[11]

In spite of royal ordinances of 1784 and 1785 that went beyond the Code Noir and gave slaves the legal right to denounce abuses committed by slaveowners and plantation administrators, the judiciary was reluctant to convict guilty slaveowners or hand down appropriate sentences. In some instances, the courts ignored strong, convincing, and condemnatory evidence collected from French administrators and slaves against slaveowners accused of cruelty to slaves, and dismissed the cases. The cases that came to light (only a minority did) involved cruelty to both male and female slaves, but females were disproportionately represented, and the range and nature of acts of cruelty against them were greater than in the case of male slaves.[12]

In 1736 the female slaveowner Audache of Léogane, Saint-Domingue, retrieved a young slave girl she owned from prison (which suggests that she may have been caught at *marronnage*—the most common cause of imprisonment among slaves), had her put in the stocks, and whipped once she was back on the plantation. The following day Audache ordered that the slave be given the *trois piquets* punishment, which involved being tied to three posts face down and whipped. With the complicity of one Lazare, Audache began to torture the slave. Lazare dowsed her with gunpowder, which he also spread on the cane trash surrounding her, while Audace set the pile ablaze, meaning to scorch rather than to consume her. As the slave struggled hopelessly to free herself, Audace placed her feet on the slave's shoulder "so that the fire could burn her stomach." Audace then had her taken to the kitchen, where she applied aloe and quicklime to the slave's wounds. The slave was tortured in this manner for five days, until another slave reported the matter to the authorities. As Lucien Peytraud noted, however, there is no indication that the guilty parties were ever brought to justice.[13]

Peytraud stated that the judiciary intervened increasingly on the side of slaves, but the cases he cited show that this intervention was, at best, limited. Besides, he was not able to provide a comprehensive picture of judicial rulings as his study of slavery does not go beyond 1789. One of the cases he highlighted occurred in 1746, when the state confiscated a female slave from her owner, Foucault, fined him 2,000 *livres* for her upkeep in addition to 3 *livres d'amende,* and prohibited him from owning slaves in the future on grounds of poor treatment. In another example, dating from 1760, the wife of a brigadier named Veigne was condemned by the judiciary in French Guiana to serve a life sentence for beating a slave woman (of whom she was jealous) to death. The incident occurred when her husband, the manager of the estate on which the slave woman lived, was absent. The slave was owned by one Descoublans. The action that the brigadier's wife took was a deliberate and unprovoked act which amounted to premeditated murder. French archival documents indicate that by imposing life imprisonment, the authorities apparently meant to set an example, but Veigne wrote a letter to them requesting that the king of France pardon his wife, Jeanne. The governor of Guiana appeared to have been somewhat sympathetic. He stated that he was not especially concerned about Jeanne's plight but noted that Veigne, a father of children who were potentially good workers, had been an honest servant of the king for six years, during which he foiled plots and desertions from the garrison. In any case, the punishment Jeanne received was no compensation for the slave woman's life, and there is no certain evidence that she remained in prison.[14]

Among the actions of slaves who sought protection from their owners, the one brought against Sieur Dessource of Le Cap, Saint-Domingue, provides further evidence of cruelty. In 1771 Dessource set fire to his slave driver Janne, torched the feet and legs of two female slaves, Fanchette and Jeanette, and then had them buried alive. In addition, Dessource torched the feet and legs of another female slave, who was pregnant, and placed her in solitary confinement in the plantation dungeon, where she died. That Dessource assaulted his slave driver in the presence of other slaves may have had the effect of creating solidarity among the slaves and emboldening them to approach the authorities. In this case, the judge's response could not have satisfied the aggrieved slaves: he confined them to prison for their own safety as well as that of "the aggressor."[15]

The fourteen male and female slaves who lodged a complaint with Saint-Domingue authorities in 1788 against their owner, Lejeune—the wealthy coffee planter from Plaisance—received no justice either, but their case reveals a disturbing pattern of cruelty against women slaves in particular. So severe did the slaves consider Lejeune's actions that they asked to be voluntarily imprisoned rather than return to the plantation. An official investigation corroborated their account. Lejeune set a male and female slave on fire, and he torched the feet and legs of two female slaves, whom he accused of poisoning a female slave during delivery and of attempting to poison him with a powder. This he did in order to extort a confession. He then placed the women in solitary confinement in the plantation prison, the infamous *cachot*. A subsequent investigation, based on analysis of the powder in question, showed that the women were innocent. The king's doctor, a state-authorized physician, found that the powder was a mixture of tobacco and rat dung. Both C.L.R. James and Carolyn Fick noted that the investigators, two magistrates of the state, found the two women chained and barely alive, with parts of their bodies in a state of decomposition. In spite of the weight of the evidence against him, including further testimony by the fourteen slaves, Lejeune was acquitted, a decision based on concerns about the security of whites and the need to instill fear in the hearts of the slaves. As Lejeune himself warned, "Remove this brake and the slave will attempt anything." Interestingly, his slaves viewed the judicial system as a means of redressing their grievances. Surely it is of significance that they filed their complaints before the courts a few years after the introduction of the royal ordinances of 1784 and 1785. That the judicial process did not yield the results they must have hoped for must be seen against the fact that they dared to test the system.[16]

Lest it appear that slaveowners in Saint-Domingue had a monopoly on brutality, the Sommabert case proves otherwise. On February 15, 1827, the Conseil Privé of Guadeloupe considered the case of a slaveowner and former artillery officer, François Rivière Sommabert of Moule. Sommabert had refused to reimburse Marie, a former slave who, at the request of authorities, cared for one of Sommabert's slaves, Jean-Philippe, at a cost of 160 francs for a period of thirty-two days. Sommabert was also accused of murdering the slave woman Mélie, a fugitive who was caught on a neighboring plantation, and of other crimes against slaves including torture, assassination, confinement, and deprivation of food. Of all the heinous acts that Sommabert committed, his treatment of Mélie was the most horrendous, according to an administrative report. Sommabert beat her severely; then he attached her to the millworks and ordered all the slaves present to beat her with a stick. He then trampled her, jumped on her chest, punctured her stomach, and burnt her in hay up to her chest. After she died, Sommabert ordered that she be buried far away from the slave burial grounds. As this was not normal practice, it may be that Sommabert wished to conceal the evidence of wrongdoing while making an example of her.[17]

Reports from the coroner following exhumation of Mélie's body, as well as testimony from police authorities and Sommabert's *économe* and slaves, confirmed the conditions under which Mélie and other slaves died, and formed the basis for charges against Sommabert and his wife and accomplice, Lady Rivière. A year after the Conseil Privé's sitting, administrative correspondence indicates that Sommabert was remanded in custody. In a letter of February 6, 1828, the governor of Guadeloupe informed the Minister of Marine and Colonies that, in spite of government surveillance, Sommabert had attempted to escape on several occasions with the help of family members. Although the prison warden in Pointe-à-Pitre, the capital of Guadeloupe, had refused a significant bribe to release him and reported the matter to authorities, the governor seemed resigned to the fact that Sommabert would eventually escape, as the prison buildings were not very secure. This raises a question as to whether the same fears existed about the possibility of slaves escaping from prison. In any case, the Cour Royale of Martinique cleared Sommabert of all charges in 1829. The admission of slave testimony, and Sommabert's claim that he was absent from the scene when his slaves (whom he accused of carrying out his orders overzealously) beat Mélie, seem to have been the basis of the acquittal. The resolution of this case came on the eve of important amendments to the slave laws, but at the level of the judiciary, the slaves fared no better. Why was this?[18]

The laws that were introduced in the 1830s and 1840s were important in that they were designed to ameliorate slavery at a time when the political and economic climate warranted change, but they were not really effective. First, there was a change in administration in France which resulted in a more conciliatory approach to slavery. Second, the sugar-plantation economies of the French Antilles became more integrated into the world market economy and declined as a result of increased competition, particularly from new areas of production and the rise of beet sugar production.[19]

Josette Fallope has argued convincingly that the July Monarchy under Louis-Philippe ushered in a new era in 1830. She contended that the new rulers were ideologically close to the liberal principles of the French Revolution, with its emphasis on civil rights, and were preoccupied with policies aimed at lessening the tensions in slave society and resolving conflicts through dialogue and liberal solutions. Other scholars credit the July Monarchy for creating the atmosphere that eventually led to the abolition of slavery, but note that it did so out of fear of violent eruptions in the colonies and that the state sometimes violated its own policies on the slave trade. In any case, both in France and in the colonies, new liberal personnel were appointed to head government ministries, and this created an atmosphere of hope.[20]

On the economic front, the sugar economies of the French Antilles began to falter after 1830 due to local and international factors. The loss of Haitian sugar production beginning in 1804 led to the loss of French dominance on the European market. The beet sugar industry in France began to thrive in 1830, production rising from 7,000 metric tons in that year to 20,000 metric tons in 1833 and 40,000 in 1835. This impressive increase was largely due to French protective tariffs and duties placed on sugar produced in the colonies. At the same time new and more fertile areas of production such as Mauritius, India, Java, and the Philippines made the sugar industry more global and competitive. In Mauritius, for example, sugar cane cultivation expanded from 27,000 acres in the 1820s to 129,000 acres in the 1860s. Similarly, as David Northrop noted, "sugar exports rose from an annual average of 33,443 tons in the 1830s, to 100,000 tons in the 1850s and 1860s." However, increased globalization led to a fall in French colonial sugar prices. From 139.90 francs per 100 kilograms in 1830, colonial sugar prices dropped to 107.18 francs on the Paris market in 1839. The colonial economies were therefore characterized by crisis in the 1830s. In these circumstances the viability of the slave system was questioned, particularly after 1833, when the 1831 ban on the French maritime slave trade was taken seriously for the first time. For about fifteen years, the French had resisted British demands to board and search French ships suspected of trading slaves illegally, but the July Monarchy reluctantly conceded in order to promote good diplomatic relations with England, which it needed to counterbalance other forces in Europe. With the abolition of British slavery in 1834, French abolitionists were motivated to redouble their efforts in the struggle to end French slavery. Indeed, it was in 1834 that the Société pour l'abolition de l'esclavage was founded in Paris with the aim of monitoring slave conditions and ending slavery. During a debate on colonial budgets in 1836, one of its members, Lamartine, called for the immediate emancipation of the slaves. As these are the circumstances under which new slave laws were introduced, it seems probable that the July Monarchy tried to reach a compromise between abolishing slavery, as the liberals would have liked, and keeping it on grounds of economic necessity. This means that while supporting the planters, the July Monarchy would also become more responsive to criticisms of their excesses.[21]

This was a period when accounts of cruelty to slaves surfaced in antislavery publications such as the *Anti-Slavery Reporter,* a French newspaper. In an issue dated February 23, 1841, it noted that slaveowners had poisoned and mutilated slaves. It reported the eyewitness account given by one Favel Gourand, who said that six bulls, egged on by six whites, gored a slave to death on the plantation Marquise de Bellegrade in Martinique. Neither the authorities nor the judiciary endeavored to stop the incident, he claimed.[22] In France the Minister of Marine and Colonies was aware of the criticisms leveled against slaveowners and the judicial system, but there was a tendency at this time for the Ministry to view the problem in terms of differences in interpretation of slave law. In a circular sent to colonial governors in November 1841, the Minister complained that slaveowners were out of hand and that unlimited detention and certain corrective measures they used to punish first offenses at *marronnage* were incompatible not only with the laws of morality and humanity but with a sound interpretation of the slave laws. "It was never understood," he wrote, "that the master possessed, in any sense of the word, the person of the slave; it is solely the labor of the slave that has been allotted to him." The Minister was aware of the laws in the Code Noir that gave slaveowners the right to chain slaves, but insisted that such measures were meant to deal with serious offenses that threatened the security of the plantation and not simple infractions. Given amendments that were introduced after 1685, the Minister held the opinion that the Code Noir regulation on discipline had been superseded. He believed that a laudable humanitarian sentiment had begun to take effect among "the great majority" of slaveowners, as evidenced by inspections showing that most *cachots* had been abandoned while others "were either destroyed spontaneously by slaveowners, or at the urging of the Procureurs du

Roi and their deputies." By adopting a broad interpretation of the slave laws and relying upon uncritical reports from magistrates who visited the plantations, the Ministry was somewhat out of touch with the actual situation of the slaves, however.[23]

Although attitudes toward the law among white colonists remained fairly uniform and the slaves' recourse to the judiciary remained circumscribed, scholars should still proceed cautiously. Slaveowners resisted change, but they faced an increasingly determined and resilient slave population that was willing to test the limits of the slave system and profit from the cracks in white hegemony that became more evident in the 1830s and 1840s, when administrative officials began to monitor conditions on the plantations. For the slaves surveillance of plantations and "protection" by public officials did not come without a price. Word spread quickly in slave society and the fate of slaves who lodged complaints with the authorities was known, but they still persisted. In 1840 a group of six female and male slaves from Saint-Pierre, Martinique, lodged a complaint with the Procureur du Roi, after initial complaints to their female owner about the abuse they and other slaves suffered at the hands of their plantation overseer were disregarded. For their efforts, the slaves were imprisoned overnight. With their hands tied behind their backs, they were taken under police escort back to the plantation the following day, there to be whipped in front of the plantation gang.[24] Similarly, Schoelcher related the case of a slave woman and her daughter from Moule, Guadeloupe, who complained about excessive whipping, which produced, in the woman's case, cuts and welts that made mobility difficult. The medical report which he examined also showed that the woman received fifteen to twenty strokes and her daughter, twelve to fifteen. Thus the decline in the maximum number of strokes did not lead to a decline in the abuse of slaves. The persistent complaints lodged by slaves show that they were conscious of the intent of the law, however.[25]

COMBATING PHYSICAL ABUSE

In March 1840 the actions of Marie-Claire, a slave on the plantation Mondelice in French Guiana, showed how the slaves interpreted the intent of the law and acted accordingly. The management of Mondelice exempted Marie-Claire from work on account of the number of children she had, four of whom had reached adulthood. This act was in keeping with incentives to encourage natural reproduction among slaves, as we saw in the previous chapter. The manner in which she attempted to use her free time was the crux of the problem, however. According to the overseer, Vidal de Lingendes, Marie-Claire was one of several slaves who absented themselves regularly from the plantation. French archival sources indicate that some of these slaves were maroons; others had been granted the same "privileges" as Marie-Claire. The overseer complained that they remained in the city for extended periods without permission and turned to vagabondage at night. The situation was such that only the ailing slaves responded to the call to return to the plantation for morning prayers. When the thirty-year-old *régisseur,* Auguste Nicolas Reine, ordered that all slaves on the plantation should attend morning and evening prayers, Marie-Claire was apparently the only one to disregard his directive. Upon her eventual return, the overseer ordered that she be given five strokes for refusing to comply with orders. When she complained to Reine about the punishment, he ordered that she be given another nine strokes. Marie-Claire continued to press the matter, however, and denounced Reine in the presence of the plantation's slaves. For this, he ordered that she be given twenty-nine additional strokes. She was also incarcerated in the plantation prison but was released a few hours later upon the request of her husband. The morning after she was released she left the plantation without permission, walked for four hours to Cayenne, the capital, and exposed her predicament publicly and loudly before several magistrates and friends of her absentee owner. She also identified several witnesses who could corroborate her account.[26]

The Procureur Général heard about the case through Anne Marie, Marie-Claire's daughter. A hired-out slave, Anne Marie was working as a domestic in his household, and she raised the matter at dinner in the presence of his guests. The Procureur Général visited the plantation and advised Reine to conduct an investigation. A perturbed Reine claimed that Marie-Claire had eluded even the light tasks which she had been required to perform on the plantation, and had suffered no ill effects from the whipping. He also lamented that "the entire city of Cayenne had been made aware of the case because of her actions," and insinuated that the Procureur Général was biased because of his intimate relations with Marie-Claire's daughter. In any case, the Procureur Général reported the incident to the governor, who complained about infringement upon his jurisdiction, but who nevertheless followed administrative procedures and informed the Minister of Marine and Colonies in Paris.[27]

In the case that ensued, Reine was indicted for inflicting inhumane punishment on a slave. The court considered Article 225 of the French criminal code, but also noted that Article 42 of the Code Noir gave masters the right to punish slaves. The court was told about the "crimes" committed by Marie-Claire and informed that the punishment was administered gently with her clothes on and posed no danger to her health. That she was able to walk a distance of more than three miles after the whipping suggested to the court that her injuries were not severe. It was also revealed that she requested permission to see the nurse on the Beauregard Plantation but did not indicate that she had been whipped and was treated for another illness. There was no testimony from the nurse, but the court was presented with medical certificates submitted by two doctors, Segono and Roux, who examined Marie-

Claire and reported that in spite of her advanced age, she was in good physical shape.[28]

The court's judgment was that Reine could be blamed for not restraining his anger, for being inconsiderate, and for having disrespected the instruction of the absentee proprietor of Mondelice by beating with such severity a slave woman whose age, status as a mother of several children, and long, dedicated service to her owner warranted better treatment. Even so, the case was dismissed. At the heart of this case was the fact that whipping was not a violation of the Code Noir, and that the number of lashes Marie-Claire received was considered inconsequential. The thinking was that forty or so ordinary lashes, administered lightly by slave drivers to elderly slaves in order to set an example, were probably less barbarous than ten lashes applied severely as in maritime discipline. The Minister of Justice in Paris supported the judgment rendered based on the Code Noir and saw no need to send the case to a higher court. He wrote, "The magistrates of this colony have therefore decided that the 45 lashes given to the black woman Marie-Claire have not exceeded the rights of punishment conferred to masters over their slaves under Article 42 of the edict of 1685 which means that no law has been violated."[29]

Marie-Claire lost but her case caused judicial officials in French Guiana to consider whether the legal maximum of twenty-nine lashes was an appropriate law, as well as to come face to face with the perception of the judiciary as being racist. Within the French Caribbean as a whole, however, rulings remained arbitrary, uneven, and unpredictable.[30] Take the case of Jules Dispagne, the *gérant* of the Estate Massy-Massy in the district of Vauclin, Martinique, who was accused of physically abusing the female slave Himitée to the point where she was incapable of working and of whipping her illegally in July 1845. In a letter to the Minister of Marine and Colonies that year, the governor of Martinique revealed that Dispagne was charged for punching Himitée in the face—breaking one of her teeth in the process—and causing bleeding to her head, eyes, and mouth. A few hours later on the same day, July 13, Dispagne had Himitée tied by the hands and feet to a ladder and given five strokes. He then kicked her in the shoulder. As her movements apparently impeded the whipping, he sent the slavedriver, Hypolite, to collect a wooden plank, which was placed between her stomach and the ladder. In this position, she was given an additional ten strokes. In the governor's opinion, Dispagne had therefore violated Article 42 of the Code Noir and several articles of the colonial penal code, but the Code Noir did not really apply since there was no mutilation in this case. But the governor may well have interpreted the treatment of Himitée as torture, in which case Article 42 would be relevant. What was at issue, above all, was really the 1840 regulation abolishing the whipping of women.[31]

Like Marie-Claire, Himitée was exempted from work on account of hav-

ing nine children, among them a daughter, Adeline, who had an intimate relationship with Dispagne. This relationship was at the root of the problem, for
it was through conversation with her daughter that Himitée learned intimate
details of Dispagne's life, which she then spread indiscriminately around the
plantation house, thus embarrassing him and undermining his authority. This
led Dispagne to unleash his anger on Himitée, whose clothing he seized, dragging her in front of the plantation house, where the physical abuse took place.
Dispagne admitted guilt but sought to demonstrate that his actions were not
excessive. The use of the wooden plank, he claimed, was for Himitée's own
good in that it prevented the whip from striking her in the pelvic region. As
for the punches to her face, he claimed that this was an accusation made only
by Himitée and her sister Joséphine (Zozo), a witness. However, he was contradicted by the slave driver and another slave who assisted with the whipping. Even so, the governor assured the Minister of Marine and Colonies that
Himitée had not really been physically harmed by the whipping. He claimed
that both she and the witnesses acknowledged that the whipping was gently
administered. That Dispagne put Himitée in the plantation prison and denied her appropriate care following her ordeal seemed not to have been of
concern to the judiciary. Nor for that matter was Himitée's claim that the ordeal caused her to miscarry. Considering her age (which was not stated), the
expert opinion of "men of letters," and the testimony of witnesses that she did
not mention her pregnancy prior to, during, or after the whipping, the judiciary cast this issue aside. The issue of illegal whipping remained relevant. The
defense fought hard to show that Dispagne did not disregard the law by abusing his power as a slaveowner. But the court found him guilty of illegal and
excessive whipping, sentenced him to sixteen days in prison, and imposed a
fine of 200 francs as well as court costs. This judgment, the governor believed,
would have a sobering effect on the slave system.[32]

The case of the Jaham brothers of Martinique suggests that the governor
was mistaken. The two attracted public attention in France in December 1845,
when the barbarity to which they subjected their slaves came to light. Among
the atrocities that twenty-two-year-old, Martiniquan-born Octave de Jaham
and his brother Charles were accused of was the repeated whipping of the
slave woman Hortense, better known as Rosette, who was four months pregnant when the incident took place, in July 1844. In a letter to the governor of
Martinique, the Procureur Général related how, following a whipping with a
rigoise (cowhide), which drew blood and caused cuts and bruises, Octave de
Jaham had Rosette chained and had lemon juice and pepper rubbed into her
wounds.[33] With her face on the ground and her hands strapped behind her
back, the whipping was administered to her naked body. According to Pujo,
the Procureur du Roi who prosecuted the Jahams in the assizes court in Saint-
Pierre, this was the second such punishment Rosette had endured within a

matter of days for allegedly returning too late from Saint-Pierre, where she had been sent to sell charcoal.[34] The records do not indicate the reasons for her delay, but it is possible that market conditions or her physical state were factors. Sale of her full load of charcoal would likely have been her objective, for the alternative—transporting the remaining quantity back to the plantation at Morne-Bénit in the district of Camp-Flore, a walking distance of one and a half hours—would not have been attractive. But of course defiance on her part cannot be ruled out, especially as her children had also suffered at the hands of the Jahams. She had suffered a miscarriage prior to her current pregnancy as well, and the material condition of the slaves on the plantation was atrocious. Also, *marronnage* and illness were endemic. Rosette may have been aware that her financial transactions were important to the struggling young Jahams. To provide the plantation community with ground provisions, they had purchased the provision estate from Desfontaines, a marine commissioner, only in December 1844. Under these conditions, being forced to return to market after a debilitating punishment and torture may have inspired intransigence rather than fear. Indeed, it was Rosette herself who registered a verbal complaint against Octave de Jaham, the younger of the two brothers, with the Procureur du Roi at Saint-Pierre. Administrative correspondence between Pujo and the Procureur Général reveals that the judiciary did not take Rosette's case seriously. Pujo told his superior that the investigation got off to a slow start because the instructional judge was late in handing him the file, and begged his forgiveness. Although several warrants had been issued for the Jahams, he added, Octave had remained at large since the beginning of the trial. But Pujo revealed his hand when he claimed that on July 12, when Rosette registered her complaints, he did not regard them as being very serious. He therefore based his first report on the premise that the whipping had no effect on Rosette's health.[35]

As Pujo read out the charges in court, the commissioner of police called for silence, a response to the audible disquietude manifested by the black and mixed-race individuals present. This was due to the fact that the Jaham brothers had also mistreated two of Rosette's children—Jean-Baptiste, eleven, whose earlobe Charles de Jaham cut off and forced him to eat with yam, and who died in chains a little before the trial began; and Vincent, five, who spent several weeks in hospital in Saint-Pierre recovering from whippings administered by Octave de Jaham himself, and by others upon his orders. Worst of all, the Jaham brothers stood accused of gross negligence of their slaves, some of whom—the young ones—they forced to consume a mixture of human and animal waste.[36]

At the trial, which spanned eight sittings, there was testimony from medical specialists, colonists, and slaves. Desportes, the medical doctor who examined Rosette, testified that he had found several definitive traces of whipping along with body movements that suggested a life of suffering. There were re-cent deep scars on Rosette's buttocks and on her lower right thigh. These were in addition to old traces of whipping. In general, Desportes found Rosette to be in poor health and suffering from stomach illnesses. However, he concluded that the whipping was probably not excessive though perhaps administered in anger and without restraint, which explained why she required hospital treat-ment.[37]

Another medical doctor, Martineau, testified that he and his colleague, Lafaye-Deguerre, carried out an autopsy on Rosette's child, Jean-Baptiste, on the wishes of Octave de Jaham, who allegedly suspected that poisoning was the cause of his death. He examined the contents of the stomach but ignored the head and feet. Therefore, he did not notice traces left by chains, although there were marks on the thighs. Thus, he attributed the death to indigestion. In his turn, Lafaye-Deguerre told the court that he did not examine Jean-Baptiste's head, which was wrapped with fabric, or pay attention to the rest of the body. Rather, he studied the organs, noticed the marks on the thighs, which he attributed to punishment the youth suffered around four days prior to his death, and concluded that death was the result of an ear infection.

Doctor Fazeuille, who wrote the medical report, found no reason to doubt the findings of his colleagues. He pointed out that the body was interred with-out a coffin in clayey soil, and that exhumation took place five weeks after the death. He could not remember whether the head was wrapped, but noted that it would have been impossible, given the state of decomposition, to recognize the ears. As for the cause of death of the young male slave Gustave, whom the Jahams had chained along with Jean-Baptiste, Fazeuille attributed it to dysen-tery rather than mistreatment at the hands of his owners.

These are the circumstances under which Rosette and her son Vincent were called upon to testify, not as a legitimate witnesses but as slaves. In a resolute voice punctuated by tears and sobs, Rosette spoke of the trauma she underwent as the tragic circumstances under which her children lived and died unfolded. Her testimony revealed that Jean-Baptiste and Gustave were punished for not gathering enough animal feed, and she recounted how she herself suffered along with them at the hands of the Jahams, even though she had neither stolen from them or turned to *marronnage*. She admitted that she had advised her children to steal from their owners, but only to satisfy their hunger. And she contrasted the Jahams' treatment with her life on the estate under the management of Desfontaines, whom she characterized as a good slaveowner. The prosecution countered that the Jahams fed the children well and accused Rosette of being insolent and lazy.

Under questioning, Vincent admitted that he stole from Octave de Jaham, who did not provide him with sufficient food. Upon request, he identified the type of chain used to fetter him, distinguishing it from a chain used on cattle.

He also recognized and explained the use of the apparatus made of guava wood that was placed around his neck to prevent him from crossing the hedges leading to the provision garden. The Jahams labeled Vincent's testimony as false. However, the male slave Edouard, whom the Jahams sold back to his previous owner, Desfontaines, during the trial, testified against them. While a slave of the Jahams, he told the court, he was given Saturdays off in place of food rations—a violation of the Code Noir. His testimony, and that of Montdésir, a male slave owned by the Jahams, confirmed the charges against the accused. Several other individuals, including colonists (such as the woman Delille, a neighbor of the Jaham brothers who sang their praises and claimed to have no knowledge of the crimes they were accused of) and slaves, gave testimony. It was then left to the Procureur du Roi, Pujo, and Cicéron, the counsel for the Jaham brothers, to make their summations.

As the trial neared conclusion, the governor of Martinique told the Minister of Marine and Colonies that Jaham admitted knowing that Rosette was pregnant, a fact that did not deter him from ordering a first whipping and personally administering a second consisting of twenty-six lashes. After a long deliberation, however, the court set the Jahams free—by a unanimous decision, as Antoine Gisler pointed out. It seems certain that the court did not give much weight to the testimony of the slaves. Also, the reports on the autopsy performed on Jean-Baptiste ought to have raised suspicions about the impartiality of the medical examiners, but this was not the case.[38] Thus, whereas in Virginia the community and the behavior of the slaves themselves had a bearing on judicial rulings, racial solidarity among whites in the French Antilles and the siege mentality that fostered it led to rulings that almost always went against the slaves.[39]

Not-guilty verdicts like that of the Jaham brothers and others likely brought on a sense of resignation among some colonial officials who appeared to have been sympathetic to the slaves' plight. The manner in which the police superintendent France documented an incident that occurred in Martinique in July 1844 is evidence of this resignation. A nursing mother of twins, the female slave Adélaïde was caught napping while she watched the children of other slaves. For her negligence she was given the *quatre piquets* punishment, whipped with the *rigoise,* and thrown into the bullpen with her children. She escaped during the night, however, and made her way to Fort-Royal, where she sought help from the women of the Désouches family. The women were moved to pity at the sight of her wounds but took no active role in helping her. She then turned to the Procureur Général, who interrogated her, placed her in protective custody in prison, and arranged a visit to the doctor the next morning. In France's view, however, it would only be a matter of two months or so before her wounds would heal and she would be forced "to return to the plantation of her oppressor."[40]

France's cynicism aside, and the vagaries of the slave system notwithstanding, it seems somewhat bizarre that Adélaïde would have been punished so severely for an offense that appeared to have caused no harm. It is not unusual for nursing mothers to be tired, and the fact that her owner could add two infant slaves to his property should have put her in a favorable position. To put her and her children at risk of being trampled by animals seems irrational to say the least.

As if to nudge the judiciary into action, France wrote to the Procureur Général on June 31, 1845, to say that the continuous acts of violence committed against slaves by their owners were "reminiscent of torture during the Middle Ages that oppressed humanity." In the same letter, he indicated that the slave woman Polixène, owned by Rampon Sainte-Claire of district Rivière-Salée, had just filed with him a complaint of barbarous treatment against her owner. She complained that Sainte-Claire subjected her to daily whippings, which accounted for the cuts on her buttocks, and to branding as a result of *marronnage*—a charge she rejected on the grounds of having to escape on account of inhumane treatment. France told the Procureur Général that he was taking the liberty of sending Polixène to him in the hope that he would authorize her to be examined and treated by a doctor. In a postscript likely designed to strengthen the slave's hand, France indicated that Polixène was the mother of a free eight-year-old child, which qualified her under law for manumission. What followed was a series of written exchanges between France and the office of the Procureur Général which revealed that local authorities forced Polixène to return to the plantation of her owner, where she received a new round of whippings for having lodged a complaint with France. She was re-imprisoned for her own safety, but was made to return to her owner, who promised the Procureur Général that she would henceforth be treated humanely. As to the charge of *marronnage,* Sergeant Bedout told France that Sainte-Claire had accused Polixène of stealing a silver fork, which caused her to abscond. After two months at large, she was caught on the plantation Fleury and transported to her owner, who gave her the *quatre-piquets* punishment, whereby both her hands and feet were tied to a ladder and she was whipped. Even though it was later discovered that it was a child in Sainte-Claire's household who had lost the fork, Sainte-Claire continued to regard Polixène as a rascal.[41]

Tensions between slave women and plantation personnel sometimes led to open confrontation, as was the case in 1845, when the slave woman Colombe clashed with Julien O'Neil, the *économe* of the plantation Lagrange in the district of Marigot, Martinique. The problem began on October 11 at about nine o'clock in the morning, when O'Neil followed Colombe into the plantation garden and accused her of being lazy. Swiftly and firmly, Colombe responded that she was a hard worker. Displeased with this retort, O'Neil struck her with a whip, which he carried on this occasion, along with a iron-tipped rod. Not content to remain silent in the face of authority, Colombe told O'Neil that he did not have the right to beat slaves in such a manner for nothing. So incensed was O'Neil at Colombe's intransigence that he began to whip her. Colombe fought back. She seized his arm and attempted to wrestle the whip away from him. In the struggle that ensued, O'Neil attempted to free himself from Colombe's grip, tearing his clothing in the process. In his fury, he struck her in the face with his iron-tipped rod, cutting her lower lip. He then ordered that she be arrested and placed in solitary confinement on the plantation. She was deprived of food until seven o'clock that evening. The following morning, de Compignan, the plantation overseer, ordered that she be given twenty-nine lashes. Her pleas that she was breast-feeding her four-month-old infant fell on deaf ears; her clothes were removed, and de Compignan's order was carried out. Not content to leave it at that, de Compignan ordered that an iron ring be placed around her ankle and attached to a chain weighing four kilograms.[42]

The chain was meant to punish her and restrict her mobility, but it was no deterrent for Colombe, for it was in this state, two days later, that she left the plantation. Accompanied by Frédéric, a male slave who carried her infant in his arms, she headed for Saint-Pierre. But her chains gave her away. When interrogated en route, she could not produce the pass from her owner that slaves who were away from the plantation were required to possess. Slaves in this situation would be summarily returned to their owners, but Colombe refused to reveal her owner's identity and was consequently imprisoned as a fugitive. It was from prison that she drew attention to her condition, and lodged a complaint with the Procureur Général of Saint-Pierre, who ordered that her chains be removed and an investigation be launched. O'Neil testified that he gave Colombe only one lash and that her lip wound was the result of a punch. Save for the slave driver, the other slaves who witnessed the fight contradicted O'Neil's version of events. As for de Compignan, he insisted that he had acted within the boundaries of the law.[43]

Baffer, a substitute for the Procureur Général, blamed Colombe for responding to O'Neil in a tempestuous manner, but believed that it was the slave's recognition of the illegality of O'Neil's actions that caused her to fight back. He deplored the altercation that took place in the presence of the plantation slaves. Although he acknowledged de Compignan's right to discipline slaves, he found his treatment of Colombe, "a weak woman and sucking infant's mother," excessive and revolting. He applied the Mackau Law of 1845 (which abolished the whip for women) to this case, and pronounced O'Neil and de Compignan guilty without attenuating circumstances. O'Neil was fined 101 francs, and de Compignan 150.[44]

In a judgment rendered in February 1846, the Cour Royale of Guade-

loupe fined Crosnier, the *gérant* of the plantation O'Connor in the district
of Capesterre, five hundred francs for a catalog of acts against male and female slaves, including whippings, extended detentions in the stocks, and torture by fire. Some of these acts highlight the fact that, as in the case of Marie-
Claire of French Guiana, there was no consideration for the age of slave
women, nor for motherhood. Among the charges Crosnier faced in 1846 was
that of locking up the sixty-year-old slave woman Sophie in a naked state for
three consecutive nights. Crosnier also ordered and participated in the *quatre-
piquets* punishment of the elderly slave woman Clarisse. Upon Crosnier's orders, Clarisse's son, Martin, was one of four slaves who held down the naked
slave while the slave driver administered the whipping.[45]

Five hundred francs was also the fine levied by the courts in Guadeloupe
against Leprince of Pointe-Noire for working the elderly and sick slave woman
Themie beyond endurance. In 1846, when the judgment was rendered and the
judiciary sought to protect Themie, it was too late. She was taken to hospital
in Basse-Terre, where she died two hours later.[46] Similarly, the Cour Royale of
Martinique fined Lehimas, manager of a sugar plantation in the district of
Prêcheur, 500 francs for detaining slaves beyond the legal limit. Lehimas's
crimes were really more serious. Lehimas had promised the pregnant slave
woman Jenny a whipping because he blamed her for the absence of her daughter, Rienette, a domestic in the service of the plantation household. So it must
have been with some trepidation that Jenny, a mother of nine children, returned to the fields fifteen days after she delivered. Lehimas confronted her
in the presence of the plantation gang and reminded her of her daughter's
continued absence. To stave off the whipping, Jenny sought the help of Des-
bordes, mayor of Prêcheur, who accompanied her back to the plantation and
intervened on her behalf. But his efforts came to naught on this occasion, for
that night Lehimas beat her about the head and face with his fist and had her
placed in the stocks overnight. The next morning he gathered her children together and forced them to watch as he removed her clothing, had her tied to
a ladder, and ordered the slave driver to administer a whipping. This was the
experience that caused Jenny to file a complaint with the authorities, as a result of which Lehimas's mistreatment of other slaves came to light.[47]

Besides fining them the judiciary sometimes deprived convicted slaveowners of their slaves. In 1847 the testimony of the female slave Marguerite
helped convict her owner, Fouré of French Guiana, of cruel treatment of at
least four slaves. The judiciary gave Fouré two months to sell them off, failing
which they would become the property of the state.[48]

In the last years of slavery, as an increasing number of cases revealed acts
of cruelty against slaves by their owners, different branches of the law began to take firmer action, but the results remained fairly predictable. It was
through the active intervention of the police in French Guiana, for example,

that Gabriel Dernier was arrested for the attempted murder of Justine, a slave woman owned by his mother. In 1846 Dernier was charged with willfully firing shots at Justine and causing wounds to her buttocks and legs. The governor of French Guiana told the Minister of Marine and Colonies that two doctors, Roue Simon and Auguste Roue, confirmed that Justine was shot from a distance, but that the wounds were not serious. Nevertheless, he argued that the charges against Dernier were justified inasmuch as the shots "could have ended up in a more dangerous place, Dernier not having calculated the distance." Although Dernier claimed that the gun went off accidentally, he must have been aiming in the direction of the slave since the shots were fired from a distance. The governor told the Minister that the case was proceeding but that he had to wait twenty days for a second medical report. He did not explain the purpose of the second report, but he promised to do his best to ensure that the well-being of the slaves was respected. Archival documents contain no evidence that the case was pursued to conclusion, demonstrating once again the legal system's reluctance to convict slaveowners.[49]

During the same period colonial authorities expelled slaves whom they considered dangerous or whose character was "turbulent." On mere suspicion of acts of poison, assassination, or subversive activities, the authorities usually imprisoned slaves, compensated their owners, and deported them to Puerto Rico, a Spanish colony, or to Senegal in West Africa. There were those who questioned the legality of deporting slaves to Puerto Rico, given that Article 76 of a local ordinance stipulated only Senegal. But Puerto Rico remained the authorized destination of most deportees. Interestingly, the Spanish colonies were also the choice of legal authorities in Antigua in the seventeenth century while Virginia was the favored destination between 1802 and 1819.[50]

In its deliberations of July 9, 1827, the Conseil Privé of Martinique considered the case of the slave woman Desiré, who was declared a derelict in a judgment rendered on May 19 and June 1, 1827. This allowed the woman Lachaume of Fort-Royal to purchase her for 261 francs, a bargain. Lachaume also paid 154 francs 56 *centimes* in prison costs, and then proceeded to use Desiré as a hired-out slave. However, the Procureur Général and the Superintendent of Police of the district of Lamentin, where the slave resided, declared her dangerous; she was suspected of poisoning one Arnaud. The authorities therefore returned Desiré to prison pending arrangements to deport her to Puerto Rico and compensated her owner, as was the custom. The accusation against Desiré could well have been groundless since administrative reports employed the term "perhaps" in determining her guilt. But the fear of poisoning made slaves vulnerable.[51] Interestingly, slaves suspected of poisoning, though found not guilty, were deported from Virginia in the 1740s.[52]

Suspicion that the slave woman Adélaïde, along with two male slaves, Louis and Guanguin, plotted to assassinate Sieur Asselin and other white colonists in Carbet, Martinique, in 1827, resulted in their imprisonment and deportation. Here too the evidence against them was insufficient to warrant a court trial. Nevertheless, the colonial state compensated their owners, much as if they were considered condemned slaves, and deported them to Puerto Rico. Similarly, in a letter addressed to de Rosily, the Directeur de L'Interieur, the slaveowner Clauzel of Case-Pilote, Martinique, claimed that one of his female slaves, Aline, was dangerous to his family and to other slaves. He explained that deportation orders had already been issued for her by the director's predecessor, who was unable to expedite them because she had run away. "Now that she is in prison in Saint-Pierre," he continued, "I am requesting the same favor." In his response, the director pointed out that the slave woman had remained at large for a year before being apprehended and could be characterized as dangerous. As she was not accused of poisoning or similarly threatening behavior, however, there was no reason to deport her. Since the original deportation order would have condemned her to a life in Senegal without her infant son, Aline may have decided to abscond in order to preserve her family. Indeed, the authorities were cognizant of Article 47 of the Code Noir, which prohibited the breakup of the slave family, and thought it unwise to accede to Clauzel's request.[53]

In 1828 there were well over twenty-five slaves in the Fort-Royal prison slated for deportation. Many of them were accused of poisoning and assassination. To the authorities, their presence may have been an indication that slaveowners were using deportations to rid themselves of unwanted slaves. Also, some slaves apparently courted deportation, preferring to risk the unknown rather than remaining in slavery in the French colonies. Since the colonial treasury paid compensation, their owners had nothing to lose. Thus it is probably not coincidental that on November 5, 1829, the Conseil Privé of Martinique set up a commission to study the problem. The commission met in December that year and examined several cases, but could find little by way of concrete details regarding the crimes committed by slaves whose owners wanted them deported. This situation may not have changed much over time. In 1838 the owner of two estates in Martinique—one in Sainte-Anne, the other in Vauclin—requested the deportation of several of his slaves, including the slave women Clara and Elisé, whom he suspected of poisoning slaves and animals.[54]

Other women ended up in prison besides those slated for deportation and those attempting to flee their owners. Slaves could be arrested for contravention of any of the laws in the Code Noir, and for a host of other acts that the authorities considered criminal. For disorderly conduct the police in Marigot Saint-Martin, Guadeloupe, arrested the slave woman Cateau in March 1828. She spent ten months in prison, during which her owner, who clearly did not want this rebel, did not reclaim her. In December she was sold at public auction to one Questel for 133 francs—a song. Unknown to Questel, Cateau had been suffering from an illness she contracted in prison that was not disclosed at the auction. Upon Cateau's death shortly after the sale, he demanded a reimbursement. However, the Directeur Général de L'Intérieur of Guadeloupe told the governor that Questel, like others, knew of Cateau's demeanor and had sufficient time to examine her before the sale. On these grounds Questel was denied reimbursement. In 1837 the Directeur de L'Interieur of Guadeloupe informed the Conseil Supérieur that the slave woman Nanette, who was arrested for vagrancy, was still in prison. Her ownership appears to have been in doubt. An investigation showed that in 1823 de Lachariére, her owner, turned her over to Pierre Démoin, who had hoped to cure her of a disability. It is not certain that he did. What is clear is that he left his estate to the unmarried Prudence Démoin (who may well have been his daughter), who claimed Nanette under the terms of the will that Baudouin, the executor, probated. But Nanette never appeared on the census of slaves owned by Démoin, which means that the transaction was never made legal. Mindful of the cost incurred for Nanette's incarceration, the prison warden wanted the matter settled so that the state could be reimbursed. He announced that if her owners did not reclaim her, he would acquire ownership in order to discharge her debt, an euphemism for putting her at auction. Since there was an absence of "recognized heirs" in this case, the Conseil Supérieur stayed the judgment. The governor of Guadeloupe then ordered the trustee of Basse-Terre to accept Nanette as a state warden, which surely meant a life of labor in public works.[55]

Throughout slavery the length of time slaves remained in prison was a source of tension between colonial officials and slaveowners. Imprisoned slaves made no contribution to their owners. On the other hand, it was not in the economic interest of the state to keep them in prison indefinitely since reimbursement for prison costs, even when required of slaveowners, was never certain. If the state resorted to auctioning the slaves, it could expect only meager returns as there were known risks involved in purchasing prison slaves, who were often ill and prone to rebellion. But the state was caught in a bind: it could not afford to anger slaveowners by refusing to imprison slaves who ran afoul of the law and were considered a threat to the slave system; nor could it afford to maintain slaves indefinitely without resolution. As early as 1726, administrative reports indicate that the state was burdened with maintaining slaves in prison at the behest of their owners. In an 1819 circular, the governor of Guadeloupe complained that slaves, especially from outlying areas, remained in prison over extended periods during which they were subject to arbitrary whippings. However, he was less concerned about the treatment of slaves than about the cost of maintaining them. Indeed, he asked the *commandant* to notify colonists in all districts that detentions lasting beyond six months would no longer be permitted unless slaveowners sought and received special permission for an extension. The governor specified that such demands would be thoroughly scrutinized before certification could be granted and his approval obtained. This measure was essential to ensure that unclaimed slaves could be declared *épaves* (derelict slaves), who could be sold at auction, the returns accruing to the state. The fact that such restrictions had to be placed on prison stays indicates that slaveowners used state prisons as a means of convenience.[56]

In September 1828, the Procureur Général in Martinique had to justify the prolonged detention of slaves when it was revealed that a mixed-race slave, Jacquer, who had been arrested on January 11, 1827, and should have been released on March 11, 1828, remained in prison. Throughout his imprisonment, his owner, Capoul, paid for his keep. Therefore, the Conseil Privé of Martinique decided to reimburse Capoul, who had attempted to retrieve the slave from prison on several occasions, the sum of 486.66 *livres*. Jacquer was one of several such slaves in the Saint-Pierre prison, many apparently incarcerated on the orders of the Procureur Général. According to an administrative report, such detentions were "illegal and truly costly to the colonial treasury." The report cited another case in which the colonial treasury had to reimburse one de Saint-Albin for the value of his slave. It is not clear whether the slave died in prison or was executed, but the Conseil Privé was warned that such reimbursement could become a regular occurrence. In response to the report, the Procureur Général blamed prolonged detentions on his predecessors. However, the problem was clearly deeper, as the case below demonstrates.[57]

In June 1832 the slaveowner Semoine Mandet of Moule, Guadeloupe, petitioned the governor on behalf of one of his female slaves, Justine, who remained in the Pointe-à-Pitre prison for two years awaiting deportation following her condemnation on suspicion of poisoning. When Mandet discovered that Justine had become pregnant while in prison—the likely result of sexual abuse—and was said to be of good conduct, he had a sudden change of heart and requested her return on humanitarian grounds and expressed a desire to forget the past. He also seized the opportunity to request an exemption from paying prison costs by arguing that the state had benefited from her labor in public works. In the correspondence that the case generated, the Procureur Général rightly accused Mandet of being self-serving, noting that his real interest was the possession of Justine's unborn child, to which he had legal claim as her owner. The governor was aware that the charges of alleged poisoning against Justine had failed through lack of evidence, but he believed that there was a danger in reintegrating her into her owner's slave force, meaning that he considered her a rebel. Nevertheless, he yielded to the wishes of the Conseil Privé to free Justine, provided that Mandet would settle the full debt. But the council had the last word on the matter. Although it unanimously approved the governor's decision, in the end it ruled that Mandet should pay only half of the cost of Justine's incarceration in view of the fact that she had been part of the state chain gang. Had it insisted on the full amount, the matter could have dragged on, leaving the state to care for a mother and child.[58]

Detentions such as that of Justine were probably the exception rather than the rule by the nineteenth century, a time when prison stays were generally short—three months or less—but sustained detentions remained a reality. For assault and battery on a free woman named Lucile, twenty-five-year-old Rose, a married slave seamstress, received fifteen days in prison. On June 26, 1847, Rose allegedly followed Lucile—a former rival for the affections of her husband—hurled insults at her, and then attacked her physically at the riverside, shredding her clothes to rags in the process. At the trial, Rose portrayed Lucile as the aggressor against whom she defended herself, but witnesses did not corroborate her version of events. In this case, the judiciary applied Article 34 of the Code Noir, which prohibited slaves from assaulting free persons. There can be little doubt that slaves were aware of this regulation, but such assaults were usually against other black and mixed-race individuals, which may indicate that slaves did not view them as being legitimately free.

There are a significant number of cases of altercations between slaves and free persons, but the data are in very poor condition and do not always indicate the ethnic background of the latter. Given the gravity of assaults against whites, their racial backgrounds were usually given when they were set upon by blacks, both slave and free. So in 1833, when the eighteen-year-old slave woman Nicole, a seamstress from Saint-Pierre, struck the lawyer Vergeron, she was fined 20 francs and sentenced to forty-eight hours in prison. It is likely that if Vergeron were white, the sentence would have been more stringent.[59]

This chapter shows that slave women were cognizant of their vulnerability under law, irrespective of the changes that were introduced in the 1830s and 1840s. It also demonstrates that they did not view the lack of direct access to the courts as a barrier to litigation. Certainly, the material presented here lends credence to Gilbert Pago's undocumented assertion that slaveowners were surprised by the level of complaints filed by slave women following the banning of whipping under the Mackau Law.[60] That the courts generally ruled in favor of slaveowners is no reflection on slave women. The ways in which they dealt with the suffering and degradation they experienced on the plantations, in prison, and in facing banishment should serve as valuable lessons in how the human spirit can triumph in the face of adversity. Surely, to feel pity for slave women and nothing more would be to downplay the most important element that kept them going—their indomitable spirit of resistance.

7

Women and Resistance

IN THE French Caribbean, slave women resisted slavery in the same ways that men did as well as in ways which gender and the differential allocation of tasks made possible.[1] Most often, both sexes pursued similar goals insofar as they worked to destroy slavery or to live within the system on their own terms. In this respect, the struggle waged by males and females was complementary by nature. That it was so is all the more intriguing when one considers that under slavery women suffered multiple oppressions—from slavery itself and from men, black and white, slave and free. This chapter explores women's individual and collective resistance to slavery.

It should come as no surprise that the patterns of resistance of slave women in the French Caribbean were largely the same as those of males. As we saw in chapters 3 and 4, while gender played a role in the allocation of tasks, European views of females as fragile beings did not apply to African women. What mattered was not sexual differentiation but the need for hard, intensive labor. African women were thus seen as slaves rather than women and were given just as heavy tasks as men.

The disregard of gender distinctions placed women in roles alongside men in most plantation operations, depending on the needs of each plantation. This social dynamic gave rise to common forms of resistance to slavery in spite of the additional oppression of black women by black men. Slavery was, in other words, the common enemy. Both women and men worked in field gangs, experienced the harshness of the slave driver's whip, and were likely to participate in the plotting and execution of all forms of resistance. Both worked in the slaveowner's household as domestics and engaged in poisoning as a means of resistance. But some gender-specific aspects of plantation labor, like gender itself, provided women with unique ways to resist slavery. In chapter 4, we saw that only women were nursemaids and midwives and that accusations of infanticide were directed solely at them. Gender made it possible for women to restrict fertility and control reproduction through abortions and other techniques, although it is improbable that such actions always constituted resistance. After all, not all slaves were revolutionaries. The forms of female resistance highlighted below—armed revolt, *marronnage,* the use of poison, and work avoidance and withdrawal—were among the most prevalent in slave society. The data on these forms of resistance, though not always conclusive, also permitted a greater exploration of the subject than would have been possible for other, more subtle forms of resistance, such as insolence and verbal altercations with slaveowners, to which scholars of the French Caribbean have paid little attention. What should be emphasized is the variety of responses possible in the continuum along which resistance occurred from armed rebellion to acts of accommodation. Surely, the most prevalent forms of resistance were not necessarily the most effective nor the most important.

To get at the slaves' perception of their own condition, one can draw on some of the literary works on the French Caribbean that are an authentic representation of the Caribbean historical experience. An analysis of the actions of the female protagonists in these works points up the importance of adopting a broad perspective on resistance. Télumée Miracle appears to accept domination and brutality at the hands of her mate, Elie, in *The Bridge of Beyond*, a novel which chronicles the struggles of four generations of Guadeloupian women from slavery to modern times.[2] Though she suffers her misfortune largely in silence and experiences a nervous breakdown as a result, Télumée transcends the turmoil which surrounds her and establishes an identity of her own while Elie falters. Likewise, Délira Délivrance seems oblivious to her subjugation by her husband, Bienaimé, in *Masters of the Dew*, a novel which deals with bitter feuding among peasant families in independent Haiti over land and water during a period of extensive drought.[3] But it is Délira who ensures a smooth transition from a society plagued by conflict to one in which men and women who were former adversaries strive for the common good. Lastly, timid but resolute Madame Christophe in *The Tragedy of King Christophe*—a play about the rule of Henri Christophe, a former slave, compatriot of Toussaint-Louverture, and one of the early rulers of independent Haiti—consistently reminds the tyrannic King Christophe about the importance of Africa and the need to remain grounded in its traditions. Just before committing suicide, King Christophe chooses to return to his roots and, in a final act of defiance, asks to be buried in Africa.[4] These examples demonstrate that, as was the case during slavery, what appears on the surface to be docility is often a very subtle, calculated, and conscious form of resistance. It is imperative that a multidimensional perspective be adopted in assessing the resistance of slave women.

ARMED RESISTANCE

Armed revolt was an important dimension of women's resistance to slavery in the French Caribbean, even though few women actually participated in combat. This kind of resistance can best be explored in the context of the

1790s, a period of great upheaval in the French colonies. The perennial rest-lessness of slaves notwithstanding, these colonies remained fairly stable and economically profitable slave societies from 1635, when Guadeloupe and Mar-tinique were settled, until 1791, when slaves in Saint-Domingue rose up against their owners in a bid for freedom, upholding the ideals of "liberty, frater-nity and equality" which were the trademark of the French Revolution of 1789. "These were," in the words of Antoine Métral, "no longer timid salves. Women, children and the elderly had all experienced the perils of slavery for a considerable period, and regarded war as indispensable to liberty."[5] The slaves' bloody and protracted struggle for freedom, which lasted until the end of 1803, revealed policy contradictions that led the French National Conven-tion to declare the abolition of slavery in the French colonies on February 4, 1794. In April 1794 French commissioners Victor Hugues and Chrétien were scheduled to make the declaration in the colonies and to set up a provi-sional council to govern the islands. In the interim, the English, on whom the French had declared war in February 1793, seized the opportunity to occupy Martinique and Guadeloupe and thus maintain slavery.[6] The British were successful in Martinique. Hugues was able to use his expeditionary force of 1,500 men and an enthusiastic slave population to repel the British invasion in Guadeloupe after a seven-month struggle which ended in December 1794.[7] Thus, while slaves in Martinique remained under British occupation and in slavery, those in Guadeloupe and French Guiana lived in a state of quasi-free-dom. This freedom was threatened, however, by Napoléon Bonaparte, ruler of France, who by 1799 was determined to restore the authority of France in all the colonies. In essence, this meant the restoration of slavery in Guadeloupe and French Guiana and a redoubling of efforts to subdue Saint-Domingue. In March 1802, under the Treaty of Amiens, Britain returned to France posses-sion of Martinique and other French colonies it had occupied since 1794. The French decided to retain slavery in Martinique. It was only a question of time before the other colonies were brought back into the fold. On May 6, 1802, General Richepance landed with 3,400 men at Pointe-à-Pitre, the capital of Guadeloupe, with orders from Napoléon to reestablish slavery.[8] Having virtu-ally no hope of winning in Saint-Domingue, Napoléon spared no effort in sub-duing Guadeloupe. On May 20, 1802, slavery and the slave trade were reim-posed there.[9]

During the revolutionary wars in Saint-Domingue and Guadeloupe, women participated in the fighting. In Saint-Domingue, Marie-Jeanne, wife of the black general Lamartinière, "took her share in the defence."[10] There may well have been others. Women formed part of the rebel stronghold lo-cated in the heights of the Cahos Mountains, close to the shores of the Arti-bonite River, where the slave leaders Toussaint-Louverture and Jean Jacques Dessalines stored their weapons and spoils, and planned and executed their fighting strategies.[11] In Guadeloupe slave women, along with men and children, formed part of the forces of Louis Delgrès, a mixed-race colonel born in Martinique who led a slave army against General Richepance and the French forces. They were also part of the forces of Joseph Ignace and Palerme—Delgrès's commanders who led factions of the army after it split to fight the French on several fronts to maximize its chances of success. Most of the fighting took place in Basse-Terre, the southern part of Guadeloupe. On May 12, 1802, one of the major battles fought under the slave commander Palerme took place at Dolé, an important post in the hands of the rebels; white women and children, whom the slaves had rounded up on plantations, were being held there.[12] Here at Dolé, the mixed-race slave woman Solitude, though pregnant, battled her way into history by participating in all the fighting.[13]

With regard to the armed struggle in Saint-Domingue, Antoine Métral described how, under the bayonets of General Leclerc, who led the French troops, slave women transported weapons by leaping from rock to rock until they disappeared into the woods.[14] At Guadeloupe slave women also transported ammunition, food, and supplies, served as messengers, cared for the sick, acted as cover for men under fire, and chanted revolutionary slogans which kept spirits high in the insurrectionary forces of Delgrès, Palerme, and Ignace. On May 10, 1802, as the battle intensified, whites in Basse-Terre, fearing massacre, barricaded themselves in their homes. The silence which characterized the city was, according to the Guadeloupian historian Auguste Lacour, broken only by "the gallop of horses ridden by officers carrying orders and the singing of the French National Anthem, by female slaves who transported bullets and other ammunition to artillery units."[15] Slave women transported ammunition in the fiercest of battles, and risked their lives in shielding their men.[16] Their chants motivated the slave troops. Lacour highlighted this aspect of women's contribution when he wrote, "It was not their fault if their fathers, their sons, their mothers and their lovers were not endowed with superhuman courage. When a bullet whistled above their heads or a bomb exploded near them, they sang loudly, holding hands while making their hellish rounds interrupted by the chant: 'Vive la mort!' ('Long live death!')."[17]

During the wars in Saint-Domingue and Guadeloupe, women demonstrated a striking strength of character. Undaunted by the practice of the French army in Saint-Domingue of burning slaves alive and throwing them to the dogs as a way of crushing the spirit of the resistance, women displayed as much courage as men. According to C.L.R. James, "When Chevalier, a black chief, hesitated at the sight of the scaffold, his wife shamed him. 'You do not know how sweet it is to die for liberty!' And refusing to allow herself to be hanged by the executioner, she took the rope and hanged herself."[18] Similarly, a mother whose daughters were weeping while on their way to the scaffold comforted them with the words, "Rejoice! Your wombs will not beget slaves."[19] Antoine Métral has reinforced this view of slave women by noting that during the war, "the weaker sex became the stronger. Young women without voicing a single complaint either in the streets or at the public squares, went valiantly before the scaffold. By their moving examples, they encouraged those who were hesitant in dying for liberty. Some were seen to display a surprising character trait by smiling in the face of death in the presence of their masters whose desire for vengeance was thereby thwarted."[20] Astounded whites attributed the demeanor that slave women adopted in facing death to the indoctrination provided by an association to which the women belonged, rather than to the cause of liberty.[21]

There are also indications that during the early stages of the war in Guadeloupe, when casualties were high, some black male slaves fled and were admonished to follow the example of women who demonstrated incomparable zeal.[22] Women's enthusiasm for the struggle never waned, even when defeat seemed inevitable.

In 1802 Louis Delgrès's major artillery unit was set up on the left bank of the Rivière-des-Pères flanked by Fort Saint-Charles, which the slaves held. The French troops positioned themselves on the right bank. Despite stiff resistance the French troops crossed the river and engaged Delgrès's army. Though the rebels were able to retain strongholds such as Dolé after inflicting heavy casualties on Richepance's forces, Delgrès was cognizant of the superior technology of the French. His strategy of retreating to Fort Saint-Charles after engagements was effective in the initial stages, but it backfired as the fort became a target for French bombardment. As the fighting intensified, Delgrès and his slave army barricaded themselves in the fort to which Richepance later laid siege. Richepance appealed to Delgrès to surrender and offered him a pardon, but Delgrès stood his ground. On May 22, however, after he realized that the battle could not be won, Delgrès abandoned the wounded in the fort, taking with him about 400 men and a number of black women, all of whom remained active in the resistance.[23] Some of these women remained with Delgrès while others joined the forces of Palerme and Ignace. On their way to Pointe-à-Pitre from Basse-Terre, Ignace's forces burned and pillaged and scored initial successes against the French. Around May 24, Ignace staked out a position on the plantation Belle Plaine in the community Abymes, three kilometers north of Pointe-à-Pitre, but abandoned it a day later for the fort at Baimbridge, on the outskirts of Pointe-à-Pitre. The fort proved easy to penetrate, and Ignace and the men and women he led became easy targets for a section of the French forces commanded by General Nicolas Gobert. It is believed that Ignace was killed along with 675 of his followers on May 25.[24] Most of those taken prisoner were shot in Pointe-à-Pitre, 150 of them on October 27 alone. The women who accompanied Palerme fared little better. Routed by the French, Palerme's people fled into the hills.[25]

Delgrès took his last stand on the extensive plantation Danglemont, where the battle of Matouba was fought on May 28, 1802. Unable to match the well-armed French, Delgrès resolved to commit suicide and take as many French troops with him as possible by setting fire to barrels of gunpowder he distributed among his troops. Gunpowder was spread along the approaches to the main entrance of the plantation. Delgrès also placed gunpowder within firing range of his two defensive positions in the plantation Great House. According to Oruno Lara, the women "were even more enthusiastic about dying" than the men.[26] After shouts of "Vivre libre ou mourir!" (liberty or death), Delgrès and about five hundred men, women, and children were killed when the gunpowder exploded. French casualties were put at four hundred. Some rebels escaped into the surrounding forest and became maroons, but the defeat of Delgrès brought organized resistance to an end. An *arrête* of July 16, 1802, reimposed slavery in Guadeloupe.[27]

Women who appeared before the military tribunal which tried the captured rebels received no special considerations and were given the same sentences as men. For example, the tribunal sentenced the mixed-race slave woman Solitude to death. Solitude was pregnant, and Jacques Adélaïde-Merlande notes that "the execution had to be postponed. She was executed on November 29, after her delivery." Arlette Gautier's explanation that the French army "awaited the birth of the child so that it would have a slave in due time" is plausible.[28] Other women also received the death penalty, including Marthe-Rose (Rose-Toto), Delgrès's mistress, who had been at Fort Saint-Charles with him. A native of Saint Lucia, one of the French islands occupied by the British in 1794, Marthe-Rose suffered a broken leg during the evacuation of the fort and appeared before the tribunal on a stretcher. Accused of influencing Delgrès to resist and of inciting slave soldiers to kill white prisoners held in the fort, Marthe-Rose was hanged publicly. With the rope around her neck, she is said to have remarked to onlookers, "Having killed their king and left their country, these men have come to ours to bring trouble and confusion. May God judge them!"[29]

In February 1831 women appeared before similar tribunals in Martinique, following a slave uprising in Saint-Pierre that was aimed at torching and pillaging the town and massacring its white inhabitants. This was a period when, according to Procureur Général Arsène Nogues, slaves became unusually restless, insolent, and insubordinate, setting revolutionary words to, and singing in public, *La Parisienne*, a military patriotic tune composed in Paris in 1830 for the July revolution. For the words "march against their cannons" the slaves substituted "march against the colonists."[30] They also wrote the inscription "la liberté ou la mort" on a French tricolor which they removed from the Place Bertin—the main square—and placed it at the entrance of the église du

Mouillage on the evenings of February 5 and 6. Beginning on February 7, they set fires all over Saint-Pierre; on February 9 alone they torched several houses in the city as well as eight plantations, bringing the total to eleven plantations. The same evening some slaves armed with cutlasses came down from the hills to join others in a general insurrection against slavery and set fire to cane fields. The planters were terrified and drew comparisons with the slave uprising several years before in Saint-Domingue. The French newspaper *Have* printed a letter from a colonist who called Saint-Pierre the most miserable place on earth due to its succession of bankruptcies, interest rates of 50 percent on loans when available, and the haste among planters who had the means to ship their wives and children to the United States and France for safety. These were the circumstances under which Governor Dupotet declared a state of siege and called out the militia, the police force, other troops, and the French marines. Massive force and superior arms were used to quell the rebellion on February 10.[31]

Several women were accused of participating in the 1831 insurrection. Of particular interest to French authorities were the slaves owned by the absentee sugar planter Madame Dariste, whose estate on the outskirts of Saint-Pierre was administered by a Frenchman named Bosc. Police investigation of the activities of slaves on the Dariste Plantation charged that Pauline, a Guadeloupian-born slave woman owned by Bosc, not Dariste, had concealed the plot from authorities. The accusation stemmed from the fact that Bosc kept Pauline as a concubine and had several children with her. With shock and dismay, the authorities alleged that Bosc was implicated in the plot and that he shielded some of the male rebels from arrest. Weapons were found hidden in the huts of several female slaves on the plantation. These events led to the arrest of Bosc on charges of complicity, and of Pauline, who was alleged to have been party to his knowledge of the slave rebellion and was, by this association, guilty. French authorities claimed that Bosc was motivated by the desire to end slavery and marry Pauline, an act that would free her and her children. Without acknowledging the other means by which enslaved black women and their children could be liberated, or the possibility that he may have been duped by the slaves, the authorities seemed content to label Bosc's actions as a crime of passion.[32]

On May 2, 1831, a special session of the assizes court convened in Saint-Pierre to judge the 250 male and female slaves accused of participating in the insurrection. After nearly two weeks of hearings, most of them, including Jeanne, Coralie, Victoirine, Séraphine, Monique, Louise, Sophie, and Lucette, were set free for lack of evidence, but 50 slaves were tried. Twenty-six were condemned to death while the others received diverse penalties. In his report to the Minister of Marine and Colonies in Paris, Governor Dupotet mentioned that a slave woman (Pauline, perhaps) received twenty-nine lashes.[33] He made no mention of Bosc, but French newspapers reported that the charges against him were withdrawn and that he was acquitted.[34]

In Martinique slave women also participated, directly or indirectly, in an uprising which occurred in May 1848, when the expected abolition of slavery did not materialize. Slave unrest touched several communities in the west and south of the island. Most alarming were events in Saint-Pierre on the evening of May 22, when twenty houses were burned, two white males were killed, and thirty-two people, mostly whites, were burnt alive in a house to which rebellious slaves laid siege. According to public rumor, the house was the location of an arms depot belonging to whites. An insurance claim filed by Lauriette, one of the twenty homeowners, amounted to 30,250 francs, 50 centimes, and it highlighted both the gravity of the situation facing the whites and the urgency of freeing the slaves. On May 23, Brigadier General de Rostoland, the provisional governor of Martinique, yielded to the unanimous wish of the Provisional Municipal Council of Saint-Pierre and declared the abolition of slavery, which was made official on June 4.[35] Thus by their own actions the slaves accelerated the process of emancipation.

The circumstances surrounding the death of the thirty-two people are unclear. It is known that several members of Désabaÿs's family were also among the victims. Désabaÿs had helped to crush resistance movements in Grand-Anse in the 1830s and, like the de Sanois family, in whose house he took refuge, he was despised by mixed-race individuals and slaves. Given that he was scheduled to testify in court on May 23 against Pory Papy, the mixed-race deputy mayor of Saint-Pierre who was popular among the slaves and who was sympathetic to their demand for emancipation, the siege may well have been designed to silence him. But the fire that resulted from the struggle between the rebels and the occupants of the de Sanois house may not have been intentional, as it was Monsieur Désabaÿs who fired a shot that killed one of the assailants. Some sources claim that an exchange of gunfire followed. Others indicate that the slaves set the house ablaze. Among the thirty-two victims were twelve mixed-race slave women who were domestics. Whether these women provided information about the contents of the house to other slaves is not known, but in slave society gender could be manipulated to serve revolutionary ends.[36]

Women also successfully deployed their sexuality in resistance against slavery. Prostitution was a fact of Saint-Domingue slave society, and some slave women used it to support resistance. Malefant, a soldier who fought with the French army in Saint-Domingue in the 1790s, observed that there was "a particular type of prostitution solely associated with slave girls and women.... They entered soldier's camps shamelessly and exchanged sexual favours for bullets and gunpowder."[37]

MARRONNAGE

The contributions that women made to armed struggle were therefore significant and varied, and their participation in flight reinforces this conclusion. In the French Antilles more males than females participated in slave flight or *marronnage*. But, although the proportion of women fugitives was a little less than 50 percent, their number is still significant. Explanations of this pattern of resistance remain largely male centered and unsatisfactory. Orlando Patterson argued that male slaves "were better able to bear the vicissitudes of such an undertaking." Similarly, Michael Craton declared that "runaways had to have the stomach, as well as the arms and skill, to fight on the move and the knowledge, ingenuity, and hardihood to live off the bush." Gautier, on the other hand, attributed the lesser participation of women to their lesser mobility in Africa, their relations with whites, and the advantages they derived from these.[38]

These issues are more complex than they appear. Women may have been less mobile than men in Africa, but in both Africa and the Caribbean they were the primary agricultural producers.[39] It is likely that this was also the case in maroon communities in the Caribbean. Therefore, they would have been valuable, even essential, to cultivation particularly in the case of *grand marronnage* (running away to form a permanent and independent community in the forest) if not in *petit marronnage* (running away for short periods, which many planters considered tantamount to absenteeism). Gautier linked mobility to maternity, suggesting that the spectre of women chained along with their children in the fields—"a ghastly and effective scene in restraining the desire of a mother to run away no matter the degree of opposition to slavery"—served as a powerful deterrent to would-be fugitives. Indeed, slaveowners imposed this form of punishment on runaway slave women who were caught, as we shall see. If we agree with Patterson that the Caribbean was a "theatre of European imperial horrors," however, it is not far-fetched to suggest that women were not strangers to, or intimidated by, punishment and suffering. Thus Vanony-Frisch may well be right in stating that neither child care nor the unforeseen dangers which characterized *marronnage* deterred women.[40]

Advertisements in colonial newspapers and prison records provide startling revelations about female fugitives. Black and mixed-race females fled from their white, black, and mixed-race owners, chained and unchained, with and without their children. The race and sex of the slaveowner were immaterial in slave women's decision to abscond. Also, neither pregnancy nor the age of their children seem to have prevented some women in the French Caribbean from fleeing, but women without children were more likely to flee. In

1788 one of the fugitives in the Petit-Bourg prison in Guadeloupe was the eighteen-year-old black woman Adélaïde, who was owned by Julienne, a free mixed-race woman from Pointe-à-Pitre. In the nineteenth century, several female fugitives advertised in the *Gazette de la Martinique* belonged to black and mixed-race owners as well. Such was the case of Émélie, a twenty-five-year-old Congolese, who in October 1803 was believed to be in Fort-de-France or Gros Morne with other Congolese, hiding from her mixed-race female owner, Rose. In 1804 Christine, a black slave woman, fled from her owner, Mathurine, a free black woman from the district of Trinité.[41]

A slave who escaped wearing chains was a dead giveaway, but even so chains did not deter women. Some may have found ways to rid themselves of such an encumbrance (with the help of a blacksmith, no doubt), but many remained at large in this state for extended periods. In late 1805 Madeleine, a twenty-year-old mixed-race female slave, fled in chains in Martinique. About six months later, in March 1806, her owner offered a reward of two *moëdes* for her capture. Also in Martinique the black women Clémence, forty, and Marie-Rose, who was owned by the widow Madame Prospert, fled in chains in late 1805. The iron collar Clémence wore was described as being "long and sturdy." Magdeleine, a black slave woman, also ran away from her owner, Monsieur Mathieu of Saint-Pierre, wearing an iron collar around her neck.[42] Slave women wearing chains fled with their children as well. France, a police superintendent in the French colonies, reported that in 1844 the slave woman Coralie of Guadeloupe was still wearing chains when she, along with her seven- or eight-month-old child, was captured as a fugitive and imprisoned. Coralie told prison officials that she preferred to die with her child than return to her owner, Jules Dispagne. She resisted his efforts to reclaim her with all her might, but Dispagne ignored her screams and prevailed in the end. He openly disregarded bureaucratic procedures, whipped her in the presence of other prisoners, and had a chain gang of slaves transport her and her child back to his plantation. Arlette Gautier used this case to state that slave women's refusal to succumb to the sexual advances of their owners may have led to physical abuse. This may have been so, but in Coralie's case the data do not go that far.[43]

In French Guiana, Anne-Marie Bruleaux and her coauthors wrote, "Pregnant women as well as those carrying babies in their arms took to marronage." This pattern was strikingly similar in the rest of the French Antilles. Some women left with infants only seven or eight days old. Marie, aged thirty-eight, took three children aged seventeen, four, and two years old with her into *marronnage* in Saint-Domingue. Similarly, Blandine, thirty-five, and her daughter Adélaïde fled together. In 1788 Victoire, a fugitive, and her infant son were inmates of the Pointe-à-Pitre prison in Guadeloupe. A reward of ten *gourdes* was offered for the capture of Robertine who, though pregnant, absconded in Guadeloupe with her two daughters, four-year-old Lise and five-year-old Clémence, in 1826. At Martinique two domestic slaves, Sarah and her son William, absconded from their owner, General Kipple, who offered eight *gourdes* for their capture in 1803. Régis, a thirty-year-old seamstress originally from Mozambique, took off with her eighteen-month-old daughter in 1806. In 1809 Michael Catherine, a mixed-race slaveowner, offered a handsome reward for the capture of Gertrude, who ran away with her four children, ranging in age from one to eight years old. Gertrude took a trunk and other personal effects with her, a sure indication that she did not intend to return. Of the forty-two female fugitives in Vanony-Frisch's sample (1768–83) of the Lepreux Plantation in Guadeloupe, seven left their children behind, however. One of these was Bénée, a thirty-one-year-old creole slave who had run away several times and who left without her two-year-old son, Séverin.[44]

Female *marronnage* was not restricted to any particular age group, although adult women constituted the majority of refugees. In the French colonies generally, most fugitives were between seventeen and thirty-five years old, but there were also younger fugitives and others of advanced age. In most cases, women were recaptured and imprisoned. At Martinique in 1838, the police caught the fugitive slave women Véronique (Vonique), a forty-year-old creole, and Félicité, a twenty-five-year-old black creole, and imprisoned them at Fort-Royal. At the same time, several other fugitive women of color were imprisoned at Saint-Pierre. Among them were the mixed-race Urane, the black woman Adélaïde, who was pregnant, and Marguerite. Rose, a young fugitive inmate in the Fort-de-France prison in 1803, was so new to the colony that she did not know how to pronounce her owner's name. Likewise, a recent arrival from Africa who had not yet been given a French name, took to *marronnage* in 1805. She wore rings in both nostrils and spoke neither French nor Creole. The authorities could not and did not always indicate the age of fugitives, but descriptive adjectives such as *vieille* (old), though deceptive given the concept of age in past centuries, provide useful hints. For example, the "old *Négresse*" Angélique, a fugitive in the Fort-de-France prison in 1804, was described as speaking in garbled tones. The authorities used the same words to describe the fugitive slave woman Marie, held in the Basse-Terre prison in Guadeloupe in 1810.[45]

In the seventeenth and eighteenth centuries, slave women in the French Antilles generally ran away alone or in groups, mostly with other women and not with their husbands. This led Jean Fouchard to conclude that "female slaves organized their marronage only among women." Some women sought work in the cities. In 1805 Martonne, a thirty-two-year-old, mixed-race, French-speaking female owned by an usher in Fort-de-France, was one such slave. Sixteen-year-old Bélérie was another. Described as "very white" in color, she was suspected of selling merchandise in Fort-de-France, where her aunt resided. Although she had been at large only for a month in May 1806, her owner offered a reward for her capture and promised her leniency if she returned, as well as the option of choosing a new owner herself. No reward was offered for the black slave woman Elénore, aged forty, who sold merchandise all over Martinique in 1806. Still others sought refuge at the outskirts of large plantations or worked for free blacks who owned small plantations. Such was the case of Rose, who ran away for more than a year; for six months she worked for the black planter Lafoucault on the plantation Lilancour in northern Saint-Domingue. On August 17, 1769, a group of slave women abandoned a Saint-Domingue plantation, but not before attempting to persuade another group of women, whose function was the pounding of millet and other domestic labors, to join them. It is not yet clear why women began to run away without their menfolk, but some historians have speculated on the possible breakdown of the slave family in which males no longer played a leading role. The explanation is more complex, however, because there are cases in the eighteenth and nineteenth centuries where women and men fled plantations together. In 1803, for example, Judith, a thirty-nine-year-old, mixed-race slave fled with Pierre, a black male slave passing as free.[46]

Throughout the slave period in the French Antilles, women formed part of the maroon bands that engaged in open confrontation with the slave system. The existence of such bands dates back to the early stages of plantation slavery in the seventeenth century, but their makeup has sometimes sparked controversy among scholars. In the mid-seventeenth century, Françisque Fabulé of Guadeloupe is said to have led as many as four hundred maroons, divided into groups of twenty-five to thirty slaves each. Léo Elisabeth has disputed this figure by arguing that it was beyond the capacity of a single individual to lead so many bands, and that attempts to capture the fugitives netted only six to seven of them. What is revealing, however, is the fact that the colonial government considered a truce with Fabulé necessary in order to dissuade other slaves from practicing *grand marronnage*. This tactic was not successful, however. During the period 1803–45, authorities in Guadeloupe sent several expeditions against bands composed of fifty or more fugitives, led by the infamous Grand-Papa, a maroon for more than forty-five years. Other bands were led by Nocachy, a "very mischievous subject" who was caught after seventeen years in the mountains in Petit-Bourg, Guadeloupe.[47] In the 1790s, several bands of male and female fugitives terrorized the cities of Saint-Domingue, incited unrest among other slaves, and plagued the French army. In 1793 the French fought several fierce battles with some of these groups around Le Cap, in the north of the island. In this region alone, according to Fouchard, "there were fourteen thousand Maroon women willing to accept an amnesty then in the offing. This figure is astonishing, but authentic."[48] There is no evidence that these maroons were led by a woman or that they pursued a struggle separate from that of males.

In French Guiana as well, male and female maroons formed many bands. During the years 1802–1806, one of the most infamous bands was led by a male named Pompée, who two decades earlier had established a stable, agricultural maroon community called Maripa on the left bank of the Comté River, above Brodel Hill. Besides Pompée's sixty-year-old wife, Gertrude, other female fugitives in the band included Rosine, aged sixty-seven, and Adeline and Ester, both aged forty—all former slaves of the Sigogne Plantation, which they subsequently set afire. Using the forest and waterways as cover, Pompée and his band successfully fought troops sent from Cayenne until the 1820s. Administrative reports also indicate that at least three expeditions were sent against the maroon community Ajoupa, whose members included Suzanne, wife of the maroon chief Linval, Catherine, and several other women.[49]

When caught escaping or condemned for assisting others to become fugitives, female slaves could be whipped, placed in iron collars, branded with hot irons, or executed. Article 36 of the Code Noir prescribed that fugitive slaves who remained at large for a month should have their ears cut off and be branded on one shoulder with the fleur-de-lis. If such fugitives ran away again and stayed away for a month, they were to have their hamstring cut and be branded on the other shoulder. A third attempt to escape or an unauthorized absence brought execution.[50] The Antigua slave act of 1702 was somewhat similar, but in the French Antilles some slaves were executed for fewer than three attempts at *marronnage,* especially if they were considered dangerous. Fugitive women, however, had to be concerned about dangers other than punishment. The prospect of being raped, for example, was real and may explain why women, unlike men, left more often in twos, with a brother, or even disguised as men. In some cases, women also changed their identities. In July 1803 an advertisement in the *Gazette de la Martinique* revealed that thirty-year-old Dauphine had been a fugitive since September 1802. Described as "a very mischievous subject," Dauphine had previously been a fugitive from June 27, 1798, to March 1802—a period of almost four years, during which she bore a child. To cover her tracks, she changed her name to Angélique and passed as free.[51]

Planters normally exercised flexibility in administering punishment for *marronnage* and other offenses, as it would have been difficult to maintain a robust slave force and be assured of full monetary compensation from the state otherwise, but women were usually punished as severely as men. They were killed, disfigured, and humiliated for acts of *marronnage.* In 1724 the Conseil Supérieur of Martinique condemned a slave woman to death for a third act of *marronnage*. During the execution, the cord around her neck broke, but her executioner resorted to strangulation, considered an act of mercy, despite pleas for clemency from onlookers. Marie Jeanne, a female who was part of a maroon band at Malegrou in Guadeloupe, was killed in another manner. In February 1743, while bathing in the Rivière des Parès, she was seen by Dugez, an administrator of the plantation called de Brinon, which belonged to de Sennecterre and his partner La Sègue. Dugez attempted to recapture Marie Jeanne, who either defended herself or called for help. Dugez stabbed her twice with a sword, disemboweling her.

"To make this deed more hideous," the historian Lucien Abénon wrote, "it has been suggested that the negress was pregnant, but this is uncertain. Informed by Dugez of the murder, La Sègue commended him and ordered that the head of the negress be cut off and exposed on a pike opposite to her hut," a common method in the Caribbean and the Americas of displaying the remains of rebels that was intended to deter would-be imitators. Two months later, as Dugez went out alone to examine the cattle and the cooperage, he disappeared and was never heard from again. Later interrogation of the plantation slaves—which resulted in the deaths of nine males and the whipping and branding of a female slave with the fleur-de-lis—revealed that he had been killed by the slaves of de Brinon, although de Sennecterre attributed the plot to an unnamed European, believing that slaves were incapable of masterminding such a plot. Abénon argued convincingly, however, that de Brinon slaves were responsible for the disappearance of Dugez, which showed that "there was solidarity among them and that they were conscious of the effects of their action," or of *marronnage*, on the slave system.[52]

Slave women, like slave men, were sentenced to state galleys to row seagoing vessels for acts related to *marronnage*. Consider the case of the mixed-race slave women Aï and Agnès, owned by Sieur Edouard Henry, who hid and fed for three months the fugitive male slave Elizée, and provided him with the means to escape from Martinique by boat. Twice a runaway and also accused of stealing, Elizée, owned by Sieur Faugas, was executed in Saint-Pierre in 1815. For her part, Aï was given twenty-nine lashes in public, branded with a hot iron on the right shoulder with the letters G.A.L., denoting perpetual servitude in the king's galleys. Agnès was given the same sentence, but was remanded in custody in the new prison in Fort-Royal pending further investigation.[53]

The children and relatives (mostly female) of habitual maroons—*mauvais sujets* (mischievous subjects) in plantation parlance—were sometimes placed in chains in retaliation for the acts of family members. A planter also resorted to this form of punishment to head off *marronnage*. In 1832 Xavier Tanc, a magistrate in Guadeloupe, observed that slaveowners made a captured fugitive woman, or a slave woman suspected of intending to run away, wear a large chain around her neck or foot with one of her children attached. Tanc "saw a little girl about six years old dragging this heavy and irksome burden with torment as if the crime . . . of the mother was justification for punishing this young child in such a barbarous manner. At that age, her fragile frame and delicate flesh were all battered."[54] In 1846 the Cour Royale of Guadeloupe imposed a fine of five hundred francs on Crosnier, an administrator on a plantation in Guadeloupe who had committed several acts of cruelty against slaves, including chaining and whipping the slave women Hermenie and Belonie solely because their children had run away. The case of the planter Achille Wermin d'Aigrepon of French Guiana, who chained the mothers and sisters of fugitives, was also typical. In 1827 the judiciary in French Guiana charged d'Aigrepon with cruelty to such women, including Marie Thérèse and Denise, who were given up to two hundred lashes per day pending the return of their relatives from *marronnage*. Although d'Aigrepon sent his brother to face the charges rather than appearing in his own defense, he claimed that Denise, an elderly slave woman, poisoned herself out of desperation. However, slave testimony revealed that Denise had no teeth and could not have extracted the poisonous juice from the manioc pulp. Upon her death, d'Aigrepon ordered that her head be severed and placed on a pole outside her hut, in the same manner as that of her seventy-five-year-old husband, Jacinthe, who had previously been accused and punished for *marronnage*. The court banned d'Aigrepon from French Guiana for ten years.[55] The age of this slave couple raises questions about the authenticity of the accusation leveled against them, in spite of the fact that age was not a barrier to *marronnage*. But this case shows how *marronnage* could be used as a pretext by slaveowners to terrorize slaves. The impact of such terror on the slave woman's psyche can only be imagined. Slave women, however, continued to engage in *marronnage* and other acts of resistance to slavery, demonstrating that punishment, however barbaric it may have been, was not a certain deterrent.

POISON

Besides armed revolt and *marronnage,* women also engaged in poisoning as a form of resistance. Auguste Lacour's characterization of poisoning as "a political act"[56] fits the situation for Guadeloupe in 1802, but also applies to other French colonies in that the slaves were conscious of the devastating impact poisoning had on slavery and the planter class. Maurice Satineau noted that slaves in Guadeloupe and other French colonies engaged in acts of poison prior to the Code Noir of 1685. Poison was thus one of the earliest forms of resistance to slavery. Difficult to detect, it was also one of the most popular forms of resistance, as Gwendolyn Mildo Hall stated.[57] Slaves targeted their owners, other slaves, and animals, into whose nostrils they are said to have inserted poisonous wood. Père Labat related an incident which occurred on the Saint-Aubin Plantation in Martinique around 1697, when more than thirty slaves died painfully and in rapid succession owing to "malice on the part of a slave who poisoned the others after observing that the master showed favouritism to another slave." The slave allegedly confessed to his owner that the poison he placed in alcohol was derived from a plant.[58] The fact that Labat severely punished his own slaves for their alleged involvement shows that even members of the clergy subscribed to the theory of sabotage. However, French sources show that it was only in the early eighteenth century—a time when the volume of slaves imported from Africa began to increase markedly, and with it, incidents of poison—that slaveowners became greatly concerned about poison cases.

In 1712 Governor Phélypeaux of Martinique was alarmed by the prospect of a slave revolt, which had loomed in the air for two years, and by talk of "black poisoners" whose aim was to kill animals and people. As a result of increasing death rates in the eighteenth century among planters, slaves, and animals in Guadeloupe, Martinique, and Saint-Domingue, French authorities issued a series of ordinances to curb poisoning. Some ordinances applied to all the colonies, others only to individual colonies. In Guadeloupe an ordinance dated May 10, 1720, prohibited both male or female slaves from treating sick people except in the case of snakebite. The penalty for an infraction was death.[59] Slave medical practitioners, male and female, used a wide range of herbal remedies to ward off snakebites and other illnesses. The skills were passed on from one generation to the next and derived from African tradition.[60] Planters viewed such practices as a façade for the rampant use of poison. Slave healers therefore became prime targets for anti-poison legislation. Epidemics and epizootic outbreaks were responsible for many deaths in the French Antilles, but doctors were ill-equipped to study them, and the plantocracy used them as a basis for convicting and punishing slaves. For example, Governor Phélypeaux knew that droughts and the material condition of slaves caused more deaths than poisoning, but did not criticize slaveowners who took drastic countermeasures against those they suspected.[61] European doctors in the French colonies, known as the "king's doctors," held official positions and performed medical operations.[62] They distinguished themselves from local healers and diviners, whom they considered quacks, although these people sometimes held important posts, owing, no doubt, to the lack of doctors. Yvan Debbasch observed that it was easy for European doctors "to conceal their ignorance behind the diagnosis of poison" and "give masters the answers they wanted to hear."[63]

In February 1724 a royal ordinance applicable to the French colonies was introduced, which characterized poisoning as the most detestable crime and the most dangerous for Europeans. It proclaimed that all slaves suspected of administering, concocting, or distributing poison, lethal or nonlethal, would be put to death. Similarly, a Martinique ordinance introduced on May 18, 1724, outlined measures to prevent poisonings, "which have become more frequent in the last several years."[64] That a declaration dated February 1, 1743, called for the strict application of the various ordinances in the French Caribbean shows that poison remained a serious concern.[65] In 1749 the governor of Martinique published an ordinance denouncing poisoners. A comprehensive report of 1762, which dealt with poison in Saint-Domingue from around 1712, blamed carnal relations between white male slaveowners and female slaves for much of the poisonings. In 1763 the governor of Guadeloupe ruled that anyone who bought poison or who instructed slaves in the medical arts, surgery, pharmacy, or knowledge of plants and tropical roots was guilty of poisoning. The death penalty was also to be administered to slaves on whose persons drugs were found and to diviners who distributed amulets. This ruling was very similar to a series of local ordinances that were introduced in Saint-Domingue in 1780. These ordinances sought to curb poisonings by tightening regulations governing the preparation, distribution, and sale of drugs. For example, only the king's pharmacist had the right to sell arsenic. Also, pharmacies were required to lock up drugs and sell them only to other pharmacies and to surgeons. In addition, pharmacists and surgeons were prohibited from allowing blacks to prepare drugs. In the nineteenth century, several local ordinances in French Guiana prohibited the injection of poison into rivers, a source of food and drinking water.[66]

In spite of the stringent measures adopted, the use of poison as a weapon among slaves against their enemies continued down to the end of slavery. In 1726 an administrative report noted that there were few estates in Martinique that did not suffer the effects of poison. In October 1741 Governor Champigny of Guadeloupe and his assistant Delacroix wrote about slaves who brought planters to ruin through acts of poisoning. They pointed out that

> a number of slaves and animals are dying of poison. We cannot attribute this to anything else but the abuse which some slaves make of the knowledge they possess of herbs and juices of certain plants. They concoct powders and drugs from them which they distribute to other slaves as a remedy. They are, to be sure, remedies which they sell publicly without disclosing the composition [and are used for] exacting their vengeance against masters, against whites who cross them in their dealings and against their comrades whom they bear ill will.[67]

In the French Caribbean, poison was used mostly against animals and other slaves rather than against slaveowners. According to French sources, this was because the slaves believed that whites were less susceptible to African poisons.[68] There may have been other factors involved, though. Few slaves had unlimited access to the slaveowner's household, so it was easier for them to vent their frustrations on cattle, mules, horses, and (rarely) other slaves. The loss of slaves and animals was a serious blow to any planter. Testimony by a female slave revealed that the rampant cases of poisoning in Le Cap and Fort-Dauphin in Saint-Domingue in 1756 were the work of slaves.[69]

Debien reproduced several letters written between 1765 and 1774 by François Lory de la Bernardière, an absentee planter from Nantes who owned the Cottineau Plantation in Fort-Dauphin, Saint-Domingue, which show that planters were frequently concerned about poison. Lory consistently asked his managers to find the slaves responsible for poisoning other slaves—an act of resistance designed to bring slaveowners to economic ruin—and make an example of them. Jeannit, a male slave on the neighboring Loiseau de Montaugé Plantation, who had a female slave companion, Boukmann, on the Cottineau Plantation, became the prime suspect. Lory offered Jeannit's owner compensation to have the slave executed, and then turned his attention to Boukmann, aged forty-two, and her niece, Marie-Louise, aged twenty-six, whom she allegedly trained in the art of poisoning. Accused of being a professional, Boukmann was imprisoned in solitary confinement, as was her niece, much to the pleasure of Lory, who claimed that in spite of his concerns about poison, he was still inclined to believe that the deaths were due to epilepsy. Lory's uncertainty leaves the impression that disease may have been a factor, but once a suspected poisoner was identified, however arbitrarily, nothing else mattered. Boukmann was executed and burned in 1773. Marie-Louise was spared because of her age and working potential, but in a letter of 1774 to his manager, Lory expressed the fear that she might poison the plantation slaves by putting herbal concoctions in *tafia*. He advised that she be carefully watched by the boiler, the head slave driver, and the manager himself.[70]

Poison is said to have been responsible for the near extinction of some plantations in Martinique during the eighteenth century. Debbasch presented statistics taken from administrative reports and secondary sources which showed a massive loss of slaves and animals on several plantations in the French Caribbean dating from 1757, enough to put a dent in the fortunes of plantation owners and even cause a cessation of business. However, because of the large number of slave deaths involved, Debbasch doubted the reliability of these statistics. Debbasch drew attention at the same time to some striking cases of poisoning. In 1746 a Martiniquan planter, Dessales, lost 102 head of cattle, 37 mules, and 25 slaves in a three-month period.[71] As late as 1822, authorities in Martinique indicated that poisonings were still on the increase. As a result, the governor introduced an ordinance on August 12, establishing a military court that allowed no appeals. The only sentence it handed down was decapitation, which had to be carried out within thirty-six hours.[72]

As chapter 4 showed, women formed part of the domestic entourage on every plantation, which gave them access to the slaveowner's kitchen and opportunities to poison food. However, the paranoia over poisoning in the French Antilles during the eighteenth century led to false accusations and wrongful convictions of many male and female slaves, including cooks and nurses. In 1723 Blondel de Jouvancourt, an intendant in Martinique, reported that criminal proceedings against a female slave accused of poisoning resulted in a one-year prison term pending further investigation. De Jouvancourt also mentioned that two slave women received the death penalty for poisoning a white female, L'Escourt. One of the slave women, Marie Ann, made a public confession prior to facing her executioners, but de Jouvancourt was made aware of this development only after the sentences had been carried out. He did not indicate the circumstances that led to the confession, but Governor Phélypeaux noted that, in some cases, executioners extracted confessions from slaves by applying hot irons to the soles of their feet hourly, making walking impossible for up to six months. Sugar was poured on other slaves, who were then left in designated spots where they were stung from head to toe by insects. "Under these circumstances," Phélypeaux wrote, "it is not surprising that confessions of poison and sorcery are obtained." In 1726 the Conseil Supérieur of Martinique sentenced a slave woman to death for poisoning her female owner, who died eighteen hours after consuming a chocolate drink. The slave did not admit to the deed, but the authorities claimed that the evidence against her was very strong.[73] On August 15, 1782, the overseer of the Bonrepos Plantation, in the Cul-de-Sac region of Saint-Domingue, reported that he caught the plantation washerwoman about to dump poisonous powder into his water jars. Surprised in the act, the woman ran, throwing the powder away. The overseer became convinced that the slaves, whom he had found difficult to govern for a year, wanted to murder him and his family.[74] Labat warned that female domestics often plotted to kill their owners and advised planters to employ an outside surgeon, a nonresident who could come to the plantation in the mornings or whenever needed.[75]

The cases of poisoning that came to light in the nineteenth century, and the manner in which slaveowners responded to them, reveal a continuous cycle of violence stemming from frustration on the part of a planter class trying unsuccessfully to stamp out poisoning. After the failure of the 1802 slave revolt in Guadeloupe, all black nurses at the military hospital in Pointe-à-Pitre, where rising mortality among General Richepance's troops was attributed to poison, were rounded up and shot. According to Lacour, many had reportedly come down from the hills specifically to seek employment at the hospital with the intention of poisoning French soldiers. The French commander, Pillet, gave the order to execute the black nurses only after he became suspicious that they were part of a larger slave plot which included *gens de couleur libres*—people of African and European ancestry usually called free coloreds—in the military, all from Sainte-Anne near Pointe-à-Pitre. The rebels called for the death of the French military and began their revolt on October 6, 1802, but were crushed within a few days.[76] In Saint-Domingue, slave women may also have targeted the military. The National Guard, which camped on the Galiffet Plantation in the northern part of the island during the early years of the war of liberation, experienced high mortality. According to Métral, soldiers died in droves after repeatedly drinking water from a well into which the slaves had dumped copper utensils.[77] Whether the slaves knew that copper in the water supply would become toxic is uncertain. Indeed, the water could have been contaminated before by other agents. However, the act of dumping appears to have been deliberate and would likely have been the work of slave women.

Executions, immolation, and deportations were common forms of punishment for poisonings in the nineteenth century. After sustained interrogation of male and female slaves in 1806, authorities in Martinique sentenced a thirty-year-old creole slave woman, Émile, to be burnt alive and ordered that her ashes be thrown to the wind for putting ground glass in the food of the Empress Josephine, wife of the Emperor Napoléon. Born and raised in the empress's household, Émile, a Catholic, admitted to serving her owner a dish, but claimed that the suspicious substance, tested by a member of the tribunal during the course of the investigation, was sand. Thères, another female slave implicated in the plot, was to undergo further investigation, but Jeseph, a male, was discharged.[78]

In the decades leading up to emancipation in 1848, trials of slave women for poisonings and requests by slaveowners to deport suspects from the French colonies were quite common. Many of the slaves awaiting trial in Martiniquan prisons in 1827 were women accused of poisoning. They were mostly elite slaves and included Rosette, a "reputed poisoner," and Marceline, an *hospitalière*. That same year the planter Sainson-Sainville requested the deportation of one of his female slaves, who belonged to a family of poisoners and whom he blamed for poisoning several of his animals. In appealing to state authorities to rid him of this slave, Sainson-Sainville argued that, in spite of the regulations against deporting slaves from the French colonies to foreign territory, "we are not . . . obliged to keep dangerous slaves." In this case, the state agreed. In 1844 another planter, Georges Despointes of Lamentin, Martinique, also sought to have a slave woman Élise, an elderly *hospitalière* whom he suspected of poisoning his animals, declared a dangerous slave and expelled. However, the Procureur du Roi, having found no merit to the accusation, released her from prison and sent her back to her owner, rather than pursuing a case that might have led to deportation.[79]

In French Guiana in 1831, Michel Brémond and Michel Favard, owners of the Caroline sugar plantation in Roura, asked the authorities to deport three slaves whom they accused of poisoning. This request led to one of the most detailed investigations of poison in the French Caribbean, and illustrates the possibilities open to slave women to poison food. It also shows the damage that slave women with a reputation for poisoning could do to the slave system. The slave at the center of the investigation was Magdeleine, a fifty-five-year-old domestic and local surgeon on the Caroline Plantation. In a letter to the authorities, Brémond stated that Magdeleine used her ability and intelligence to seduce her owners, who awarded her the post of head cook. In this role, she was the custodian of the keys and was responsible for the care and preparation of food for the plantation household. In addition, she was in charge of surgery on the plantation. She enjoyed the "complete confidence" of her owners and of other domestics in the household, who were awed by her excellent management skills; other slaves were envious of her position within the slave hierarchy. As surgeon Magdeleine was, as Brémond noted, in possession of lethal drugs that she could have used to poison over an extended period without drawing suspicion to herself. Indeed, Magdeleine's position enabled her to keep a tight rein on other domestics and to voice her opinion on who should occupy the post of manager, which her son-in-law, the slave Mirtil, had occupied for thirty years. When Mirtil was replaced by Quenessou, a European, and the slave woman Estelle was given the position of housekeeper, Magdeleine sought to rectify a potentially threatening situation by eliminating the new appointees and by ensuring, in particular, that no whites remained in a managerial position on the plantation. She carefully chose the moment to poison Quenessou and Estelle, who experienced vomiting, convulsions, and colic a few days after Favard left for France. Quenessou accused Magdeleine of poisoning him and abandoned the plantation as a result, but this was not the end of the story. Mirtil requested that he be reinstated in the post of manager. Brémond refused, however, and instead named another white, named Rimal. Eight days after Rimal began work, he began to show the same symptoms as his predecessor and was treated at the hospital at Cayenne. Rimal, who had no history of illness in the colonies and was well acclimatized to the Roura district, recovered and returned to the plantation, but became sick again within days, half an hour after drinking coffee prepared by Magdeleine. In the end, he was advised by Chrétien, a white foreman on the plantation, to leave while he was still alive since it was obvious that the slaves "did not want a white manager on Caroline." Frightened, helpless, and barely able to walk, Rimal was taken to Cayenne vowing never to return to Caroline. Thus, Magdeleine was able to ward off, albeit temporarily, "the threat which the white manager represented to her authority on the plantation."[80]

Without raising a cutlass against her owners or appearing to lash out at the system, Magdeleine had assessed the various players on the plantation, the relations between them, and her own capacity to act and test the outer limits of the system. She created a world of her own in which she and other slaves could live on their own terms, but she and they were still vulnerable to the vagaries of the slave plantation system. Testimony from plantation owners in the region, police commissioners, and slaves revealed that Magdeleine was widely feared and considered untouchable, but the authorities had the last word. French archival records indicate that Magdeleine admitted giving Quenessou "la tissane" but denied that any poisonous ingredients were added to it. Neither she nor her children, Boy and Virginie, who were deemed to be accomplices, were brought before the courts, as there was insufficient evidence to convict them. However, the Conseil Supérieur of French Guiana, which made the local laws, voted unanimously to expel her and her children from the colony for security reasons, but refused to pay their owners indemnity so as not to set a precedent.[81]

Magdeleine was not the last slave woman in French Guiana to strike fear into the hearts of slaveowners concerned about poisoning. In 1843, when sudden and unprecedented deaths among the 120 slaves on the sugar plantation Marianne reached a height, Pompone, notorious among *piayeurs* (poisoners in local parlance), and her son, Adrien, were blamed. As the situation worsened, twenty-eight-year-old Adolphe Thomas Fourier, a French manager at Marianne, asked to be relieved of his position and was, after months of pleading, replaced by one of the absentee co-owners, Quinton Dupin of France. However, mortality continued to mount. Adrien was arrested and released due to insufficient evidence, and Quinton Dupin was left without a solution until Crispin, a slave, informed him that unless Fourier was arrested and brought to justice for cruelty against the slaves of Marianne, the death rate would not decline. Pompone, Adrien, Crispin, and other slaves then provided authorities with details of Fourier's actions that led to his arrest. Thus the slaves changed the focus of the investigation from poison to abuses against slaves. In sittings that lasted from November 23 to November 26, 1843, the Cour d'Assises considered eight charges against Fourier. In November 1839, for example, Fourier struck the slave woman Chereze with a cable and kicked her in the stomach, after accusing her of not working fast enough. She died on May 30, 1840. Pompone was the primary witness for the prosecution, but the jury, composed of whites and mixed-race individuals, did not find her testimony credible and acquitted Fourier. A French newspaper described how Fourier's friends surrounded him and rejoiced at the verdict, but the white spectators who attended the trial left the courtroom perturbed that the planters in the colony no longer seemed invulnerable.[82]

MALINGERING, WORK AVOIDANCE, AND WORK STOPPAGE

Women resisted slavery in countless other ways, including insolence, a worthy topic that has been neglected by scholars. Women, more so than men, engaged in verbal altercations with slaveowners, especially females. As early as 1712, Governor Phélypeaux of Martinique reported that a black person had insulted his wife in public. At Guadeloupe the magistrate Xavier Tanc noted that in 1832 the female owner of a fifteen-year-old mixed-race slave, who "was always given to making remarks," gave her a beating for being insolent. In 1848, a few months before the end of slavery in the French Antilles, the slave-owner Paguenaut of French Guiana gave the slave woman Delphine eleven strokes with a branch (one of which struck her in the vagina) for insulting his wife. The authorities charged Paguenaut with cruel and inhumane treatment against Delphine, who was seven months pregnant when the incident occurred. However, the doctor who examined her reported that the whipping had caused no ill effects. This finding, in addition to the fact that the whipping did not exceed the legal limit of twenty-nine strokes, resulted in a dismissal of the charges against Paguenaut.[83]

The widely held view that slave women killed their own infants as a means of resisting slavery has been taken up in chapter 4. As we saw, midwives and expectant mothers faced corporal punishment when infants died at birth because planters interpreted such deaths as infanticide. However, neither the threat of punishment nor the incentives that planters granted women to encourage reproduction yielded positive results. Pregnant women were certainly guilty of malingering and feigning illness to avoid work, as can be seen in the reports from the overseer Dujardin de Beaumetz written to Barre de Saint-Venant, owner of a plantation in Saint-Domingue in the 1780s. They also used other tactics, as the following account shows. On September 5, 1788, Dujardin wrote to complain about the slave woman Françoise, "who has been in the convalescence house for centuries for an incurable ulcer and who has been ordered to conceive a female child in 10 days as compensation for her absenteeism from work."[84] Presumably, an additional slave would augment the labor force in time. It must have been with some gratification that Dujardin reported on October 7, 1789, that Françoise had conceived but her child had become a victim of "her ill will not to nourish it. She has so far escaped the whipping she deserves, but not for long, I hope."[85] Françoise obviously had no desire to reproduce, but gave the overseer the impression that she was complying with his wishes, only to show him in the end who had the upper hand.

Work avoidance took other forms and was sometimes combined with additional modes of resistance. In correspondence dated May 7, 1774, Regnault de Beaumont, son of a indigo planter in Léogane, Saint-Domingue, told his mother that he spent most of his time trying to get the eight males and six female plantation slaves to work. Once he turned his back, the slaves did nothing at all. On August 12, de Beaumont informed her that after his father lost his sight in an accident, the situation had grown worse. "Imagine what state the plantation is in," he wrote.[86] De Beaumont had come to Saint-Domingue in hopes of making a quick fortune, but he lacked the experience his father had, and the slaves no doubt seized the opportunity to exploit the situation and avoid work.

This form of resistance can also be observed among individual slaves. In 1822 the management of the Malgré-Tout Plantation in French Guiana discovered that a slave woman who ought to have been performing *samedi-nègre* (working on her own account on Saturdays) had managed to avoid Saturday work for some time while still being fed by the plantation on that day. On August 21, Hérault de Montalis, the *régisseur,* requested authorization to take her to Bathilde to clear land on Saturdays, "which she has been spending with her lover." On January 1, 1848, two issues of salt fish were deducted from the weekly rations of Catherine, a slave in the district of Approuague in French Guiana who refused to perform her duties in the field gangs. On January 11, a defiant Catherine was hit with another deduction of two issues of salt fish for refusing to keep quiet at work. The same offense drew a penalty of six days in the stocks for the slave woman Toussine, also of Approuague. Toussine spent an additional three days in the stocks for avoiding work and fighting with other members of the slave gang. Between January 1 and March 19, 1846, seven of the fifteen slaves placed in the stocks in this district were women.[87]

While refusal to work may not have been a new phenomenon in the slave societies of the French Antilles, it was prevalent among female slaves in the 1840s, when ameliorative laws forced authorities to pay more attention to such cases. Besides confinement to the stocks and deprivation of rations, some slave women were imprisoned for this offense. Such was the case of the nineteen-year-old field slave Marie-Louise of Martinique, who was sentenced to two months in prison for refusing to work and for *marronnage* in March 1841. In July 1842 Marie-Louise went back to prison for three months, this time for refusing to work and for theft. For "complete refusal" to work and "perpetual insolence," the thirty-year-old slave Rose, also of Martinique, was sentenced to three months in prison on July 14, 1842, but was returned to her owner on August 11. Add to these cases that of the eighteen-year-old slave woman Selina of Martinique, who was given three months in prison for refusal to work, insubordination, and vagabondage.[88]

Work stoppage was also a means of resistance to which slave women resorted in the French Antilles. This form of resistance was particularly prevalent toward the end of slavery as well. The correspondence of the governor of French Guiana shows that mass labor protests were effective. In 1843 he told the Minister of Marine and Colonies in Paris that the action of slaves on the sugar plantation Petit Cayenne, one of the most important in the colony, caused the administration great embarrassment and fear. The entire plantation gang of more than a hundred slaves left Marianne to lodge a complaint with the authorities about the actions of their owner, Le Sage, and to protest adverse working conditions. Fifty of the male and female slaves launched a work stoppage, while the others took to *marronnage* in the woods. Le Sage also complained to the authorities about the behavior of his slaves and demanded that corrective measures be taken. This put the administration, which feared the spread of strike action by the slaves, in a bind. However, further complaints by sixteen male and female slaves from Marianne forced authorities to launch a judicial investigation, which revealed that the slaves were overworked, underfed, and excessively punished. The administration upheld Le Sage's status as a planter and supported him, but recommended ameliorative measures. Even so, the governor sensed an uneasy truce between Le Sage and his slaves and seemed certain that there would be "further embarrassment." As he noted, "If what took place at Petit-Cayenne spreads; if, on any given day the head of the colony has several hundred slaves on his hands, it will no longer be a matter of complaints: it will be a revolt that would require the declaration of a state of siege." In acknowledging that the colonial governments' hold on power in the French colonies was tenuous, that corporal punishment had lost its power, and that "a society that owes its existence to such means is very near crumbling," the governor inadvertently hinted at the moral fortitude of the slaves and the effectiveness of their resistance strategies.[89]

WOMEN'S ASSOCIATIONS

Another way that slave women combated slavery was by banding together in associations, some of which may have been exclusively female, judging by their names. Some of the earliest known slave associations began in Martinique in 1793, as dance clubs organized along ethnic lines in urban centers. In the nineteenth century, they sprang up all over Martinique and broadened their functions and membership to become guilds whose members— male and female—pooled money to hold religious functions and funerals for members. By 1830 the city of Fort-Royal alone had seventeen such associations, matched only by Saint-Pierre, which may have had even more.[90] They became less ethnic in character, attracted many slaves from the rural areas, and named themselves after flowers. Leaders of the slave associations carried titles indicating gender, such as king, queen, woman of honor, and master of ceremonies. The queen of one such association, located in Petit-Bourg in Guadeloupe around 1845, was a slave. One of several such associations, this group was united by oath and was dedicated to aiding slaves who wanted to escape.[91] In French Guiana, the minutes of a Privy Council meeting of August 1837 acknowledged two female associations of which freed slaves were also members, noting that each had a distinct name and a leader. These associations organized entertainment evenings, principally dances with drumming. The women composed the traditional songs and competed with one another over the merits of the compositions. As in the rest of the French Caribbean, however, these associations were mutual aid societies whose activities frightened authorities.[92] Planters viewed slave associations, male or female, as vehicles for promoting crimes such as theft and for inciting rebellious behavior. In the 1830s planters in Martinique feared that "behind the pleasant appearance of a society of roses and carnations operated a band of hardened criminals, thieves and people dedicated to poisoning animals and whites." Their fear was that these groups contained elements who were preparing to massacre whites, as had been done in Saint-Domingue in 1791.[93]

Female slaves in the French Caribbean resisted slavery for the same reasons that men did and in much the same way. Slave men and women waged a complementary struggle and died together for common ideals of liberty because slavery reduced both sexes to units of labor. Drawing upon the experiences and circumstances of their occupations and using the opportunities that gender presented, women participated in all aspects of resistance, including armed revolt, *marronnage,* poisoning, and withdrawal of the labor through which planters sought to dehumanize them. The study of slave resistance in the French Caribbean, as elsewhere in the Americas, would therefore be grossly distorted without full consideration of the breadth of women's resistance and its effects.

8

Women and Manumission

MANUMISSION IS ALMOST as old as slavery in the French Antilles, where freedom, if not taken by force, could be granted by slaveowners or the state for meritorious acts and service in the militia, or achieved through marriage to free persons, as was already the case in the seventeenth century. The overwhelming majority of manumitted slaves were women and children, particularly mixed-race women. Not surprisingly, conjugal manumission was the most common form of manumission. Indeed, conjugal relations were behind most of the *libre de savane* or *libre de fait* manumissions—an unofficial and incomplete freedom granted by slaveowners mostly to mixed-race slave women and their children without the authority of the state, which means that the *libres de fait* lacked appropriate documents attesting to their free status.

In addition to these paths to freedom, slaves also acquired liberty through legislative acts, litigation, and *rachat* (redemption). The modes of manumission remained virtually unchanged during slavery, and the number of slaves who gained their liberty before emancipation in 1848 was always statistically small compared to the total population of slaves in each of the French colonies, except in some urban centers in the 1840s. This was largely due to the fact that, even under the best of circumstances, slaveowners seldom freed slaves. In addition, the French administration adopted an increasingly stringent policy toward the granting of manumission after the promulgation of the Code Noir of 1685.

SLAVE STATUS IN THE PRE-CODE NOIR PERIOD

Before 1685 there were a limited number of freed slaves in the French Antilles—mainly black and mixed-race women married to Europeans, as we saw in chapter 2. Others lived in a state of limbo between slavery and freedom that can be characterized as *libre de fait,* even though the term did not officially come into usage until the eighteenth century. Before 1685 the rules governing manumission were not yet firmly established in law. Therefore, the granting of freedom was somewhat arbitrary and usually left up to slaveowners, who generally favored mixed-race women and their children. This tendency remained a contentious issue in slave society. Indeed, French authorities circumvented the problem of status by attempting to prevent miscegenation, particularly between white males and black females. At the same time, they enacted ordinances aimed at creating strict boundaries between slave and free, white and colored.

The question of whether there was a specific law governing the determination of slave status in the French Antilles prior to 1685 has come under scrutiny. Yvan Debbasch noted that Commander de Poincy, a lieutenant general of the French Antilles who arrived in the colonies in 1639, apparently declared that mixed-race individuals were to be considered slaves. However, Debbasch agreed with Père Du Tertre that subsequent governors were lenient regarding the status of mixed-race individuals. He postulated that after approximately 1664—the period when the French colonies came back under the hegemony of metropolitan France and were no longer in the hands of proprietors—there was a retreat: mixed-race children were to be regarded as slaves belonging to their mothers' owners until the age of twenty years. As the law was not implemented, however, a natural father could immediately seek indemnity for his mixed-race child from its mother's owner, thereby freeing his offspring. Debbasch also argued that around 1680, the French colonies began to adhere to Roman-Dutch law when the Conseil Souverain of Guadeloupe authorized its usage. From then onward, colonial society developed along hierarchical lines based strictly on race. Institutionalized racism later became enshrined in the Code Noir, which closed off some avenues to manumission. While Debbasch is on solid ground with respect to the interpretation of law, institutionalized racism was already entrenched in the French colonies prior to 1680, as evidenced by local ordinances.[1]

THE CODE NOIR, CONCUBINAGE, AND MANUMISSION

The Code Noir established, for the first time, clear guidelines on manumission. Under Article 55 slaveowners who were twenty years of age could free their slaves without giving reasons or seeking consent from their parents. This shows that young people could own slaves at any age. Manumission was also possible under Article 9 of the Code Noir in cases where a male slaveowner had one or more children by a slave concubine. If such a slaveowner was unmarried, as we saw in chapter 6, he was required to marry his slave concubine in the Catholic Church, freeing her and her progeny by this act. Also, contravention of Article 47, which prohibited the breakup of the slave family if all of its members were the property of the same owner and the children were minors, required the freeing of slaves. The Code Noir notwithstanding, metropolitan and local amendments aimed at reducing the number of mixed-race individuals in society while limiting their civil and political rights were restrictive and curbed manumission.[2]

In particular, slave women and their mixed-race children—viewed as products of concubinage—became the focus of the amendments and the motivation behind legal reform, much as they were the motivation behind changes in immigration policy in the seventeenth century. In the late seventeenth century, a legislative document from Guadeloupe mentioned that for every hundred slaves freed, only about five were freed for laudable motives. The other ninety-five were favorite concubines and their children—a likely exaggeration, but an indication of the sentiments within a sector of French Antillean society. Nearly a century later, in 1765, one Saint-Mauris lamented that prevailing ordinances had failed to curb licentiousness among slaves in Martinique. He believed that concubines and their children should never be manumitted or be separated through sale. He directed his comments principally to young male planters who were considered by the white community to have debased themselves with slave concubines or to have purchased their freedom from others. Similarly, the instruction which the king of France gave to colonial administrators in 1777 emphasized that manumission should be granted with discretion. It cited domesticity as the principal cause of abuse of the laws in the French colonies and concubinage as a primary means of acquiring freedom. It called for the limiting of manumission and indicated that the consequences of having a large number of free people should be considered.[3]

In proposing new amendments, French authorities used various pretexts, among them the need to rein in colonists who disregarded the laws and to ensure that only those who qualified for manumission were freed. However, the repeated attempts to renew and tighten manumission legislation hint at failure. From 1685 to around 1830, the French administration adopted a stringent attitude toward granting manumission. A period of leniency followed but did not yield substantial results. Paradoxically, the effect of a tight French policy was an increase in the *libres de fait,* as slaveowners turned increasingly to unofficial means of manumitting slaves.

While decrying slaveowners whose relations with slave women resulted in illicit manumission, the colonial administration became entangled in its own web when a liaison between the Intendant Vaucresson and the black slave woman Babet became a public scandal in Martinique in the period 1711–13. Babet was one of three sisters called the La Palu sisters, after the name of the family who once owned them. In Saint-Pierre, the sisters ran a successful tavern and lucrative retail enterprise with merchandise obtained from buccaneers. While the sisters Marie Castelet and Catin Lamy had gained their liberty, however, Babet still legally belonged to Madame La Palu. In 1705 she petitioned Intendant Mithon for her liberty on the grounds that she was born of free parents. As she was unable to support her claim, Mithon declared her a slave and condemned her to a serve a month in prison, chained at the feet. In 1706 Babet appealed to the new Intendant Vaucresson, but his interim status prevented him from ruling on her case.

Through the help of Madame de Begue, a socialite who had an intimate relationship with Vaucresson, Marie found a way to free her sister Babet. She cultivated Madame de Begue by presenting her with expensive gifts daily, including 500 *écus* (the equivalent of the annual salary of a clergyman, or the price of two or three new slaves, according to Léo Elisabeth) and an authentic golden robe. Before long, according to Governor Phélypeaux, the three sisters, collectively and individually, began to spend considerable time with the intendant, so much so that district judges and others who had official business to conduct "had to wait three or four hours before the closed door of his cabinet opened and the three *Négresses* emerged to murmurs and whispers of scandal." A somber Governor Phélypeaux informed the Minister of Marine and Colonies in 1713 that Vaucresson had ignored strong evidence presented by a struggling Madame La Palu, the head of an established family who depended on revenue from Babet and her children to keep her going, and manumitted Babet. In spite of the public misgivings to which Vaucresson's actions gave rise, the matter might have rested there had a free Babet not insulted Madame La Palu's son, a militia officer who considered her his rightful slave who beat her with a baguette-shaped stick. Accompanied by Madame de Begue, a furious Babet complained to Vaucresson, who had the officer imprisoned without a hearing. Phélypeaux emphasized that Vaucresson's actions sent the wrong message to blacks and that residents of Saint-Pierre feared Babet and her sisters to the extent that no one dared complain (even to him) about their illicit activities, which allegedly included running a whorehouse and harboring runaway slaves. He requested that Babet's manumission be rescinded. The case dragged on for some time, but Vaucresson eventually reversed his decision and sent Babet back to slavery. Clarence Mumford argued that Vaucresson "had to protect his own skin against charges of impropriety with a Black woman," while Léo Elisabeth suggested that Phélypeaux wanted to prevent free people of color from acquiring wealth in the adult entertainment business, thus making "immorality the sole preserve of whites." Of greater importance, however, was perhaps the fear of black women and the role they could play in expanding the colored population. In other areas of the Caribbean such as Saint Kitts and Grenada, fear of the growth of the free colored population brought on restraining legislation.[4]

Two pieces of legislation followed in the wake of the La Palu scandal and became the centerpiece of French policy on manumission in the eighteenth century. In a royal ordinance of 1713, Governor Phélypeaux ruled that all slaveowners had to obtain written permission from the administration whenever they wished to free slaves. This measure permitted the governor general or the intendant to examine all claims and the justification behind them, which meant that the administration could determine what constituted a legitimate demand even though it set out no clear and precise guidelines. In 1736 a royal ordinance reinforced the 1713 law and specified severe penalties for noncompliance—confiscation and sale of the slaves with proceeds going to the Crown. The law also forbade the clergy from baptizing as free, and without proof, children of black and mixed-race women. Pierre Baude stated that priests knowingly engaged in this illegal practice. But status was sometimes indeterminate. Indeed, it is likely that there were free mixed-race women who were one or more generations removed from slavery but who had no official documents attesting to their free status.[5]

The renewal of the measures adopted in 1713 and 1736, by way of an ordinance imposed in 1768 in Martinique, shows that they "had not had the desired effects," as an administrative report put it. The report labeled reprehensible the action of those who went before priests to baptize slave children as free, and noted that such action had "dangerous consequences." It called for full compliance with the ordinances of 1713 and 1736.[6] The 1768 measure required baptizing priests to verify that the mothers of black and mixed-race children who requested baptism had obtained their freedom through legal means. Thus the authorities sought to verify not only the status of colored children but that of their mothers. Proof of status had to be obtained in writing from the governor or intendant and recorded in the baptismal registers. For their part, notaries could not legitimize any act of liberty without the permission of the governor general or the intendant. Contravention of this measure carried a penalty of a thousand *livres d'amende* and the lifting of the notary's license for a year. The 1768 ordinance also prohibited slaves from acquiring liberty outside of the French colonies. Reinforced in 1803, when such slaves were required to leave the colonies within three months or forfeit their liberty, this measure was aimed at slaveowners who apparently concocted fictitious transactions in foreign lands to free slaves for a fee.[7]

In Guadeloupe and Martinique, administrative attention turned increasingly to verification of status. In Guadeloupe a 1774 ordinance—a reworking of one passed in 1761—carried virtually the same provisions as the measures adopted by Martinique in 1789. In general, these measures sought to curb the granting of *libre de fait* status, especially to independent slaves—that is, those employed outside the owners' domain, who were said to be disruptive of public order and accused of immorality.[8]

In the first years of the nineteenth century, verification of status remained an administrative preoccupation. It is as if the measures of the 1760s and beyond were never adopted, for in 1803 tribunals and special commissions were set up in Martinique to assess titles, which all mixed-race people had to pre-

Table 8.1. Slave, Free Black and Mixed Race, and Total Population of
Martinique, Selected Years, 1696–1847

Year	Slave	Free	Total
1696	15,000	505	20,000
1700	14,566	507	21,670
1767	70,553	1,814	84,817
1776	71,268	2,892	85,779
1788	83,416	4,851	98,870
1802	79,754	6,578	96,158
1816	80,800	9,364	99,462
1831	86,300	—	109,716
1835	78,100	—	116,031
1838	76,500	—	117,569
1839	74,333	—	—
1840	76,403	—	—
1841	75,225	—	—
1842	76,172	—	—
1843	75,736	—	—
1844	76,117	—	—
1845	76,042	—	—
1846	75,339	—	—
1847	72,859	—	—

Sources: Philip D. Curtin, *The Atlantic Slave Trade: A Census* (Madison: University of Wisconsin Press, 1969), 78; Alex Moreau de Jonnès, *Recherches statistiques sur l'esclavage colonial et sur les moyens de le supprimer* (Paris: 1842), 17–22; Dale Tomich, *Slavery in the Circuit of Sugar* (Baltimore: Johns Hopkins University Press, 1990), 83.

sent to the courts within a period of three months. Failure to comply with this measure within the prescribed period resulted in those without proper papers being placed in the category *épaves*—derelicts to be sold at auction, the profits accruing to the state.[9]

The figures in tables 8.1, 8.2, and 8.3 (which should not be taken as accurate and definitive as statistics vary from source to source and verification of status remained an ongoing problem) show that the growth of the freed slave population was very slow, especially before the nineteenth century. There was never a certainty as to the actual number of freed slaves. Under a law passed on June 11, 1839, slaveowners in the French Antilles were obliged to take regular censuses of the slave population—counting births, marriages, and deaths—but they often neglected to do so, and the courts refused to impose penalties as the law required.[10]

The statistics do not give a breakdown by sex, but among the manumit-

Table 8.2. Slave, Free Black and Mixed Race, and Total Population of
Guadeloupe, Selected Years, 1700–1838

Year	Slave	Free	Total
1700	6,725	325	10,875
1720	17,184	895	24,317
1730	26,801	1,262	35,496
1753	40,525	1,300	50,959
1779	85,327	1,382	99,970
1788	85,461	3,044	101,971
1816	81,740	7,946	102,669
1831	—	97,300	119,663
1833	—	99,000	—
1835	—	96,300	127,574
1838	—	93,900	128,284

Source: Alex Moreau de Jonnès, *Recherches statistiques sur l'esclavage colonial et sur les moyens de
le supprimer* (Paris: 1842), 17–22; Philip D. Curtin, *The Atlantic Slave Trade: A Census* (Madison:
University of Wisconsin Press, 1969), 78.

Table 8.3. Slave, Free Black and Mixed Race, and Total Population of
French Guiana, Selected Years, 1695–1838

Year	Slave	Free	Total
1695	1,047	4	1,449
1707	1,401	14	1,774
1740	4,654	54	5,274
1765	5,728	21	8,129
1780	10,539	21	11,897
1807	13,474	1,040	15,483
1820	13,153	1,733	15,890
1831	19,102	—	22,862
1835	16,898	—	21,956
1838	15,751	—	20,940

Source: Alex Moreau de Jonnès, *Recherches statistiques sur l'esclavage colonial et sur les moyens de
le supprimer* (Paris: 1842), 17–22; Philip D. Curtin, *The Atlantic Slave Trade: A Census* (Madison:
University of Wisconsin Press, 1969), 78.

ted, as we have noted, women outnumbered men. Dessalles's breakdown of
the slave population of Martinique in 1753 confirms this trend in spite of
the loose categories he employed. He listed the number of free mixed-race
and black adult males as 363 and the number of free mixed-race and black
adult females as 436. The children of free mixed-race and free black women

Table 8.4. Free and Slave Population in Martinique, 1846

District	Free	Slave
Fort-Royal	10,307	12,752
Saint-Esprit	5,470	9,422
Anses-D'Arlets	2,294	4,701
Marin	4,458	10,784
Saint-Pierre	14,107	16,103
Grand Anse	3,889	8,198
Trinité	6,717	14,092

Source: ANSOM, Fonds généralités, Carton 207, Dossier 1516, July 26, 1846.

stood at 477. Thus, according to Dessalles's figures, the total freed slave population of Martinique in 1753 was 1,276, of which women constituted 34.2 percent, adult males 28.4 percent, and children 37.4 percent. Baude gave a similar gender breakdown for Martinique. His figures show that from 1701 to 1783, women constituted 60 percent of the freed slave population on average, and men 40 percent.[11]

Fallope's statistics on Guadeloupe support the evidence for higher rates of manumission among slave women. Of the 10,730 slaves freed in Guadeloupe between 1832 and 1842, 4,140 (38.58 percent) were women, 2,264 (21.09 percent) were men, and 4,326 (40.31 percent) were children. Also, of the 249 slaves with known occupations freed in Guadeloupe in 1842, 143 were women and 106 were men. These statistics lead Fallope to conclude that the matrifocal family remained the norm and that, most often, slave women were freed along with their children. Even so, Fallope's figures on women manumitted in Guadeloupe are only significant in relation to the number of males, not in relation to overall totals.[12]

The ratio of freedmen and -women to slaves in Martinique was somewhat higher than in Guadeloupe and French Guiana, which would mean proportionately larger numbers of freedwomen in Martinique than elsewhere, but this may only indicate long-term trends rather than greater liberalism. In some communities in Martinique in 1846, there was little statistical difference between the slave and free population in urban centers such as Fort Royal and Saint-Pierre, as table 8.4 shows. Taken together, the free black and mixed-race community of Fort Royal constituted 44.7 percent of the nonwhite population; slaves represented 55.3 percent. For Saint-Pierre, the corresponding figures are 46.7 percent and 53.3 percent respectively. These statistics raise questions about the relative effectiveness of the different modes of manumission. But they indicate that the rate of manumission among urban slaves was higher than that of rural slaves.

There can be little doubt that domestic slaves and concubines, whether urban or rural, were the principal beneficiaries of manumission. For dutiful service rendered to his father and mother, Guilbert-Minière of L'Artibonite, Saint-Domingue, freed the slave woman Jeanne in 1784. Among the ten slaves who were manumitted for services rendered in Guadeloupe in 1832 were the slave woman Cécille and her children. French sources are replete with examples of slave concubines who, along with their children, were granted freedom at the behest of slaveowners, and not as a consequence of legal proceedings launched either by the state or by slave women. Slave women manumitted in this way were, however, a minority among manumitted slaves. Under the terms of his 1743 will, Étienne Lefeure freed a Senegalese housekeeper, but in this case, as in others, according to Gautier, "one quickly recognizes the act of concubinage, evidenced by her mixed-race children." In 1757 Jean Barreau freed Marie-Thérèse and her two mixed-race sons; in 1760 he freed Phillippe Dupond, a black woman, as well as the mixed-race woman Marie-Victoire. Léonarde and her two female children were also to be freed after another five years of service. In 1751 in Nippes, Saint-Domingue, a slaveowner, Berquier, wished to give a twelve-year-old black girl to a mixed-race woman and her daughter, to whom he had just granted freedom.[13]

In his study of Saint-Claude, Guadeloupe, Géraud Lafleur detailed the case of the slaveowner Michel Antoine Bourdaise Demontérant, who in 1755 dictated his will in the presence of notaries just before he died. He granted liberty to the slave woman Roze (Rosine), as well as to her children and grandchildren—his own blood, in Lafleur's judgment—in addition to a small plantation called Petite Place. According to Lafleur, this was an entire matrifocal family to whom he granted liberty.[14] A similar case is that of Jacob Lesueur, a *gérant* on the plantation Bologne in Guadeloupe, who spent the considerable sum of 8,250 *livres* to liberate and support some of his slaves. In his will of 1782, Lesueur called for the freedom of several mixed-race slaves, including Pauline, twenty-seven, and her son Anasthase, four; Elisabeth, twenty-three, and her daughter Reine, five months; and four others ranging in age from five to sixteen years. When asked why he waited so long to free the slaves in question, Lesueur made the following declaration: "I declare that this disposition is an act of justice on my part based on the most respectable motives that I need not explain to anyone. However, I will be guilty before God if I do not act thus."[15]

The manumission of a slave concubine did not automatically mean the manumission of her children; nor did the manumission of slave children automatically mean the manumission of their mothers. Gautier noted that no more than about 10 percent of "favourite concubines" were manumitted as fathers preferred to free their children. As Debien put it, "Planters were not always generous, even when it involved their own offspring." In fact, "Quite often, freedom was granted to mothers to the exclusion of their children; or to chil-

dren long after their mothers had been freed." Gautier also observed a tendency among slaveowners to free their mixed-race male children without freeing their mothers. She gave the example the colonist Bernard le Jeune of
Saint-Domingue, who in 1790 had a mixed-race daughter with the slave
woman Louise. Andrault de Salle, a fellow colonist and friend of Bernard le
Jeune, considered him fortunate to have had a female child, as it spared him
the expense he would have incurred for manumission had it been a male.[16] So
although "white paternity of free colored children was frequently recognized"
in Saint-Domingue, as John Garrigus has asserted, boys had the edge over
girls.[17]

THE *LIBRES DE FAIT*

While the manumission of concubines and their offspring was widespread, the number of women and children freed legally in this way was very
limited. The reason is that most concubine manumission was of the *libre de
fait* variety, an enduring phenomenon that remained the most popular mode
of manumission until 1848. During this period (but especially in the 1830s,
when new laws came into being) the number of *libres de fait* rose apprecia-
bly as slaveowners circumvented the law and adopted a casual approach to
manumission that saved them money and allowed them to continue exploiting the slaves' labor. Male and female, black and mixed-race, the *libres de fait*
were found in every age category. They included domestics, wet nurses, elderly
women no longer active in the workforce, women who had several children,
and slaves working independently in urban centers mainly as domestics, midwives, and seamstresses who submitted regular remittances to their owners. In
addition, there were *libres de fait* who were abandoned by their owners. In
large measure they acquired their status through bequests. In sum, there were
libres de fait who were concubines and *libres de fait* who were not.[18]

The slave woman Thérèse of Saint-Domingue fell into the latter category. In 1765 her husband, Guitteau, a former slave and cook on the plantation Galbaud du Fort in Léogane, who had purchased his freedom for 1,380
livres in 1748, died and left her a small inheritance. Rather than storing her
money under her sleeping mat, as was the custom, she gave it to Monsieur
du Fort, her owner, for safekeeping, who in turn passed it on to Parison, his
gérant, before he departed for France. Correspondence between Parison and
Madame Galbaud du Fort in France indicates that Thérèse had been a *libre de
fait* for twenty years (during which her sole task consisted of performing midwifery duties for slave women alone) but asked to buy her freedom in 1767.
On April 11, 1768, Parison informed Madame du Fort that he had followed
her instructions and granted Thérèse, then fifty-six, her liberty that very day.
But it was a costly and restrictive liberty. Parison kept the 405 *livres* he had

held for her, an old mare valued at 90–100 *livres,* and a 100-*livre* bill donated by a freed slave. As for Thérèse, she remained on the plantation and was obliged to continue practicing midwifery. She was left to eke out a living from her garden plot, on which Parison expected her to cultivate manioc and other crops alongside the plantation slaves, although his misgivings about her strength and endurance suggest that this slave woman had passed her active working years. Debien pointed out that Thérèse and Guitteau were born on the plantation, married there, and held elite positions. But they were still subjected to a protracted struggle for manumission, which in Thérèse's case was not recognized by the colonial administration.[19]

Some *libres de fait* were shielded from labor exploitation in their elderly years. In his will of 1777, Hallot de Chavannes, a slaveowner in Saint-Domingue, granted *libre de fait* status and an inheritance of 150 *livres* annually for life to the slave woman Charlotte, who had served as wet nurse to two of his children. He extended the same benefits to the slave woman Michou, his daughter's former wet nurse. In her case, however, the 150 *livres* were to be paid each year in two six-month installments. Cognizant of the exploitation to which both women could be subjected, he asked that neither his wife nor any other executor of his estate (including the *gérant*) harass them or attempt to extract service from them. Thus, de Chavannes stopped short of freeing the women outright, a move that would have cost him legal and other fees. Debien observed that throughout slavery, wet nurses were generally freed more easily than other domestics, but not until they had served generations within the slaveowners' household, by which time they were usually advanced in age.[20]

Just as some Europeans sought to justify slavery and hail its benefits over life in Africa, there were slaveowners who viewed *libre de fait* status as preferable to complete freedom. In his will of July 1816, Le Pelletier de Laincourt of Guadeloupe indicated that he believed slaves to be happier with partial liberty, as it allowed them to retain their huts and slave gardens. He therefore granted *libre de fait* status to his former cook, Étienne, his wife, Scolastique, and the elderly black slave woman Monique, the wet nurse of two of his children. He acknowledged that he allowed them to live in a state of semi-freedom for many years, which permitted them to tend their gardens beyond the ordinary, and he recommended that his heirs follow his example and only draw upon their services sparingly when in need. He requested that *libre de fait* status also be granted to the black women Laurentine and Désirée when they reached age fifty, as long as they continued to serve with zeal and loyalty. Le Pelletier de Laincourt believed that the *libre de fait* route produced many excellent subjects without depriving him of their labor. Another *libre de fait* manumission was that of Sophie and her daughter Paulette. For their loyalty, the planter Moreau de Saint-Méry of Basse-Terre, Guadeloupe, granted them their liberty on August 5, 1820.[21]

Slave women responded positively to legal amendments that made *libre de fait* status leading to outright freedom more attainable in the nineteenth century. Under an ordinance implemented on March 1, 1831, the colonial state dropped the fee for liberty patents—freedom papers or certificates—which cost as much as three thousand French francs each prior to 1831. This measure facilitated freedom for slaves who had limited access to cash. However, the slaveowner still had to assume responsibility for the slave's sustenance before the state could issue a patent, an obligation which Victor Schoelcher contended discouraged slaveowners from emancipating slaves. This may well have been so inasmuch as the 231 slaves manumitted in Martinique on May 30, 1831, on the occasion of King Louis Philippe's birthday, were all recommended by white males, in spite of their eligibility. Some were males who had served in the militia, but the vast majority were women, many of them mothers who had contracted marriage with free males. The 1831 ordinance was followed by a royal decree of July 12, 1832, which permitted all categories of slaves not covered by previous legislation to bid for their freedom through sponsorship by a *patron*. The *patron* was usually the slaveowner, but others, notably manumitted women, sponsored their children. A law of June 11, 1839, allowed free relatives—spouses and biological and adoptive parents—to sponsor slaves with the approval of slaveowners. However, slaveowners opposed the laws of the 1830s, no doubt because they permitted others besides themselves and the state to manumit slaves. In spite of their ire, however, they realized that sponsored slaves could be kept in limbo and exploited for some time.[22]

The process of sponsorship held out the possibility of quick, positive results, but the colonial bureaucracy put in place to implement it was cumbersome. The coordination required between state officials at the district level, where the *libre de fait*'s bid for freedom began, and the higher levels of administration was poor and resulted in delays and inefficiency. However, all categories of *libre de fait* sought emancipation under the new laws. Indeed, the level of demand for freedom papers, as indicated by the colonial newspapers, was high. The number of slaves granted freedom in Guadeloupe rose significantly after the enactment of the 1832 law. In the period 1833–37, for instance, the number of liberty patents granted rose by a little more than 380 percent over the period 1830–33. Of the 6,839 patents granted in 1833–37, 4,033 (58.97 percent) were *libres de fait*. Josette Fallope indicated that 7,576 slaves were freed in Guadeloupe between 1833 and 1837, while Schoelcher gives a figure of 8,637—a difference of 61 slaves that does not change the statistical picture much. In Guadeloupe all districts experienced an increase in the number of slaves freed between 1833 and 1835, particularly the large urban communities of Pointe-à-Pitre and Basse-Terre. This indicates that the *libres de fait* who gained freedom were mostly urban slaves. Also, the number of slaves freed, whether *libres de fait* or not, constituted only a small minority of the total slave population. The 3,190 slaves freed in Guadeloupe in 1833—the largest number by far for any year during the decade—represent only 3.2 percent of the total slave population of 99,000.[23]

Requests for liberty by the *libres de fait* cut across age groups, but the overwhelming number of requests were made by women supported by white male *patrons,* a phenomenon that suggests the possibility of sexual exploitation, which was common in slavery. Examples of slave women and children sponsored directly or indirectly by white males after 1832 abound in the colonial newspapers. Some of these women were *libres de fait,* others were not. A typical case from 1843 featured the white male Pierre Xavier Ruffi Belleville, a plantation overseer from Saint-Pierre, Martinique, who sponsored Rosette, a washerwoman, aged forty-eight, along with her mixed-race daughter Cécile, nineteen. In Guadeloupe in 1832, the merchants and property owners Borno and Pierre-Anne Magloire, sponsored the forty-seven-year-old black slave woman Palmire and her fifteen-year-old mixed-race daughter, as well as the thirty-three-year-old black woman Paméla and her fourteen-year-old mixed-race son, Rovelas. They sponsored yet another black woman, Plasia, thirty-three, and her six-year-old mixed-race son, Oscar. In French Guiana slave women also received more sponsorship than slave men. Of the 293 slaves sponsored in the period December 31, 1831, to January 1, 1837, 97 were men and 120 were women, boys and girls accounting for 76.[24]

VIRGINIE VERSUS THE BELLECOURTS

As in the case of sponsorship, the slaves who obtained manumission through litigation were almost exclusively women and children. To their credit, women fought hard to free themselves and their kin from their owners—male and female—with triumphant results in some cases and what must have been deep disappointment and despair in others. Using Article 47 of the Code Noir, which prohibited the breakup of the slave family, they initiated court battles against their owners that demonstrated their humanity and stamina while serving as models for the slave community. It is instructive that in their struggle for family reunification, black women focused almost solely on their children, although there are cases where they fought to free their husbands as well. Thus in slavery, as in freedom, the black woman's role in the family was pivotal.

Quite often, black women who fought to reunify their families were former slaves who had to deal with three levels of justice, two in the colonies and one in France. The lower court (the Cour or Tribunal de Premier Instance) and the intermediary court (the Cour Royale) were colonial courts, while the Cour de Cassation or Supreme Court was in Paris. The Cour de Cassation, which had the last word, did not rejudge cases; its role was to ensure that the law was being interpreted and applied uniformly. When it reversed a judg-ment, it sent the case not back to the court where it originated but to a court of the same standing elsewhere. Justice was not swift; in fact, the black woman who dared to litigate could expect a protracted struggle, no matter how strong her case, no matter how stern her resolve.

Annoncine, a black woman and former slave in Guadeloupe, was one of the first to obtain a favorable judgment under Article 47, which led to the free-dom of her young daughter Adeline. Rendered in 1836 by the Tribunal de Pre-mier Instance, this judgment was upheld by the Cour Royale of Guadeloupe after a challenge by Soulès, Adeline's owner. In the court's opinion, Adeline was fourteen years old when her mother reclaimed her and thus qualified as a minor.[25]

While Adeline's case was being resolved, the most celebrated challenge based on Article 47 was being carefully monitored by slaveowners and aboli-tionists alike, though for different reasons. This was the case of the Guadelou-pean slave woman Virginie. Known as the *Affaire Virginie,* this case gained notoriety in the 1840s but began in 1832, when, for good and loyal service, Vir-ginie gained her liberty upon the death of her owner, Madame Bellecourt, a creole. As her two children, Amélie and Simon, were minors, Virginie expected them to be declared free as well. But the heirs of the Bellecourt estate refused to release them from bondage. Virginie's response was to fight the case in court. The Cour Royale of Guadeloupe, which had rendered a favorable judg-ment in the Adeline case, dismissed Virginie's case in 1838. Indeed, Schoel-cher's contention that rulings were uneven and partial on Article 47, and de-pended on the goodwill of judges, is borne out by similar challenges to Article 47, as we shall see. Undaunted by this initial setback, Virginie appealed to the Cour de Cassation, which, in a unanimous judgment of March 1, 1841, ruled that the law had to be applied in an even-handed manner and referred the case to the Cour Royale of Bordeaux. The choice of Bordeaux, a port city that thrived on the slave trade and colonial commerce and where, according to Schoelcher, the entrepreneurial class always opposed emancipatory measures, caused uneasiness among abolitionists. In particular, they were mindful of the presence among the judges of the influential Imbert de Bourdillon, a former Procureur Général in Martinique who was notorious for his anti-abolitionist stance. The court took eighteen months to hear the case. In June 1842 it upheld the Code Noir when it ruled that families could not be broken up through sale or seizure, but it did not view manumission as falling within these parameters. Virginie had lost her case, but she remained relentless in her pursuit of justice and appealed once more to the Cour de Cassation. Schoel-cher reproduced, in its entirety, the judgment rendered by Procureur Général Dupin and two other judges on November 22, 1844, and called it one of the finest in French judicial history. This ruling was a broad interpretation of the

Code Noir in that it viewed separation not only as resulting from sale and seizure but also from involuntary alienation—cases in which slaves were deprived of their children. In the court's view, the spirit of the law was such that any form of separation between a slave mother and her prepubescent children was prohibited. The need to maintain public morality, to protect the young at a vulnerable age, and to respect the rights of motherhood required a broad interpretation of the law that the Cour Royale of Bordeaux did not apply. This time, the Cour de Cassation sent the case to the Cour Royale of Poitiers, which agreed with the high court and ruled in Virginie's favor.[26]

It took Virginie almost eight years of struggle—from May 1837, when she launched her case, to November 1844, when it came to a close—to free her children. It was likely a bittersweet victory. The Cour Royale of Poitiers awarded her 15,000 francs in damages, which, in addition to court costs, the Bellecourt heirs had to pay. But her twelve-year-old son, Simon, was kicked by one of his owner's horses and died a slave, while her daughter, Amélie, was already a young woman by the time her case was resolved. The duration and nature of her legal battle raise questions about the financial and other resources available to slave women as they engaged in prolonged litigation, not to mention the emotional trauma they must have suffered. The abolitionists were sympathetic, but it is not clear how much help they provided or on what basis they selected cases to promote. Certainly, the Virginie case received wide coverage in *L'Abolitionniste français*. In the 1840s, the police superintendent, France, noted that there were more than a hundred people in the same situation as Virginie, who could not appeal to the Cour de Cassation as they had not yet taken the first step of going to the lower courts, as the law required. Besides, they lacked the resources and the support of colonial administrative officials such as mayors. Indeed, Gautier noted that mayors often had to be forced by judges to pursue such cases.[27]

The impact of the Virginie case on the French Antilles was striking in some ways but limited in others, as rulings remained uneven and sporadic. Families with enslaved prepubescent children benefited almost immediately, as the courts began to rule in their favor. This was the period when the plight of Coralie, a former slave in Guadeloupe who purchased her freedom for 2,642 *livres* in 1826, came to light. In 1847 the public learned that Coralie had attempted to reclaim her children, who had been separated from her and sold several times while they were minors. Coralie and her four young children—Agathe, Pauline, Joséphine, and Narcisse—were owned by Coquille Valencourt. In 1820 Valencourt sold Coralie, Joséphine, and Narcisse to the widow Blanchet. As Agathe, six, and Pauline, three, were minors, the sale constituted a breach of the law. Then, in 1823, Blanchet sold Coralie to one Noyer, thus separating Coralie from all of her children. Upon Blanchet's death, Ride, her heir, sold Joséphine and Narcisse to Friberg. This was in 1829, by which time Agathe and Pauline had been inherited by Valencourt's widow. She sold Agathe to Blaudin, a male, who sold her to the woman Iltier Lavergueais, who in turn sold her to a young woman, Nancy. By the time Coralie made her bid to reunite her family, she was seeking not only the freedom of her children but her grandchildren as well.

The Tribunal de Premier Instance of Basse-Terre, Guadeloupe, rejected Coralie's claim on the grounds that it came too late; her children were already adults. The Cour Royale of Guadeloupe upheld this judgment in August 1844. The judges argued that a mother who acquired freedom through redemption could not be said to have been separated from her children; on the contrary, she put herself in a stronger position vis-à-vis her children, both during and after their prepubescent years. The court considered that Coralie's daughter, Agathe, was twenty-one years old when the widow Coquille sold her to Blandin and was thus "perfectly alienable." Besides, her present owner, Nancy, was seen as acting in good faith. As for Pauline, the court acknowledged that there was a breach of Article 47, as she was only six years old when she was separated by sale from her mother. Still, the case was annulled. In this instance, the court took a backward step in light of the Virginie ruling. Coralie had a year to contest the rulings, but according to Schoelcher, the period usually elapsed without the mother taking further action and children remained in bondage as a result.[28]

As to why the Virginie case was not used as a precedent, Rouvellat de Cussac suggested that there was bias on the part of judicial officials, who had a vested interest in maintaining the slave system and colluded with slaveholders. Also, while they were resigned to freeing slave women, slaveholders were reluctant to free their children out of fear that, once freed, some would make financial claims against their white fathers. In a work published in 1847, Victor Schoelcher argued that white creole magistrates in the colonies were racists who worked to exclude men of color from the bench. He cited a number of cases where the legitimate aspirations of slaves bidding for freedom were thwarted by creole magistrates with ties to the slave system. Therefore, he would likely agree with de Cussac, who viewed the Cour de Cassation as the only institution that could administer justice and humanity in accordance with the religious principles of France. Virginie's struggle helped slave women even as emancipation loomed on the horizon, however, for it was as a result of her victory that Sophie, a thirty-year-old, African-born, black woman merchant who lived in Saint-Pierre, Martinique, won her freedom in 1848 from her absentee female owner, one Dumoret of France. Sophie successfully showed that she had been forcefully separated from her prepubescent son, who was taken to France (likely to serve in Dumoret's household) but was subsequently freed there. By order of the Procureur du Roi, Sophie was freed under Article 47 on February 25, 1848.[29]

RACHAT (REDEMPTION)

In addition to litigation, black women purchased their freedom and, circumstances permitting, fought to free their kin—mostly their own children. Self-purchase was an old feature of the slave system, but under the Mackau Law of July 18, 1845, slaves were permitted to purchase their freedom or that of their parents, grandparents, spouses, and children, as long as slaveowners and slaves could agree upon an acceptable price. Such a transaction constituted *rachat amiable*—a cordial redemption in which the slave often paid the slaveowner by installments. If no agreement was possible, a commission composed of judicial officials of the Cour Royale in each colony fixed the price. This was called *rachat forcé*—redemption by force. However, slaveowners had a period of six months to oppose a price set by the commission. In any case, a slave manumitted through *rachat* had to work for a free person for a period of five years and abide by restrictive conditions bordering on indentureship. But there were, in theory at least, safeguards against abuse.[30]

In the French Antilles, the average price fixed by the colonial commission was about 1,200 francs. This price was based on a survey estimating the market value of 432 slaves, of whom 170 were children under fourteen years of age. Carried out as a preemptive measure for purposes of indemnity, in anticipation of the possible emancipation of slaves, the estimate was bound to be controversial. According to Fallope, 1,200 francs was well over the 900-franc value of a mature adult slave, especially at a time when the price of slaves was declining due to the economic downturn in the French colonies and the pending emancipation. Similarly, Schoelcher accused the commission of being overly generous in setting prices higher than what slaveowners expected.

No systematic guidelines were used to determine prices, but sex, age, and occupation were important variables, judging by the price slaveowners charged. In 1847 the sixty-two-year-old sugar boiler Oreste, owned by the woman Amédée Maillet of François, Martinique, paid the commission 1,900 francs for his redemption. But the slave woman Joséphine paid only 300 francs to redeem her two-year-old son from Maillet. At the same time, the sixty-one-year-old field slave woman, Solitude, owned by Pierre Lagodière of Lamentin, Martinique, deposited 500 francs with the commission. But the commission fixed the price of redemption of forty-year-old Laurencine, a servant and slave of the woman Dathy Morestin of Saint-Pierre, at 1,600 francs. These examples, along with a list of other slaves whose prices the Martinique commission fixed and published in May 1847, show that males generally paid more than females, and highly skilled slaves, male and female, along with housekeepers and certain other elite domestic slaves, bore the highest cost of all. The commission pegged a thirty-year-old slavedriver, Laurent, at 2,500 francs, a thirty-one-year-old mason, Désir, at 2,000 francs, a thirty-six-year-old carpenter, Elydée, at 2,400 francs, and a forty-year-old cook, Étienne, at 2,000 francs. Except for Désir, all were owned by women, including the Countess de Grenonville of François, who may well have been reluctant to let Étienne go. Often the commission priced women and their children together without listing individual prices, but the data indicate that they were still priced lower than men.[31]

This state of affairs baffled Victor Schoelcher, who took the commission to task for its "handiwork," which he believed had the effect of discouraging slaves from redeeming themselves. Drawing upon examples from French Guiana, he argued that the price of redemption was excessive and arbitrary. There the commission estimated a fifty-nine-year-old slave woman Clérence at 1,100 francs, the seventy-eight-year-old slave woman Mélanie at 150 francs, and a sixteen-year old female at 1,700 francs. Schoelcher also pointed out that "Urbain, a poor leper who was incapable of rendering service to his mistress, and whose mother wished to deliver him from slavery, was estimated at 600 *francs!*"[32]

In support of the need to accelerate the manumission process as the end of slavery approached, the Chambre des Députés in Paris went beyond the French government and voted to allocate 400,000 francs to help slaves in the French colonies redeem themselves. This aid, which amounted to 100–700 francs per slave, was to be used to supplement redemption fees, and depended on the age and occupation of each slave. Martinique received 122,000 francs, which covered the partial redemption of 284 slaves. Of these, 100 were field slaves, 76 were domestic slaves, and 108 were slaves of diverse occupations. Of the 284 slaves, 62 (22 percent) were adult males, 87 (31 percent) were adult females, and 135 (47 percent) were children. Aside from the bias toward women and children, the selective process was aimed at cases deemed "necessary." For example, 217 of the 284 slaves (76 percent) fell under a category called *conduct, morality, industry, and labor.* Indeed, slaves had to provide the Conseil Privé in the colonies with a letter from a parish priest attesting to their good conduct. Forty-five of the slaves were listed under the category *marriage, family unification, and legitimization of children.* Interestingly, only 2 slaves were selected on the basis of abuse by their owners at a time when abuse was rampant, as the previous chapter showed. Thus there is merit to Fallope's contention that there was partiality in the granting of state aid, in that it went mostly to slaves who were inclined to marry and remain as field workers once freed.[33]

In Guadeloupe 462 slaves, of which 137 (30 percent) were adult males, 169 (36 percent) were adult females, and 156 (34 percent) were children, benefited from the colony's share of the subsidy—149,000 francs. The slaves contributed 92,523 francs toward their own redemption. French Guiana's share of the funds amounted to 23,000 francs, and slaves there contributed 13,988 francs.

The remainder of the funds—106,000 francs—went to the French colony Bourbon (Réunion), where slaves contributed 65,915 francs. These statistics show that state aid, however meager, enabled more women than men to obtain manumission through *rachat*. The significance of children, who accounted for the highest percentage of all three groups, can hardly be overlooked. Nor can the fact that some women obtained redemption along with more than one child, a common occurrence starting around 1845.[34]

In the absence of state aid, slaves still gathered the necessary *pécule* (resources) to assure their *rachat*. In Guadeloupe in 1845 and 1846, 15 slaves out of a total of 205 paid for their *rachat* without state aid. In Martinique 14 out of 295 did so. In Guiana 6 slaves benefited from state aid; 26 bought their own freedom. As in *rachat* with state aid, gender distinctions can be observed here. Women, more so than men, engaged in this type of *rachat,* no doubt because there was a greater prospect of freeing their children in the process, or soon after they procured their own freedom. But there were other women, mostly the elderly, who may have had children but who could only redeem themselves. Marianne, a fifty-three-year-old merchant and former slave of the widow Fonclair Lapeyre of Saint-Pierre, Martinique, deposited 1,100 francs at the colonial treasury in March 1847, the price set by the commission. That same year, the forty-year-old domestic slave woman, Laurencine, owned by the woman Dathy Morestin, also of Saint-Pierre, deposited 1,600 francs at the colonial treasury—the price of her freedom and that of her two children, Eugène and Roselie. And Solitude, sixty-one, a field slave owned by Pierre Lagodière of Lamentin, Martinique, paid 500 francs for her freedom. Jeannine, a fifty-nine-year-old domestic belonging to the widow Anquetil de Braincourt of Saint-Pierre, purchased her freedom for 600 francs in 1847 as well. In February 1848, just months away from emancipation, the commission fixed at 1,000 francs the price of redemption for the slave woman Eléonide (Labrune) and her one-year-old son, Phillippe (Forès), both of whom were owned by Sylvanie (Marie-Claire) of Fort-Royal, Martinique. Eléonide deposited 600 francs, and the state put up the remaining 400 francs. In this case, Phillippe was omitted from a previous declaration of liberty, which necessitated a special *arrêté* by the Procureur Général on February 2, 1848, to free him.[35]

The fact that the colonial commission had to settle so many disputes over prices suggests that slaveowners were not satisfied with what the slaves offered them. After 1845 *rachat forcé,* as opposed to *rachat amiable,* was the norm. This was also a period when most of the *rachats amiables* were between male slaves and male slaveowners. It seems curious that the fifty-six-year-old black domestic slave Sainte-Rose of Basse-Pointe, Martinique, would make it a point of counting out loud the 300 francs she gave to her owner, Rose-Adéle Jeannot, in what was listed as a *rachat amiable.*[36] A close examination of *rachat*

Table 8.5. Number of Manumissions in 1846

	Martinique	Guadeloupe	French Guiana
Voluntary (1832 law and *rachat amiable*)	637	978	135
Voluntary (1839 law)	78	7	0
Slaves in France	0	80	10
Rachat forcé (state aid)	281	34	26
Rachat forcé (no state aid)	14	16	6
Total	1,010	1,115	177

Source: *Journal officiel de la Martinique,* May 26, 1847, 1–2.

in Martinique does reveal that women slaveowners were less likely to settle amicably with slave women over redemption. In this regard, as in others, there was no special consideration for women slaves.

Using 1846 as a benchmark year, the French administration sought to demonstrate that *rachat* was a success. To do so, it compared statistics in 1846 with those of the previous five years, that is, 1839–45. As table 8.5 indicates, 1,010 slaves were manumitted in Martinique in 1846. From 1839 to 1845, the average number of slaves manumitted annually was 749. The corresponding figures for Guadeloupe and French Guiana were 577 and 70 respectively. Thus, for Martinique, the administration boasted that in 1846, there were 261 more manumissions than the annual averages for the years 1839–45. Likewise, there were 577 and 107 more manumissions in Guadeloupe and French Guiana respectively. This simple arithmetic masked the reality, which was that 1,010 manumissions in 1846 represented only 1.3 percent of the total slave population of 275,339. Besides, most of the manumissions were the result of the 1832 legislation. That the number of manumissions in 1847 were 755, a decline of 255 from 1846, confirms a pattern of slight surges following the introduction of new legislation (such as in 1832 and 1845), but no dramatic and sustained increases overall. Interestingly, Baron de Mackau also reported a strong *rachat* demand in early 1847, especially from Martinique, where more than a thousand individuals had signed up with the commission. Mackau rightly took this to be an indication that "all those slaves are in possession of either all or a part of the funds for their redemption."[37]

From beginning to end, then, manumission was limited. In a royal ordinance dated October 12, 1847, King Louis Philippe authorized the manumission of 218 urban and rural slaves—the majority of them women—of which 36 were from Martinique, 41 from Guadeloupe, 119 from French Guiana, and 22 from Bourbon. This was not so much an act of benevolence but a matter of necessity. In 1847 Baron de Mackau explained that, through repossessions, several properties had come into the hands of the colonial state, and with them slaves who were mostly field hands. As this development virtually coincided with the 1845 legislation on redemption, the state could hardly stand back from its own rulings. Mackau expressed concern about the prospect of crime and its impact on planters, but noted that a group of 126 state slaves—the first batch—had already been freed in 1846, supposedly without incident.[38]

Taken as a whole, the data on redemption strongly indicate that slave women opted for manumission without regard to their material and social condition. The case of the Martiniquan slave woman Marie Sainte Platon is unique in that it is one of the few that bring together the redemption of a slave woman and the struggle to free not only her children but her husband. It also reveals the strength and resilience slave women needed to defend their families. In 1840 Marie Sainte, forty-six, purchased her freedom for a thousand francs from the owners of the plantation Casse-cou, where she and her common-law husband, François, had been enslaved since birth. The couple had thirteen children and grandchildren. She was duly provided with her freedom papers. The drama began when Marie Sainte and François legitimized their union in the Catholic Church, after they sought and received permission from Desvergers de Chambray, a co-owner and representative of the plantation who had authorized Marie Sainte's *rachat.* None of the sixteen other co-owners of Casse-cou opposed the marriage. What one of them, Madame de la Pommeraye, came to oppose was Marie Sainte's subsequent bid to free her husband, children, and grandchildren. Under the terms of an ordinance dated June 11, 1839, a slave who contracted marriage with a free person attained the status *libre de droit,* as did the children they had previous to the marriage. In any case, three of their children, Marie Luce, sixteen, Hedwige, fourteen, and Anatole, ten, had been separated from Marie Sainte upon her *rachat* and should have been freed under Article 47. On the basis of these decrees, Marie Sainte brought her case before the Tribunal de Première Instance of Saint-Pierre. On May 26, 1846, Judge Maynier ruled in her favor and freed all the parties. But this was not the end, for Madame Pommeraye and five of the other co-owners appealed the decision. The case eventually went to the Cour Royale, which declared the marriage null and void. Marie Louise then took the case to the Cour de Cassation, which ruled in her favor in 1847, five years after she first brought her case to court. The high court chided the Cour Royale for hearing the case, as it had been brought by a minority of the co-owners—the other co-owners, by their abstention, signaling their agreement with the initial judgment. The court went on at length about the marriage of Marie Sainte and François, which suggests that opposition to his freedom hinged on its legitimacy. However, the court deemed the marriage viable under the Code Noir, even though only Desvergers de Chambry, who acted on behalf of the other co-owners, had given consent and not all seventeen of them. The marriage could not be annulled, either for lack of proper consent or for failure to observe formalities. With a legitimate marriage, the manumission of the slave family was guaranteed under the law of June 11, 1839, and this included all offspring of the couple, whether they were prepubescent or not. Therefore, the application of Article 47 was superfluous in this case.[39]

The picture of slave women and manumission that emerges from the historical literature of the French Antilles is nothing short of remarkable. For how else could one characterize the fact that, even on the eve of emancipation in 1848, women of all ages, principally mixed-race as in previous times, continued to manifest a strong desire for freedom. The list of requests for freedom found in the colonial newspapers of 1848 is proof of this desire. One might argue that the ninety-two-year-old black creole slave woman Agnès, and the eighty-one-year-old domestic slave woman, Tété, also a creole, were freed by their owners, Allou Daniel of Rivière-Pilote and Pierre Maucouduit of Saint-Esprit, Martinique, in 1848 for purposes of expediency, as they were too elderly to be productive workers. But they were not compelled to accept their freedom, which they did. That women seized the opportunity to use the law—a tool designed primarily to oppress them—to gain manumission must certainly mean that they saw the law as a means of turning the tables on their oppressors. And they did so admirably, courageously, and with a sense of dignity that should make their descendants proud.

Conclusion

THE ERECTION OF statues of Solitude (pregnant) and Joseph Ignace in Abymes, Guadeloupe, in 1999 is as much a recognition of the important role that women played during slavery as perhaps it is a conscious attempt on the part of Guadeloupians to come to grips with a past that has often been suppressed if not denied. Coming as it did almost two centuries after these rebels resisted French attempts to reestablish slavery in Guadeloupe in 1802, this act of commemoration is socially and politically significant in a country that is still an overseas department of France situated in a region where almost all of the other territories have achieved political independence. The same is true of other parts of the French Antilles, especially Martinique, where in 1998—the sesquicentenary of the abolition of slavery in the French colonial empire—authorities erected statues of maroon slaves in Diamant, Lamentin, and Trois-Îlets. These statues are not as prominent as those of Victor Schoelcher or that of the Empress Josephine in the savanna in Fort-de-France, now beheaded and defaced. Like those in Guadeloupe, Haiti, Guyana, Jamaica, and Barbados, however, they testify to the fact that enslaved black women and men fought valiantly against a system of oppression—slavery—which sought to dehumanize them.

Like the monument to Solitude and Ignace in Guadeloupe, this study has attempted to bring slave women out of the shadows of the slave plantation world and into full view, where they belong. In pursuing this act of retrieval, it has focused on the work lives of slave women and the means by which they resisted slavery. At the same time, it has pointed up the correlation between work and resistance on the part of women, and the complementary nature of resistance, while paying attention to specific ways in which women resisted slavery.

In the 1950s Kenneth Stampp wrote, "Slavery was above all a labor system."[1] In the 1980s, Jacqueline Jones would write, "If work is any activity that leads either directly or indirectly to the production of marketable goods, then the slave women did nothing but work."[2] While slave women engaged in other activities besides work, Jones's statement emphasizes the extraordinary contribution of labor that slave women made. In the French Antilles, as we have seen, women's labor was all encompassing and exploited in much the same way as men's labor, because both sexes were objects of subordination and were degraded by slavery. Women, like men, did field work, domestic chores, and work related to the manufacture of sugar. Women's work in the slave quarters, whether as wives, mothers, or small-scale producers, also buttressed the slave system and worked to the advantage of the planter class and commercial export production, though in some cases the slaves were able to use domestic production to further their own ends. In some aspects of plantation life a gendered division of labor existed as men monopolized the skilled tasks, leaving the bulk of the hard, back-breaking tasks to women. It was these day-to-day tasks, more so than others, that kept the plantations in business. Planters and their managerial staff recognized this fact and catered to women out of self-interest, but still subjected them to harsh and cruel treatment both to maintain production levels and to ward off challenges to the slave system.

In the French Antilles, women's responses to their position within the occupational structure of the slave plantation system, and to slavery itself, were multidimensional. The evidence shows that they struggled against slavery individually and collectively in the same ways that men did, and with equal vigor and determination. Women participated in all forms of resistance, although their roles in combat were limited. In this respect, the role that Solitude played was unique. Like slaves in other parts of the Americas, the slaves in the French Antilles attempted to carve out living spaces for themselves, never failing to realize that the common enemy was slavery. Much can be learned from probing women's resistance further. The level of *marronnage* among women was higher than historians have anticipated. As many stayed away from the plantations for considerable periods and had children while at large, it would be interesting to probe their lifestyles during these periods of absence. In advertisements offering rewards for their capture and arrest, their usual place of residence would often be mentioned, or some dubious connection to kin. It seems likely from the documentation that women hid other women. But they would also have required the help of blacksmiths to remove their chains, and possibly assistance from other males, in order to keep evading capture. In the nineteenth century, rewards were offered more frequently for female fugitives than male. Also, the offer of clemency and the option of choosing a new slaveowner—what might on the surface be considered a magnanimous gesture—appears to have been directed almost solely at female fugitives.

Scholars need to devote more attention to areas of women's resistance such as insolence and insubordination. This study has shown that these aspects of resistance were sometimes but not always tied to *marronnage*. Women engaged in verbal confrontations with slaveowners and their representatives, tackled them physically, and flatly refused to work, drawing deductions of salt fish rations and suffering other penalties as a result. As there was recidi-

vism in some cases, the defiance of slave women appears to have been deliberate and warrants further probing. Apart from their participation in sit-down
strikes, work slowdowns, and work stoppages, men seemed not to have engaged in these other forms of resistance. This is curious since men and women
did much the same work. If men did indeed engage in insolence and insubordination, it would be interesting to compare their actions with those of women.

Although the Code Noir was basically gender neutral, and women faced
the same penalties as men for *marronnage* and other breaches of conduct in
slave society, this study posits that, overall, women were more likely to be subjected to disciplinary action than men. This means that gender influenced the
frequency and intensity of discipline. Punishments involved not only unlawful
and excessive whipping but imprisonment and confinement in the stocks on
the plantations as well. Liberties could be taken against all slaves, usually
without repercussions for slaveowners, but it is possible that the perception
that women would be less likely to fight back resulted in their being disciplined more often and more excessively. Certainly, there was no consideration for womanhood, motherhood, or the black family. Indeed, women were
stripped in front of their children, whipped, and humiliated. Slave men were
virtually powerless to protect them from physical, sexual, or other forms of
abuse, and this fact could not have been lost on slave women. It is little wonder
that it was women for the most part who engaged their owners, albeit indirectly, in judicial battles without the certainty of positive outcomes.

This study demonstrates that slave women were keenly aware of changes
in the law and their impact on slave society. Keeping track of the numerous
ordinances, local and metropolitan, with a bearing on slaveholding is difficult
enough for the modern historian in an age of information much less for the
slaves. As is the case for most people today, they may not have had direct access to the laws in published form or understood the nuances of language in
the numerous articles that constituted the typical ordinance. But slave women
must have kept their ears to the ground and focused on the essence of the
law and the manner in which it affected them as slaves. Indeed, Colombe's
response in the face of assault by plantation management, though physical,
points in this direction. Thus the ways in which slave women, if not men, made
use of the law on a broad scale is fertile ground for future research. The legal
actions taken by Virginie and other women in the French Antilles were not
available to slaves in the British Caribbean. Therefore, this study opens the
door, it is hoped, to numerous possibilities for comparative approaches to slavery, including forms of manumission such as the *libre de fait* or *libre de savane*
manumission that were peculiar to the French colonies. In Barbados in the
eighteenth century, the slave woman Old Doll claimed that she and her three
daughters had been promised their freedom once her owner, Elizabeth New-

ton, returned to England. Newton drew up no legal papers, however, so Old Doll's claim could not be substantiated.[3] But in the French Antilles she and her family may well have been considered *libres de fait*.

Many other aspects of the lives of slave women in the French Antilles are broached by this study that would benefit from full-fledged research. The relationship between black and mixed-race slave women, and between them and white women are two such aspects. It would be interesting to find out what tensions, if any, existed between black and mixed-race slave women since the latter, along with their children, were the ones who benefited most from manumission. They were also slaveowners, as this study has demonstrated. Today phenotype in the French Antilles, especially in Martinique, is of crucial social importance—more so than in the British Caribbean. To what degree this phenomenon is a legacy of the past is an interesting question.

Slavery in the French Antilles lasted a little more than two centuries. During that time, as this study has shown, slave women waged a struggle against the institution that brings to mind Norrece Jones's study of slavery in South Carolina and his concept of "total war," although in the French Antilles the war was intermittent, often of low intensity, and did not involve all slaves.[4] Many aspects of the experience of slave women remain deeply disturbing, especially those that involved cruelty by slaveowners meted out in a manner and on a scale bordering on the macabre. But this study was not designed to elicit pity or sympathy; it is important to remember that, in spite of their ordeal, slave women in the French Antilles demonstrated courage, stamina, strength of character, bravery, resilience, and the will to survive against all odds. The descendants of these slave women, and others, can draw valuable lessons from their experience. While essentially a black experience, it was also a human experience with all of its tragedies and triumphs. Set against the modern Caribbean, where the will to survive is taken as a given, the experience of slave women is as relevant as ever. In a day and age when the young in particular have a tendency to give up rather quickly, knowledge of this experience can serve to motivate and inspire them to persevere. Without the driving force of this experience, it goes without saying that this work would not have been written.

Notes

Introduction

   1. Barbara Bush, *Slave Women in Caribbean Society 1650–1838* (Bloomington: Indiana University Press, 1990); Arlette Gautier, *Les Soeurs de solitude: La Condition féminine dans l'esclavage aux Antilles du XVIIe au XIX siècle* (Paris: Éditions caribéennes, 1985); Marrietta Morrissey, *Slave Women in the New World: Gender Stratification in the Caribbean* (Lawrence: University Press of Kansas, 1989). Also see Bridget Brereton's review of Bush's *Slave Women* in *Journal of Caribbean History* 24, no. 1 (1992): 115–20, and her review article, "Searching for the Invisible Woman," in *Slavery and Abolition* 13, no. 2 (1992): 86–96.

   2. See Lucille Mathurin-Mair, *The Rebel Woman in the British West Indies* (Kingston: Institute of Jamaica, 1975); Bridget Brereton, "Text, Testimony and Gender: An Examination of Some Texts by Women on the English-Speaking Caribbean from the 1770s to the 1920s," in *Engendering History: Caribbean Women in Historical Perspective*, ed. Verene Shepherd et al., 63–93 (New York: St. Martin's Press, 1995); Verene Shepherd, "Introduction," in *Women in Caribbean History*, ed. Verene Shepherd, xvii–xx (Kingston: Ian Randle, 1999); Hilary Beckles, "Sex and Gender in the Historiography of Caribbean Slavery," in Shepherd, *Engendering History*, 125–40.

   3. For a detailed discussion on the meaning of gender, see Karen Anderson, *Teaching Gender in U.S. History* (Washington, D.C.: American Historical Association, 1997), 1–56.

   4. Bernard Moitt, "Behind the Sugar Fortunes: Women, Labor and the Development of Caribbean Plantations during Slavery," in *African Continuities*, ed. Simeon Chilungu and Sada Niang (Toronto: Terebi, 1989), 403–26; Bernard Moitt, "Women, Work and Resistance in the French Caribbean," in Shepherd, *Engendering History*, 155–75; Hilary Beckles, *Natural Rebels: A Social History of Enslaved Black Women in Barbados* (New Brunswick, N.J.: Rutgers University Press, 1989), 2, 25–54; Bush, *Slave Women*, 33–50.

   5. *Le Code Noir ou recueil des règlements rendus jusqu'à présent* (Basse-Terre: Société d'histoire de la Guadeloupe, 1980), 33–34.

   6. Morrissey, *Slave Women*, 4.

1. Black Women and the Early Development of the French Antilles

   1. See Lucien Peytraud, *L'Esclavage aux Antilles françaises avant 1789* (Paris: Hachette, 1879), 51; C. A. Banbuck, *Histoire politique, économique et sociale de la Martinique sous l'Ancien Régime* (1635–1789) (Paris: Librairie des sciences politiques et sociales, 1935), 24.

   2. Jean-Baptiste (Père) Du Tertre, *Histoire générale des Antilles habitées par les Français*, 4 vols. (1671; reprint, Fort-de-France: Éditions des horizons caraïbes, 1973), 1:3–11. All translations from French are the author's unless otherwise noted.

   3. Du Tertre, *Histoire*, 1:3–15; Jacques Petit Jean Roget, "Saint-Christophe, première des

isles françaises d'Amérique," in *Bulletin de la Société d'histoire de la Martinique,* no. 24 (1981): 3–20.

4. Richard S. Dunn, *Sugar and Slaves: The Rise of the Planter Class in the English West Indies, 1624–1713,* (Chapel Hill: University of North Carolina Press, 1972), 119.

5. Gordon K. Lewis, *Main Currents in Caribbean Thought* (Baltimore: Johns Hopkins University Press, 1983), 64.

6. Ibid.; Peytraud, *L'Esclavage,* 20.

7. Clarence J. Mumford, *The Black Ordeal of Slavery and Slave Trading in the French West Indies 1625–1713,* 3 vols. (Lewiston, N.Y.: Edwin Mellen Press, 1991), 2:362; Peytraud, *L'Esclavage,* 5; Banbuck, *Histoire,* 24.

8. Peytraud, *L'Esclavage,* 5.

9. Du Tertre, *Histoire,* 1:19; M. Philippe Barrey, *Les Origines de la colonisation française aux Antilles* (Le Havre: H. Micaux, 1918), 144; Dunn, *Sugar and Slaves,* 119.

10. Barrey, *Origines,* 154.

11. S. L. Mims, *Colbert's West India Policy* (New Haven: Yale University Press, 1912), 45–46.

12. Mumford, *Black Ordeal,* 1:137.

13. Franklin W. Knight, *The Caribbean: The Genesis of a Fragmented Nationalism* (New York: Oxford University Press, 1990), 62; Peytraud, *L'Esclavage,* 4–7.

14. Knight, *The Caribbean,* 64.

15. Du Tertre, *Histoire,* 1:59; Peytraud, *L'Esclavage,* 8.

16. Barrey, *Origines,* 155.

17. Peytraud, *L'Esclavage,* 8–9; Banbuck, *Histoire,* 310; Mumford, *Black Ordeal,* 2:363.

18. Du Tertre, *Histoire,* 1:61.

19. Peytraud, *L'Esclavage,* 9.

20. Dunn, *Sugar and Slaves,* 71.

21. Philip D. Curtin, *The Atlantic Slave Trade: A Census* (Madison: University of Wisconsin Press, 1969), 61.

22. Dunn, *Sugar and Slaves,* 127; Curtin, *Atlantic,* 59.

23. Dunn, *Sugar and Slaves,* 146.

24. Ibid., 124; Anne-Marie Bruleaux et al., *Deux Siècles d'esclavage en Guyane française, 1652–1848* (Paris: L'Harmattan, 1986), 13–15; "Notice statistique sur la Guyane française," in *Notices statistiques sur les colonies françaises* (Paris: Société d'études, 1843), 1–9; Du Tertre, *Histoire,* 3:2–4.

25. Du Tertre, *Histoire,* 1:66–72, 78–79, 104–105; Lucien Abénon, *La Guadeloupe de 1671 à 1759,* 2 vols. (Paris: L'Harmattan, 1987), 1:1, 16.

26. M. L. E. Moreau de Saint-Méry, *Description de la partie française de l'isle Saint-Domingue,* 3 vols. (Paris: Société d'histoire des colonies françaises, 1958), 1:45; Jacques Petit Jean Roget, "La Société d'habitation à la Martinique: Un Demi Siècle de formation, 1635–1685," 2 vols. (Ph.D. diss., Université de Lille III, 1980), 2:1001.

27. Gabriel Debien, *Les Engagés pour les Antilles (1634–1715)* (Paris: Société de l'histoire des colonies françaises, 1952), 253.

28. Maurice Satineau, *Histoire de la Guadeloupe sous l'Ancien Régime, 1635–1789* (Paris: Payot, 1928), 11, 116.

29. The worth of currencies used in the French Antilles during slavery is hard to estimate because value depended on the metallic content of coins and the level of demand for them, which was usually high. An additional difficulty is the lack of standardization in currency exchange before the law enacted on August 30, 1826, that made the French franc the predominant currency. During slavery, there were colonial currencies as well as currencies from France and from foreign countries, mainly Spain and Portugal. In the eighteenth century, the colonial *livre*

tournois was worth about 20 *sols;* 1 *sol* was worth about 12 *deniers* or about 12 cents (U.S.). The expression *"livre d'amende"* was used when fines were imposed, hence *"amende."* French currencies used in the colonies included coins such as the *écu,* made of gold and silver, and the *sou,* made of copper. Spanish *doublons* and *escudos* were popular, while the Portuguese *moëdes* enjoyed wide circulation. An *écu* was worth about 9 *livres,* a *moëde* about 66 *livres.* See Alain Buffon, *Monnaie et crédit en économie coloniale: Contribution à l'histoire économique de Guadeloupe, 1635-1919* (Basse-Terre: Société d'histoire de la Guadeloupe, 1979), 47-66; E. Zay, *Histoire monétaire des colonies françaises d'après les documents officiels avec 278 figures* (Paris: 1892), 44-45.

30. Archives Nationales (Paris) Colonies (hereafter AN Col.), C 8A 15 F347, November 20, 1704; David Barry Gaspar, *Bondmen and Rebels: A Study of Master-Slave Relations in Antigua* (Baltimore: Johns Hopkins University Press, 1985), 183-84.

31. Gautier, *Soeurs de solitude,* 31-32.

32. Ibid., 20-25.

33. Bush, *Slave Women,* 8.

34. Liliane Chauleau, *La Société à la Martinique au XVIIe siècle, 1635-1713* (Caen: Ozanne, 1966); Roget, *Société;* Abénon, *Guadeloupe.*

35. Chauleau, *Société,* 207.

36. Roget, *Société,* 2:1007.

37. Gaston-Martin, *Histoire de l'esclavage dans les colonies françaises* (Paris: Presses universitaires de France, 1948), 112-13; Debien, "Les Engagés," 257; Du Tertre, *Histoire,* 2:447; Banbuck, *Histoire,* 295.

38. Moreau de Saint-Méry, *Description,* 1:40, 47, 104; Roget, *Société,* 1:606-10.

39. Debien, "Les Engagés," 175; Satineau, *Histoire,* 68.

40. Debien, "Les Engagés," 181.

41. Gautier, *Soeurs de solitude,* 31-32.

42. Chauleau, *Société,* 98. These "hospitals" served more as institutions for the indigent than as health care establishments.

43. Banbuck, *Histoire,* 287-88; Peytraud, *L'Esclavage,* 196; Satineau, *Histoire,* 68.

44. Debien, "Les Engagés," 181-83.

45. Ibid., 183.

46. Ibid.

47. Moreau de Saint-Méry, *Lois et constitutions des colonies françaises de l'Amérique sous le vent de 1625 à 1785,* 6 vols. (Paris, 1785-1790), 1:434: "Ordonnance du roi, portant que le nombre des engagés sera à Saint-Domingue, égal à celui des Nègres, à peine de confiscation de l'excédent de ces derniers," September 30, 1686; Peytraud, *L'Esclavage,* 14-15; Satineau, *Histoire,* 97.

48. Peytraud, *L'Esclavage,* 15.

49. Ibid.; Moreau de Saint-Méry, *Lois et constitutions,* 1:581.

50. Satineau, *Histoire,* 78; Debien, "Les Engagés," 241.

51. Satineau, *Histoire,* 70; see also Du Tertre, *Histoire,* 2:454-55.

52. Henri Bangou, *La Guadeloupe,* 3 vols. (Paris: L'Harmattan, 1987), 1:59; Chauleau, *Société,* 182.

53. Gabriel Debien, "Les Premières Femmes des colons des Antilles, 1635-1680," in *Revue de la Porte Océane,* nos. 89-90 (1952): 8, 11-12.

54. Roget, *Société,* 2:958.

55. Ibid., 2:949.

56. Archives Départementales de la Martinique (Fort-de-France, Martinique) (hereafter A D-M, Martinique), série MI, 5mi. 89, "État nominatif et général des citoyens et les habitations de la Martinique, 1664-1764."

57. Gautier, *Soeurs de solitude,* 71.

58. A D-M, "État nominatif et général des citoyens et les habitations de la Martinique, 1664–1764."

59. Moreau de Saint-Méry, *Description,* 1:57.

60. Abénon, *Guadeloupe,* 1:30–31.

61. Abdoulaye Ly, *La Compagnie du Sénégal* (Paris: Présence africaine, 1968), 49.

62. Abénon, *Guadeloupe,* 1:31–32, 50.

63. Ibid., 1:55.

64. Ibid., 1:46–50.

65. Ibid., 1:32, 39–40.

66. AN Col., C 8A 10 F255, Copie d'une lettre écrite par le Gouverneur d'Antigue à M. D'Amblinom, October 6, 1698.

67. Bush, *Slave Women,* 13.

68. Peytraud, *L'Esclavage,* 196–97.

69. Debien, "Les Engagés," 207.

70. Moreau de Saint-Méry, *Description,* 1:83–84.

71. Bush, *Slave Women,* 13.

72. Moreau de Saint-Méry, *Description,* 1:45; Satineau, *Histoire,* 95.

73. Peytraud, *L'Esclavage,* 16; Debien, "Les Engagés," 254–55.

74. Debien, "Les Engagés," 205.

75. Moreau de Saint-Méry, *Lois et constitutions,* 1:119: "Règlement de M. de Tracy, Lieutenant Général de l'Amérique, touchant les blasphémateurs et la police des Isles," June 19, 1664; Satineau, *Histoire,* 74.

76. Moreau de Saint-Méry, *Lois et constitutions,* 1:180: "Ordonnance de M. de Baas, touchant les religionnaires, les juifs, les cabaretiers et les femmes de mauvaise vie," August 1, 1669.

77. Debien, "Les Engagés," 205–206.

78. AN Col., C 8A 9, F 73, March 11, 1695; Debien, "Les Engagés," 207; Peytraud, *L'Esclavage,* 201.

79. Pierre Dessalles, *Histoire des Antilles,* 5 vols. (Paris: Libraire-Éditeur, 1847), 3:291; Orlando Patterson, *Slavery and Social Death* (Cambridge: Harvard University Press, 1982), 215; Chauleau, *Société,* 191; *Code Noir,* 33–34.

80. Debien, "Les Engagés," 251–55.

81. Kenneth Stampp, *The Peculiar Institution* (New York: Random House, 1984), 5.

2. The Atlantic Slave Trade, Black Women, and the Development of the Plantations

1. See, for example, John Thornton, "Sexual Demography: The Impact of the Slave Trade on Family Structure," in *Women and Slavery in Africa,* ed. Claire C. Robertson and Martin A. Klein, 39–48 (Madison: University of Wisconsin Press, 1983); John Thornton, "The Demographic Effect of the Slave Trade on Western Africa, 1500–1850," in *African Historical Demography,* ed. Christopher Fyfe and David McMaster, 2 vols. (Edinburgh: Centre of African Studies, University of Edinburgh, 1981), 2:691–720; John Thornton, "The Slave Trade in Eighteenth-Century Angola: Effects on Demographic Structures," in *Canadian Journal of African Studies* 14 (1980): 417–27; Walter Rodney, *West Africa and the Atlantic Slave Trade* (Cambridge: Africa Research Group, 1974), 3–27; J. D. Fage, "The Effect of the Export Slave Trade on African Populations," in *The Population Factor in African Studies: Proceedings of a Conference Organised by the African Studies Association of the United Kingdom, September 1972,* ed. R. P. Moss and R. J. A. Rathbone, 15–23 (London: University of London Press, 1975); Patrick Manning, *Slavery*

and African Life (New York: Cambridge University Press, 1990); J. E. Inikori, "Underpopulation in Nineteenth Century West Africa: The Role of the Export Slave Trade," in Fyfe and McMaster, *African Historical Demography*, 2:283–313.

2. Du Tertre, *Histoire*, 3:179.

3. Mims, *Colbert's*, 286–309; Mumford, *Black Ordeal*, 1:187; Ly, *Compagnie*, 53; Satineau, *Histoire*, 88–89.

4. Du Tertre, *Histoire*, 1:457–60.

5. Philip Curtin, *The Atlantic Slave Trade: A Census* (Madison: University of Wisconsin Press, 1969), 84–87; Robert Stein, *The French Slave Trade in the Eighteenth Century* (Madison: University of Wisconsin Press, 1979), xiv; Robert Louis Stein, "Measuring the French Slave Trade, 1713-1792/3," *Journal of African History* 19, no. 4 (1978): 515–21; Paul E. Lovejoy, "The Volume of the Atlantic Slave Trade: A Synthesis," *Journal of African History* 23 (1982): 473–77. A more recent review of the literature on the volume of the Atlantic trade is provided by Serge Daget, *La Traite des Noirs* (Rennes: Editions Ouest-France, 1990), 151–73.

6. Alfred Martineau and Louis-Philip May, *Trois Siècles d'histoire antillaise: Martinique et Guadeloupe de 1635 à nos jours* (Paris: Société d'histoire des colonies françaises, 1935), 120; Du Tertre, *Histoire*, 2:26; Chauleau, *Société*, 97–98.

7. Stein, *French Slave Trade*, 109.

8. AN Col. C8 1, Governor de Baas to Minister Colbert, June 25, 1670, cited in Mims, *Colbert's*, 170. See also Mumford, *Black Ordeal*, 1:157–59.

9. AN Col., C 8A 3 F316, Blénac to Minister, June 18, 1684.

10. AN Col., C 8A 3 F278, Blénac to Minister, February 3, 1683.

11. AN Col., C8A 5 F425, Extrait de la recette et dépense faites aux iles de l'Amérique pendant l'année 1689, 1689; AN Col., C8A 5 F364, Relation de ce qui s'est passé à la prise de St. Eustache, May 1, 1689; AN Col., C 8A 5 F239, Copie d'une lettre écrite à M de Blénac et M. Dumaritz de St. Christophe, 1689; AN Col., C8A 5 F258, Blénac to Minister, November 12, 1689; AN Col., C 8A 5 F398, Compte que rendre M. Du Maitz de Goimpy de la recette et dépense faites suite à l'occasion de la prise de l'Île St. Eustache, December 6, 1689.

12. Jean Mettas, *Répertoire des expéditions négrières françaises au XVIIIe siècle*, 2 vols. (Paris: Société française d'histoire d'Outre-Mer, 1978–84); Mumford, *Black Ordeal*, 1:159, 180, 186; Mims, *Colbert's*, 171; Chauleau, *Société*, 102.

13. AN Col. C8A 18 F58, Mémoire de Monsieur Gabaret, Lieutenant pour le Roi au gouvernement général des Isles de l'Amérique et gouverneur particulier de la Martinique, June 3, 1711; AN Col. C 8A 17 F123, Vaucresson au Ministre, July 22, 1709; AN Col. C 8A 19 F204, Phélypeaux au Ministre, August 12, 1713.

14. Abénon, *Guadeloupe*, 1:53; Satineau, *Histoire*, 90; Bruleaux et al., *Deux siècles*, 16–19; Gabriel Debien, *Plantations et esclaves à Saint-Domingue* (Dakar: Publications de la section d'histoire, Université de Dakar [now Université Cheikh Anta Diop], 1969), 49.

15. Jean-Baptiste Bourgeois, *Opinion de Jean-Baptiste Bourgeois, habitant planteur de S. Domingue sur les moyens de rétablir les colonies* (Paris, 1794), 11.

16. Alex Moreau de Jonnès, *Recherches statistiques sur l'esclavage colonial et sur les moyens de le supprimer* (Paris, 1842), 17–29; Curtin, *Atlantic*, 19.

17. Walter Rodney, *How Europe Underdeveloped Africa* (Washington, D.C.: Howard University Press, 1974), 105; Rodney, *West Africa and the Atlantic Slave Trade*, 13; K. G. Davies, *The Royal African Company* (New York: Atheneum, 1970), 300; "Description d'un navire négrier" (pamphlet found among unclassified papers, file 027, at the Bibliothèque des Frères de Saint-Louis de Gonzague, Port-au-Prince, Haiti), n.d., 4–8.

18. Herbert S. Klein, "African Women in the Atlantic Slave Trade," in Robertson and Klein, *Women and Slavery*, 32.

19. Ibid., 29–30.

20. Ibid., 30.

21. Davies, *Royal African Company,* 299; Klein, "African Women," 117.

22. Colin Palmer, *Human Cargoes: The British Slave Trade to Spanish America 1700–1739* (Urbana: University of Illinois Press, 1981), 121–22.

23. Barry Higman, *Slave Populations of the British Caribbean 1807–1834* (Baltimore: Johns Hopkins University Press, 1984), 115–16.

24. Joseph E. Inikori, "Introduction," in *Forced Migration: The Impact of the Export Slave Trade on African Societies,* ed. Joseph E. Inikori (New York: Africana Publishing Company, 1982), 23.

25. Paul E. Lovejoy, *Transformations in Slavery* (New York: Cambridge University Press, 1983), 62–63.

26. Curtin, *Atlantic,* 19; Stein, *French Slave Trade,* 74, 79–80.

27. David Geggus, "Sex Ratio, Age and Ethnicity in the Atlantic Slave Trade: Data from French Shipping and Plantation Records," in *Journal of African History* 30 (1989): 25–26.

28. Philip Curtin, *Economic Change in Precolonial Africa* (Madison: University of Wisconsin Press, 1975), 155; John Thornton, *Africa and Africans in the Making of the Atlantic World, 1400–1680* (New York: Cambridge University Press, 1992), 107; Lovejoy, *Transformations,* 159–83; Manning, *Slavery and African Life,* 142–47; Bernard Moitt, "Slavery and Emancipation in Senegal's Peanut Basin: The Nineteenth and Twentieth Centuries," *International Journal of African Historical Studies* 22, no. 1 (1989): 27–50.

29. Curtin, *Atlantic,* 169.

30. Labat, *Histoire,* 1:456; Roget, "Société," 2:952.

31. Xavier Tanc, *De l'esclavage aux colonies françaises et spécialement à la Guadeloupe* (Paris, 1832), 14–15.

32. Victor Schoelcher, *Des colonies françaises: Abolition immédiate de l'esclavage* (1842; reprint, Basse-Terre: Société d'histoire de la Guadeloupe, 1976), 24.

33. Nicole Vanony-Frisch, "Les Esclaves de la Guadeloupe à la fin de l'Ancien Régime d'après les sources notariales, 1770–1789," *Bulletin de la Société d'histoire de la Guadeloupe,* nos. 63–64 (1985): 91.

34. Ibid., 3–4, 78.

35. François Girod, *Une Fortune coloniale sous l'Ancien Régime: La Famille Hecquet à Saint-Domingue, 1724–1796* (Paris: Annales littéraires de l'Université de Besançon, 1970), 102–103.

36. Gabriel Debien, "Sucrerie Bréda de la Plaine-du-Nord (1785)," *Notes d'histoire coloniale,* no. 100 (1966): 26; Debien, *Les Esclaves,* 67.

37. David Patrick Geggus, *Slavery, War and Revolution: The British Occupation of Saint-Domingue, 1793–1798* (London: Oxford University Press, 1982), 243, 291–92; Debien, *Les Esclaves,* 97.

38. Beckles, *Natural Rebels,* 19.

39. Michael Craton, *Empire, Enslavement and Freedom in the Caribbean* (Princeton: Markus Wiener, 1997), 207.

40. Curtin, *Atlantic,* 19.

3. Women and Labor: Slave Labor

1. Dunn, *Sugar and Slaves,* 226.

2. Du Tertre, *Histoire,* 2:488.

3. David Brion Davis, *Slavery and Human Progress* (New York: Oxford University Press,

1984), 42; Robin Blackburn, *The Making of New World Slavery: From the Baroque to the Modern 1492–1800* (New York: Verso, 1999), 64–76.

    4. Roget, *Société*, 2:1120.

    5. Antoine Métral, *Histoire de l'expédition des Français à Saint-Domingue* (Paris: Éditions Karthala, 1985), 14.

    6. Jean-Baptiste (Père) Labat, *Nouveau Voyage aux isles de l'Amérique*, 6 vols. (Paris: Guillaume, 1722), 4:177; Lewis, *Main Currents*, 66.

    7. Rose Price, "Pledges on Colonial Slavery, to Candidates for Seats in Parliament, Rightly Considered," cited in Michael Craton and James Walvin, *A Jamaican Plantation: The History of Worthy Park* (Toronto: University of Toronto Press, 1970), 191; Stampp, *The Peculiar Institution*, 7; "Slavery No Oppression or, Some New Arguments and Opinions against the Idea of African Liberty" (London: Lowndes and Christie, n.d.), 12–14 (pamphlet found among unclassified papers, file 027, at the Bibliothèque des Frères de Saint-Louis de Gonzague, Port-au-Prince, Haiti).

    8. Du Tertre, *Histoire*, 2:489.

    9. Claire C. Robertson and Martin A. Klein, "Women's Importance in African Slave Systems," in Robertson and Klein, *Women and Slavery*, 3–11; Claude Meillassoux, "Female Slavery," in Robertson and Klein, *Women and Slavery*, 49–56; Martin A. Klein, "Women and Slavery in the Western Sudan," in Robertson and Klein, *Women and Slavery*, 72–77; Manning, *Slavery and African Life*, 22.

    10. Du Tertre, *Histoire*, 2:446.

    11. Gabriel Debien, "La Société coloniale aux XVIIe et XVIIIe siècles: Les Engagés pour les Antilles (1634–1715)," *Revue d'histoire des colonies*, nos. 1–2 (Paris) (1952): 253. Bangou, *La Guadeloupe*, 1:56; Moreau de Saint-Méry, *Description*, 1:55

    12. See Noel Deerr, *A History of Sugar* (London: Chapman and Hull, 1949–50); Chauleau, *Société*, 147; Labat, *Nouveau Voyage*, 4:110–13.

    13. Higman, *Slave Population and Economy*, 1.

    14. *Code Noir*, 32; Louis Sala-Molins, *Le Code Noir ou le calvaire du Canaan* (Paris: Presses universitaires de France, 1987), 102–103; Debien, *Les Esclaves*, 148.

    15. Pierre de Vassière, *Saint-Domingue: La Société et la vie créole sous l'Ancien Régime, 1629–1789* (Paris: Perrin, 1909), 175.

    16. M. Deslandes, "Mémoire de M. Deslandes, faisant fonction d'intendant du 20 février, 1707," cited in Pierre de Vassière, *Saint-Domingue*, 166.

    17. Ibid.

    18. Marcel Reible, "Les Esclaves et leurs travaux sur la sucrerie Lugé à Saint-Domingue, 1788–91," *Notes d'histoire coloniale*, no. 173 (1976): 26.

    19. Debien, *Les Esclaves*, 124, 135–36; Antoine Gisler, *L'Esclavage aux Antilles françaises XVIe–XIXe siècles* (Paris: Karthala, 1981), 35; Jacques Cauna, *Au Temps des isles à sucre* (Paris: Karthala, 1978), 116; Justin Girod-Chantrans, *Voyage d'un Suisse dans différentes colonies d'Amérique* (Paris: Neufchâtel, 1785), 130–31; Labat, *Nouveau Voyage*, 3:210; Du Tertre, *Histoire*, 2:480.

    20. Satineau, *Histoire*, 130; Debien, *Les Esclaves*, 124, 135.

    21. Dale Tomich, *Slavery in the Circuit of Sugar* (Baltimore: Johns Hopkins University Press, 1990), 141; M. P. Lavollée, *Notes sur les cultures et la production de la Martinique et de la Guadeloupe* (Paris: Ministère de la Marine et des Colonies, 1841), 43–44.

    22. Higman, *Slave Populations*, 162.

    23. Dunn, *Sugar and Slaves*, 191.

    24. Elsa Goveia, *Slave Society in the British Leeward Islands at the End of the Eighteenth Century* (New Haven: Yale University Press, 1965), 119.

25. Lavollée, *Notes sur les Cultures,* 47–48; Debien, *Les Esclaves,* 163; Satineau, *Histoire,* 132–34.

26. Tomich, *Slavery,* 142.

27. Debien, *Les Esclaves,* 137–38.

28. Ibid., 137.

29. Pelleprat, cited in Roget, *Société,* 2:1120.

30. Labat, *Nouveau Voyage,* 1:xxvii.

31. Girod-Chantrans, *Voyage,* 142.

32. Ibid., 130, 139.

33. Ibid., 131.

34. M. Poyen de Sainte-Marie, *De l'exploitation des sucreries ou conseil d'un vieux planteur aux jeunes agriculteurs des colonies* (Basse-Terre: Imprimerie de la République, 1792), 14.

35. Debien, "Sucrerie Bréda de la Plaine-du-Nord," 26–32; Gabriel Debien, "Comptes, profits, esclaves et travaux de deux sucreries de Saint-Domingue, 1774–1778," *Notes d'histoire coloniale* (Cairo), no. 6 (1945): 21.

36. Debien, *Les Esclaves,* 137.

37. Ibid., 138; Moitt, "Behind the Sugar Fortunes," 412; Cauna, *Au Temps des isles,* 114.

38. ANSOM, Guadeloupe 107 (749), Bulletin des lois no. 1432, Saint-Claude, November 3, 1847.

39. Ibid.

40. Vanony-Frisch, "Les Esclaves," 87.

41. Michael Craton, *Searching for the Invisible Man: Slaves and Plantation Life in Jamaica* (Cambridge, Mass.: Harvard University Press), 146.

42. Hilary Beckles, *Afro-Caribbean Women and Resistance in Barbados* (London: Karnak, 1988), 17.

43. André Lacharière, *De l'affranchissement des esclaves dans les colonies françaises* (Paris: Eugène Renduel, 1836), 107.

44. Schoelcher, *Des colonies françaises,* 23–24.

45. Ibid., 23.

46. Debien, *Les Esclaves,* 158.

47. Debien, "Comptes," 22.

48. Debien, *Les Esclaves,* 161.

49. Clive Thomas, *Plantations, Peasants and State: A Study of the Mode of Sugar Production in Guyana* (Los Angeles: Center for Afro-American Studies, 1984), 8.

50. Bush, *Slave Women,* 38.

51. Labat, *Nouveau Voyage,* 3:432.

52. Dunn, *Sugar and Slaves,* 195.

53. Labat, *Nouveau Voyage,* 3:175.

54. Tomich, *Slavery,* 220, 222.

55. Dunn, *Sugar and Slaves,* 194; Debien, *Les Esclaves,* 97.

56. Eugène-Edouard Boyer Peyreleau, *Les Antilles françaises, particulièrement la Guadeloupe,* 3 vols. (Paris: 1825), 1:281–83; Veront Satchell, "Early Use of Steam Power in the Jamaica Sugar Economy 1768–1810," *Transactions of the Newcomen Society* 67 (1995/96): 222–30; Christian Schnakenbourg, *Histoire de l'industrie sucrière en Guadeloupe: La Crise du système esclavagiste (XIXe–XXe siècles)* (Paris: L'Harmattan, 1980), 1:36; Labat, *Nouveau Voyage,* 3:224; Abénon, *Guadeloupe,* 2:103; Debien, *Les Esclaves,* 166.

57. Labat, *Nouveau Voyage,* 3:202–203.

58. Ibid.

59. Debien, *Les Esclaves,* 97; Labat, *Nouveau Voyage,* 3:432.

60. Labat, *Nouveau Voyage,* 3:206.

61. Ibid., 3:208.

62. Jean-Baptiste Rouvellat de Cussac, *Situation des esclaves dans les colonies françaises* (Paris: Pagnerre, 1845), 43; Debien, *Les Esclaves,* 112.

63. *Gazette de la Guadeloupe,* May 8, 1788, 78; May 22, 1788, 86; June 3, 1788, 110.

64. Labat, *Nouveau Voyage,* 3:209; Craton, *Searching,* 203; Matthew Gregory (Monk) Lewis, *Journal of a West India Proprietor* (London: John Murray, 1834), 86.

65. Gautier, *Soeurs de solitude,* 200–201.

66. Debien, "Sucrerie," 36.

67. Labat, *Nouveau Voyage,* 3:221, 419–20; Victor Schoelcher, *Histoire de l'esclavage pendant les deux dernières années,* 2 vols. (1847; reprint, Pointe-à-Pitre: Émile Désormeaux, 1973), 1:388.

68. See Gabriel Debien, "Destinées d'esclaves à la Martinique (1746–1778)," *Bulletin de L'Institut français d'Afrique noire,* series B, vol. 22, nos. 1–2 (Jan.–April 1960): 41.

69. Labat, *Nouveau Voyage,* 3:420.

70. Some estimated that the sale of rum accounted for 10 to 33 percent of a plantation's revenues. See Robert Louis Stein, *The French Sugar Business in the Eighteenth Century* (Baton Rouge: Louisiana State University Press), 72.

71. Labat, *Nouveau Voyage,* 3:415–20.

72. Ibid., 3:442. See also, Debien, *Les Esclaves,* 184; Bruleaux et al., *Deux Siècles,* 36.

73. Debien, *Les Esclaves,* 184; Moreau de Saint-Méry, *Lois et constitutions,* 5:393: Arrêt du Conseil du Port-au-Prince, touchant les logements loués aux esclaves, et la vente du vin ou du tafia par les dits esclaves, June 20, 1772; Moreau de Saint-Méry, *Lois et constitutions,* 6:700; Moreau de Saint-Méry, *Lois et constitutions,* 5:804: Ordonnance des Administrateurs concernant le débit du tafia, December 10, 1777, and Ordonnance du Juge de Police de Saint-Marc touchant la vente du tafia, June 22, 1785.

74. *Code Noir,* 40–41; Moreau de Saint-Méry, *Lois et constitutions,* 1:68: Ordonnance du Gouverneur de la Martinique, July 13, 1648; Moreau de Saint-Méry, *Lois et constitutions,* 1:194: Arrêt du Conseil de la Martinique, April 14, 1670; Moreau de Saint-Méry, *Lois et constitutions,* 2:70: Règlement du conseil de Léogane qui ordonne de planter des vivres pour la nourriture des Nègres, May 3, 1706; Debien, *Les Esclaves,* 18; Labat, *Nouveau Voyage,* 3:211; Labat, *Nouveau Voyage,* 4:185; Du Tertre, *Histoire,* 2:481; ANSOM, Guadeloupe 107 (753), July 30, 1818.

75. Debien, *Les Esclaves,* 179.

76. Rouvellat de Cussac, *Situation,* 34.

77. Tomich, *Slavery,* 253.

78. ANSOM, Guadeloupe 107 (753), circular of lieutenant governor, July 30, 1818; Debien, *Les Esclaves,* 156.

79. Du Tertre, *Histoire,* 2:481–85; Debien, *Les Esclaves,* 183.

80. Debien, *Les Esclaves,* 180; Moreau de Saint-Méry, *Description,* 1:207; Moreau de Saint-Méry, *Lois et constitutions,* 1:180–82; August 1, 1669; Tomich, *Slavery,* 264; Rouvellat de Cussac, *Situation,* 15; Robert Olwell, "'Loose, Idle and Disorderly' Slave Women in the Eighteenth-Century Charleston Marketplace," in *More than Chattel: Black Women and Slavery in the Americas,* ed. David Barry Gaspar and Darlene Clarke Hine (Bloomington: Indiana University Press, 1996), 97–110.

81. Morrissey, *Slave Women,* 60–61.

4. Women and Labor: Domestic Labor

1. Moreau de Saint-Méry, *Description,* 1:33.

2. Cited in Jerome S. Handler, Frederick W. Lange, and Robert V. Riordan, *Plantation*

Slavery in Barbados: An Archaeological and Historical Investigation (Cambridge, Mass.: Harvard University Press, 1978), 77.

3. Debien, *Plantations,* 123.

4. Norrece T. Jones, Jr., *Born a Child of Freedom, Yet a Slave: Mechanisms of Control and Strategies of Resistance in Antebellum South Carolina* (Middletown, Conn.: Wesleyan University Press, 1990), 29; Elizabeth Fox-Genovese, *Within the Plantation Household: Black and White Women of the Old South* (Chapel Hill: University of North Carolina Press, 1988), 137–45; Pierre de Vassière, *Saint-Domingue, 168.*

5. Bernard Adolphe Granier de Cassagnac, *Voyage aux Antilles françaises, anglaises, danoises, espagnoles; À Saint-Domingue et aux États-Unis d'Amérique,* 2 vols. (Paris: Dauvin et Fontaine, 1842–44), 1:114–16.

6. *Gazette de la Martinique,* August 14, 1805.

7. Debien, *Les Esclaves,* 87; Vanony-Frisch, "Les Esclaves," 97; Moreau de Saint-Méry, *Description,* 1:59.

8. Debien, "Comptes," 21; Debien, *Les Esclaves,* 137–38; David Geggus, "The Slaves of British-Occupied Saint-Domingue: An Analysis of the Workforces of 197 Absentee Plantations, 1796–1797," *Caribbean Studies* 18, nos. 1–2 (April–July 1978): 31.

9. Labat, *Nouveau Voyage,* 3:416–17; Debien, "Destinées d'esclaves," 24.

10. Vanony-Frisch, "Les Esclaves," 89–91.

11. Debien, *Les Esclaves,* 86.

12. Vanony-Frisch, "Les Esclaves," 79, 89.

13. ANSOM, Guadeloupe 107 (749), Ordonnance du Roi qui déclare libres deux cent dix-huit Noirs du Domaine colonial, Saint-Cloud, October 12, 1847.

14. Gautier, *Soeurs de solitude,* 204.

15. Debien, "Les Esclaves," 343–47; Debien, *Plantations,* 50; Vanony-Frisch, *Les Esclaves,* 62–63.

16. Cauna, *Au Temps des isles,* 102–104; Frantz Tardo-Dino, *Le Collier de servitude* (Paris: Éditions caribéennes, 1985), 187; Morrissey, *Slave Women,* 108.

17. Girod, *Une Fortune coloniale,* 106; Geneviève Leti, *Santé et société esclavagiste à la Martinique (1802–1848)* (Paris: L'Harmattan, 1998), 307; Debien, *Les Esclaves,* 103.

18. Gautier, *Soeurs de solitude,* 209.

19. Ibid., 208.

20. Vanony-Frisch, "Les Esclaves," 89.

21. Gabriel Debien, "Un Colon niortais à Saint-Domingue: Jean Barre de Saint-Venant (1737–1810)," *Bulletin de la Société d'histoire de la Martinique,* no. 19 (1977): 65.

22. Bush, *Slave Women,* 36, 141.

23. Richard Sheridan, *Doctors and Slaves: A Medical Demographic History of Slavery in the British West Indies 1680–1834* (London: Cambridge University Press, 1985), 77–78.

24. Leti, *Santé et société,* 307.

25. Debien, "Un Colon niortais," 67.

26. Labat, *Nouveau Voyage,* 3:431; Rouvellat de Cussac, *Situation,* 491.

27. Debien, *Plantations,* 127.

28. Leti, *Santé et société,* 318–49.

29. Debien, "Comptes," 24–25.

30. Debien, *Plantations,* 126–27.

31. Reible, "Les Esclaves et leurs travaux," 23; Debien, *Plantations,* 127.

32. Debien, *Plantations,* 127.

33. Ibid.

34. Ibid., 128.

35. Reible, "Les Esclaves et leurs travaux," 23; Félix Patron, *Des Noirs et leur situation dans les colonies françaises* (Paris, 1831), 6.

36. Vanony-Frisch, "Les Esclaves," 92.

37. Ibid.

38. Gautier, *Soeurs de solitude,* 207; Vanony-Frisch, "Les Esclaves," 92.

39. Debien, *Plantations,* 124; Debien, *Les Esclaves,* 91.

40. Moreau de Saint-Méry, *Description,* 3:1219.

41. Labat, *Nouveau Voyage,* 3, 453; Debien, *Plantations,* 100; Moreau de Saint-Méry, *Description,* 1:62, 503.

42. See *Journal officiel de la Martinique,* April 16, 1834, 1; Vanony-Frisch, "Les Esclaves," 94; Gautier, *Soeurs de solitude,* 207.

43. Vanony-Frisch, "Les Esclaves," 92; Debien, *Les Esclaves,* 90.

44. Debien, *Les Esclaves,* 93; Debien, *Plantations,* 123–25; Debien, "Destinées d'esclaves," 28.

45. ANSOM, Guadeloupe 107 (749).

46. Vanony-Frisch, "Les Esclaves," 95.

47. Rouvellat de Cussac, *Situation,* 44.

48. Labat, *Nouveau Voyage,* 3:446.

49. Debien, *Les Esclaves,* 24–25.

50. Vanony-Frisch, "Les Esclaves," 97.

51. Debien, *Plantations,* 124.

52. Debien, *Les Esclaves,* 124–25.

53. Debien, *Plantations,* 124.

54. Moreau de Saint-Méry, *Description,* 77.

55. Debien, "Destinées d'esclaves," 28.

56. One *aune* was equivalent to 1.18–1.20 meters in 1840, when this ancient measure was suppressed.

57. Ann Geracimos, "A Mystery in Miniature: An Enigmatic Button Once Decorated the Uniform of Haitian Liberator Toussaint Louverture," *Smithsonian,* January 2000, 20–21.

58. Debien, *Les Esclaves,* 90.

59. Gabriel Debien, *Lettres de colons* (Dakar: Publications de la Section d'histoire, Université de Dakar [now Université Cheikh Anta Diop], 1965), 57.

60. Debien, *Lettres de colons,* 69, 73, 167.

61. Ibid., 48.

62. Debien, *Les Esclaves,* 92.

63. Debien, *Plantations,* 123; Debien, "Destinées d'esclaves," 25–31; Jean Fouchard, *Les Marrons de la liberté* (Paris: Éditions de l'école, 1972), 267.

64. Debien, "Destinée d'esclaves," 25–26; Higman, *Slave Population and Economy,* 195.

65. See *Journal officiel de la Martinique,* May 26, 1847, 1–3; Debien, *Les Esclaves,* 93; Vanony-Frisch, "Les Esclaves," 42; Girod, *Une Fortune coloniale,* 106; Gautier, *Soeurs de solitude,* 212–13.

66. Debien, "Destinée d'esclaves," 26–27.

67. Debien, "Un Colon niortais," 77.

68. *Code Noir,* 51.

69. Fouchard, *Marrons,* 374–75.

70. *Gazette de la Martinique,* October 7, 1803, 315; *Gazette de la Martinique,* June 15, 1803, 217; *Gazette de la Martinique,* September 2, 1806, 341; *Moniteur général de la partie française de Saint-Domingue,* April 14, 1792, 574; Fouchard, *Marrons,* 375.

71. *Gazette de la Martinique,* June 5, 1804, 573.

72. Gautier, *Soeurs de solitude,* 205.

73. Labat, *Nouveau Voyage,* 3:437.

5. Marriage, Family Life, Reproduction, and Assault

1. Victor Schoelcher, *De l'abolition de l'esclavage: Examen critique du préjugé contre la couleur des Africains et des sangs-mêlés* (Paris: Pagnerre, 1840), 170–71.

2. Du Tertre, *Histoire,* 2:472.

3. Pierre Paul Castelli, *De l'esclavage en général et de l'émancipation des Noirs* (Paris, 1844), 128.

4. Dugoujon, *Lettres sur l'esclavage dans les colonies françaises* (Paris, 1845), 28.

5. Moreau de Saint-Méry, *Lois et constitutions,* 1:118: Règlement de M. de Tracy, lieutenant général de l'Amérique, touchant les blasphémateurs et la police des isles, June 19, 1664.

6. AN Col., C 8A 113 F 145, Saint-Pierre, January 10, 1806.

7. Gisler, *L'Esclavage aux Antilles françaises,* 179.

8. *Code Noir,* 34–35.

9. Orlando Patterson, *The Sociology of Slavery* (London: Granada Publishing, 1973), 159–66; Bush, *Slave Women,* 86, 98; Beckles, *Natural Rebels,* 115; Morrissey, *Slave Women,* 99; Gautier, *Soeurs de solitude,* 149.

10. AN Col., 113 F 143, "Le préfet colonial de la Martinique et dépandence à M. le curé de la paroisse," December 27, 1805.

11. ANSOM, Fonds généralités, carton 630, dossier 2736, "Ordonnance du roi," Paris, June 11, 1839.

12. ANSOM, Fonds généralités, carton 372, dossier 2197, July 18, 1845; ANSOM, Fonds généralités, carton 372, dossier 2197, Paris, November 30, 1847.

13. Moreau de Saint-Méry, *Description,* 1:57.

14. Lacharière, *De l'affranchissement des esclaves,* 122.

15. Castelli, *De l'esclavage en général,* 120.

16. Dugoujon, *Lettres,* 27.

17. ANSOM, Fonds généralités, carton 372, dossier 2197, February 18, 1846; *Abolitionniste français,* nos. 1–2 (Jan.–Feb. 1844): 46; Dugoujon, *Lettres,* 28–29; Labat, *Nouveau Voyage,* 4:186.

18. Jacques Adélaïde (Jacques Adélaïde-Merlande), "Demography and Names of Slaves of Le Moule, 1845 to May 1848," *Bulletin de la Société d'histoire de la Guadeloupe,* no. 22 (1974): 6; Raymond Boutin, "Les Esclaves du Moule au XIXe siècle (naissances, mariages et décès)," *Bulletin de la société d'histoire de la Guadeloupe,* nos. 75–78 (1988): 23–24.

19. Boutin, "Les Esclaves du Moule," 23–24.

20. Adélaïde, "Demography and Names," 67–68.

21. *L'Abolitionniste français,* nos. 1–2 (Jan.–Feb. 1844): 46; Du Tertre, *Histoire,* 2:471–72; Peytraud, *L'Esclavage,* 210–11.

22. Adélaïde, "Demography and Names," 69–70; Boutin, "Esclaves du Moule," 24.

23. Baron de Wimpffen, *Voyage à Saint-Domingue pendant les années 1788, 1789 et 1790* (Paris, 1797), 33; Adélaïde, "Demography and Names," 69; Boutin, "Esclaves du Moule," 24; Patterson, *Sociology of Slavery,* 154.

24. Bernard David, *Origines,* 101–105; *Notice statistique sur la Guyane française,* 55–56.

25. ANSOM, Guadeloupe 107 (749), Ordonnance du Roi qui déclare libres deux cent dix-huit Noirs du Domaine colonial, Saint-Cloud, October 12, 1847.

26. Debien, *Les Esclaves,* 349.

27. Du Tertre, *Histoire,* 2:474–75. Du Tertre was referring to the African *pagnes,* a wrap-around skirt.

28. Du Tertre, *Histoire,* 2:476; Labat, *Nouveau Voyage,* 4:161.

29. Dessalles, *Histoire,* 3:373.

30. Labat, *Nouveau Voyage,* 4:187.

31. Abdoulaye Bara Diop, *La Société wolof* (Paris: Karthala, 1981), 47–107.

32. Debien, *Les Esclaves,* 347; *Code Noir,* 35–36.

33. Vanony-Frisch, "Les Esclaves," 59.

34. Adélaïde, "Demography and Names," 69.

35. AN Col., C8 A 66, F 31, De Fénelon to M. le Duc, Fort-Royal, April 11, 1764; Joseph Romalet du Caillaud, *Voyage à la Martinique fait en 1770–1773* (Paris, 1804), 113; Girod-Chantrans, *Voyage,* 145; Félix Patron, *Des Noirs,* 17.

36. Debien, *Les Esclaves,* 349.

37. Vanony-Frisch, "Les Esclaves," 68–70.

38. Debien, "La Sucrerie Bréda," 34.

39. Debien, *Les Esclaves,* 347.

40. Ibid., 344–45; Gabriel Debien, *Les Colons des Antilles et leur main d'oeuvre à la fin du XVIIIe siécle* (Paris: Annales historiques de la Révolution française, 1955), 265; Bruleaux et al., *Deux Siècles,* 123.

41. ANSOM, Fonds généralités, carton 630, dossier 2736, June 1843; Vanony-Frisch, "Les Esclaves," 65; Debien, *Les Colons,* 265; Boutin, "Les Esclaves du Moule," 19–21.

42. ANSOM, Martinique 33 281, "Note sur l'habitation de Hautmont, sise au quartier du Marigot, île de la Martinique," undated.

43. ANSOM, C 8A 66, F31, Fort Royal, April 11, 1764.

44. Romalet, *Voyage à la Martinique,* 113; Boutin, "Esclaves du Moule," 21–23.

45. Debien, *Les Esclaves,* 350.

46. Michael Craton and James Walvin, *A Jamaican Plantation: The History of Worthy Park* (Toronto: University of Toronto Press, 1970), 140; Craton, *Searching for the Invisible Man,* 88; Higman, *Slave Populations,* 349–50.

47. Debien, *Les Esclaves,* 130; Cauna, *Au Temps des isles à sucre,* 99; Stein, *The French Sugar Business,* 54.

48. Cauna, *Au Temps des isles à sucre,* 99.

49. Debien, *Les Esclaves,* 129–30; Debien, *Plantations,* 130.

50. Debien, *Les Colons,* 270.

51. Dazille, *Observations sur le tétanos* (Paris: Planche, 1788), 342–43.

52. Ibid.

53. Ibid., 56

54. Debien, *Les Esclaves,* 355.

55. Ibid., 130; Pierre de Vassière, *Saint-Domingue,* 253.

56. Romalet, *Voyage,* 114–15.

57. Dazille, *Observations sur les maladies des nègres, leurs causes, leurs traitements et les moyens de les prévenir* (Paris: Didot, 1776), 120, 225–26, 231, 274–75.

58. Dazille, *Observations sur le tétanos,* 212–14, 315–22.

59. Morrissey, *Slave Women,* 107–108.

60. Kenneth F. Kiple, *The Caribbean Slave: A Biological History* (London: Cambridge University Press, 1984), 120.

61. For an edited version of Thistlewood's diary, see Douglas Hall, *In Miserable Slavery: Thomas Thistlewood in Jamaica, 1750–1786* (London: Macmillan, 1989). See also Bernard Moitt,

"In the Shadow of the Plantation: Women of Color and the *Libres de Fait* of Martinique and Guadeloupe" (unpublished paper).

62. Debien, *Plantations,* 30.

63. Debien, *Les Esclaves,* 126–27, 131.

64. Debien, *Les Esclaves,* 127–29.

6. Discipline and Physical Abuse: Slave Women and the Law

1. Beckles, *Natural Rebels,* 31.

2. Peytraud, *L'Esclavage,* 28.

3. Gisler, *L'Esclavage aux Antilles françaises,* 41–42; C. L. R. James, *The Black Jacobins: Toussaint Louverture and the San Domingo Revolution* (New York: Vintage, 1989), 9–10; Fouchard, *Les Marrons de la liberté,* 111; M. France, *La Vérité et les faits ou l'esclavage à nu* (Paris: Moreau, 1846), 7.

4. Gisler, *L'Esclavage,* 41; *Code Noir,* 45–49.

5. Bruleaux et al., *Deux Siècles,* 169.

6. Tomich, *Slavery,* 242.

7. Schoelcher, *Colonies,* 89.

8. ANSOM, Guyane 107 K7 (07), Procureur Général to Governor, May 19, 1842.

9. ANSOM, Fonds généralités, carton 192, dossier 1476, Rapport à M. le Ministre de la Marine et des Colonies, sur un projet d'ordonnance du roi, relative à l'emprisonnement disciplinaire des esclaves, June 29, 1841; ANSOM, Fonds généralités, carton 207, dossier 1514, September 16, 1841.

10. Bernard Moitt, "Transcending Linguistic and Cultural Frontiers in Caribbean Historiography: C. L. R. James, French Sources, and Slavery in San Domingo, in *C. L. R. James: His Intellectual Legacies,* ed. Selwyn R. Cudjoe and William E. Cain, 136–60 (Amherst: University of Massachusetts Press, 1995); *Code Noir,* 35, 41–44, 49; Sala-Molins, *Le Code Noir,* 142–43; Elsa Goveia, *The West Indian Slave Laws of the Eighteenth Century* (Bridgetown: Caribbean Universities Press, 1970), 38.

11. De Vassière, *Saint-Domingue,* 86.

12. AN Col., F3 90 41, March 13, 1788. See also James, *Black Jacobins,* 23; Carolyn Fick, *The Making of Haiti: The Saint-Domingue Revolution from Below* (Knoxville: University of Tennessee Press, 1990), 37–38; Moreau de Saint-Méry, *Lois et constitutions* 3:674–75: Lettre à MM de Larnage et Maillart sur les mauvais traitements des maîtres pour leurs esclaves, July 15, 1741; Gisler, *L'Esclavage,* 108.

13. Peytraud, *L'Esclavage,* 328–29.

14. AN Col., F3, Fol. 149, Cayenne, June 16, 1760; Peytraud, *L'Esclavage,* 332.

15. AN Col., F3, Fol. 225, 1771; Gautier, *Soeurs de solitude,* 159.

16. AN Col. F3 90 41, March 13, 1788, Vincent de Marbois, Procureur du roi, au Ministre; James, *Black Jacobins,* 23; Fick, *Making of Haiti,* 37–38; Gisler, *L'Esclavage,* 119–20.

17. ANSOM, Guadeloupe 107 (748), February 15, 1827; ANSOM, Guadeloupe 107 (748), Paris, 1827; ANSOM, Guadeloupe 107 (748), Paris, December 25, 1827.

18. ANSOM, Guadeloupe 107 (748), Basse-Terre, February 6, 1828; ANSOM, Guadeloupe 107 (748), Paris, December 25, 1827; ANSOM, Guadeloupe 107 (748), Arrêt criminel, January 9, 1829.

19. Josette Fallope, *Esclaves et citoyens: Les Noirs à la Guadeloupe au XIXe siècle dans les processus de résistance et d'intégration (1802–1910)* (Basse-Terre: Société d'histoire de la Guadeloupe, 1992), 247–49; 286; Tomich, *Slavery,* 53–75; Schnakenbourg, *Histoire de l'industrie sucrière en Guadeloupe,* 1:118–36.

20. Fallope, *Esclaves et citoyens,* 248; Gisler, *L'Esclavage,* 145–46; Gaston-Martin, *Histoire,* 272–79, 292.

21. David Northrup, *Indentured Labor in the Age of Imperialism, 1834–1922* (New York: Cambridge University Press, 1995), 34; Tomich, *Slavery,* 62–64; Gaston-Martin, *Histoire* 264–71, 281–83; Fallope, *Esclaves et citoyens,* 248.

22. ANSOM, Fonds généralités, carton 192, dossier 1476, February 26, 1841.

23. ANSOM, Fonds généralités, carton 207, dossier 1514, November 12, 1841.

24. Gisler, *L'Esclavage,* 140.

25. Schoelcher, *Colonies françaises,* 90.

26. ANSOM, Guyane 107 K7 (7), Châtiments infligés à la née Marie-Claire de l'habitation Mondelice (Affaire Reine), 1840–1841; Arrêt rendu pour la chambre des mises en accusation de la Cour Royale de la Guyane française, séance à Cayenne, October 29, 1840; ANSOM, Guyane 107 K7 (7), Correspondence of Vidal de Lingendes, Cayenne, December 26, 1840.

27. ANSOM, Guyane 107, K 7 (7); "Châtiments infligés à la née Marie-Claire de l'habitation Mondelice (Affaire Reine), 1840–1841; ANSOM, Guyane, 107 K 7, December 26, 1840; ANSOM, Guyane 107, K 7 (7), Fort-Royal, February 19, 1841; ANSOM, Guyane 107 K 7 (7), Governor to Ministre de la Marine et des Colonies, Cayenne, November 16, 1840.

28. ANSOM, Guyane 107 K 7 (7); Arrêt qui déclare qu'il n'y a lieu à suivre [contre] le sieur Reine, Cayenne, November 3, 1840. A *lieue* was not a standard measurement, but appears to have been no less than 4,445 meters.

29. ANSOM, Guyane 107 K7 (7), Ministre de la Justice, Paris, December 14, 1841.

30. ANSOM, Guyane 107 K7, Procureur Général to Governor, May 19, 1842.

31. ANSOM, Martinique 33, 286, Fort-Royal, Governor to Minister, October 18, 1845.

32. ANSOM, Martinique 33 286, Governor to Minister, Fort-Royal, October 18, 1845.

33. ANSOM, Martinique 33, 286, November 13, 1845.

34. *Gazette des Tribunaux,* February 4, 1846, 330, found in ANSOM, Martinique 33, 286.

35. ANSOM, Martinique 33, 286, August 23, 1845, Copie d'une lettre adressée à M. le Procureur Général par le Procureur du Roi de Saint-Pierre, sous date du 23 août, 1845; ANSOM, Fonds généralités, carton 33, dossier 286, Fort Royal, November 13, 1848.

36. *Gazette des Tribunaux,* February 4, 1846, 330.

37. ANSOM, Martinique 33 286, Procureur du Roi of Saint-Pierre to Procureur Général, August 23, 1845.

38. ANSOM, Martinique 33, 286, Governor to Minister, Fort-Royal, January 10, 1846; Gisler, *L'Esclavage,* 50; *Gazette des Tribunaux,* February 4, 1846, 330.

39. Philip Schwarz, *Slave Laws in Virginia* (Athens: University of Georgia Press, 1999), 80–81.

40. France, *La Vérité,* 101.

41. Ibid., 166–67, 171–72.

42. ANSOM, Martinique 33, 285, Saint-Pierre, January 26, 1846.

43. Ibid.

44. Ibid.

45. Schoelcher, *L'Histoire de l'esclavage,* 1:326.

46. Ibid., 1:361–62.

47. Ibid., 1:387–88.

48. ANSOM, Guyane 107 K7 (16), Extrait du registre des procès-verbaux de délibérations du Conseil privé de la Guyane française, December 1847.

49. ANSOM, Guyane 107 K7 (15), Governor to Minister of Marine and Colonies, Cayenne, March 25, 1846; ANSOM, Guyane 107 K7 (15), March 23, 1846.

50. ANSOM, Martinique 42, 346 (1828–1847), Déportation des esclaves à Porto-Rico,

Paris, February 28, 1828; Gaspar, *Bondmen and Rebels,* 35–37; Schwarz, *Slave Laws of Virginia,* 107.

51. ANSOM, Martinique 42, 346, Déportation des esclaves à Porto-Rico [*sic*], Paris, February 28, 1828; ANSOM, Martinique 42 348, Extrait du procès-verbal du Conseil privé, July 9, 1827.

52. Schwarz, *Slave Laws of Virginia,* 102.

53. ANSOM, Martinique 42, 346, Paris, February 28, 1828; ANSOM, Martinique 42, 348, Extrait du procès-verbal du Conseil privé, August 8, 1827; ANSOM, Martinique 42, 348, June 20, 1827; ANSOM, Martinique 42, 348, June 22, 1827; ANSOM, Martinique 42, 346, (no day or month), 1829.

54. ANSOM, Martinique 42, 350, Extrait du registre des procès-verbaux, 1838.

55. ANSOM, Fonds généralités, carton 631, dossier 2739, Rapport à son Excellence M. le Gouverneur pour le roi, December 24, 1828; ANSOM, Fonds généralités, carton 631, dossier 2739, Extrait du registre du Conseil privé, Guadeloupe, August 18, 1837; ANSOM, Fonds généralités, carton 192, dossier 1478, Ordonnance du roi concernant le régime disciplinaire des esclaves, Neuilly, June 4, 1846, 18.

56. AN Col., C 8A 36, F204, September 17, 1726; ANSOM, Fonds généralités, carton 192, dossier 1476, Circulaire relative au séjour des esclaves détenus dans les geôles et prisons, Pointe-à-Pitre, December 30, 1819.

57. ANSOM, Fonds généralités, carton 630, dossier 2736, Extrait du registre des procès-verbaux de délibérations du Conseil privé de la Martinique, September 1828.

58. ANSOM, Fonds généralités, carton 630, dossier 2736, Extrait du registre des procès-verbaux des délibérations du Conseil privé de la Guadeloupe et dépendances, June 26, 1832.

59. A D-M, Martinique, Série U, Arrêts correctionnels (1832–1833); Police correctionnelle, audience publique du 5 mars, 1832.

60. Gilbert Pago, *Les Femmes et la liquidation du système esclavagiste à la Martinique, 1848–1852* (Pointe-à-Pitre: Ibis Rouge Editions, 1998), 46.

7. Women and Resistance

1. A version of this chapter was published as "Slave Women and Resistance in the French Caribbean," in *More Than Chattel: Black Women and Slavery in the Americas,* ed. David Barry Gaspar and Darlene Clark Hine (Bloomington: Indiana University Press, 1996), 239–258. I thank Indiana University Press for permission to use it here.

2. Simone Schwarz-Bart, *The Bridge of Beyond,* trans. Barbara Bray (Portsmouth, N.H.: Heinemann, 1982).

3. Jacques Roumain, *Masters of the Dew,* trans. Langston Hughes and Mercer Cook (Portsmouth, N.H.: Heinemann, 1947).

4. Aimé Césaire, *The Tragedy of King Christophe,* trans. Ralph Manheim (New York: Grove Press, 1969).

5. Antoine Métral, *Histoire de l'insurrection des esclaves dans le nord de Saint-Domingue* (Paris: F. Sceref, 1818), 60.

6. Jacques Adélaïde-Merlande, *Delgrès ou la Guadeloupe en 1802* (Paris: Éditions Karthala, 1986) 5–10; André Nègre, *La Rébellion de la Guadeloupe, 1801–1802* (Paris: Éditions caribéennes, 1987) 12–13.

7. Adélaïde-Merlande, *Delgrès,* 7.

8. Nègre, *Rébellion,* 114.

9. Oruno Lara, *La Guadeloupe dans l'histoire* (Paris: L'Harmattan, 1979), 126.

10. James, *Black Jacobins,* 315.

11. Métral, *Histoire,* 77.

12. Auguste Lacour, *Histoire de la Guadeloupe*, 4 vols. (Basse-Terre: Éditions de diffusion de la culture antillaise, 1976), 3:311.

13. Lara, *La Guadeloupe dans l'histoire*, 138.

14. Métral, *Histoire*, 151.

15. Lacour, *Histoire*, 3:271.

16. Ibid., 3:275.

17. Ibid.

18. James, *Black Jacobins*, 361. See also Métral, *Histoire*, 180.

19. Métral, *Histoire*, 180.

20. Ibid., 43.

21. Ibid., 180.

22. Lacour, *Histoire*, 3:275.

23. Ibid., 3:291.

24. Martineau and May, *Trois Siècles d'histoire antillaise*, 218; Adélaïde-Merlande, *Delgrès*, 147.

25. Lacour, *Histoire*, 3:331.

26. Lara, *Guadeloupe*, 154.

27. Adélaïde-Merlande, *Delgrès*, 149; Lacour, *Histoire*, 3:325–54; Martineau and May, *Trois Siècles*, 218.

28. Lacour, *Histoire*, 3:311; Adélaïde-Merlande, *Delgrès*, 152; Gautier, *Soeurs de solitude*, 251.

29. Lacour, *Histoire*, 3:398–99; Lara, *Guadeloupe*, 174; Nègre, *La Rébellion*, 150–51.

30. ANSOM, Martinique 18, 162, Cour Royale de la Martinique: Acte d'accusation, April 5, 1831; ANSOM, Martinique 18, 161, Extrait du registre des procès verbaux, May 19, 1831; Maurice Nicolas, *L'Affaire de la Grand'Anse* (Fort-de-France: Théodore Marchand, 1960), 18–19.

31. ANSOM, Martinique 18, 159, Extrait du registre des procès verbaux des délibérations du Conseil privé de la Martinique, February 10, 1831; ANSOM, Martinique 18, 159, Extrait du registre des procès-verbaux des délibérations du Conseil privé de la Martinique, May 19, 1831; *Havre*, April 8, 1831, 2; *Havre*, April 18, 1831, 3. See also Armand Nicolas, *Histoire de la Martinique*, 2 vols. (Paris: L'Harmattan, 1996), 1:343–48.

32. ANSOM, Martinique 18, 162, Cour Royale de la Martinique, April 5, 1831.

33. ANSOM, Martinique 18, 162, Governor to Minister, Fort-Royal, May 21, 1831.

34. *Havre*, July 18, 1831, 3; *Le Courrier français*, April 22, 1831, 3.

35. ANSOM, Martinique 8, 622, Copie d'une pétition faite à l'assemblée par M. Lalaurette de la Martinique au sujet des ses pertes lors des troubles du Prêcheur, Saint-Pierre, 1848; Bernard David, *Les Origines de la population martiniquaise au fil des ans 1635–1902* (Fort-de-France: Société d'histoire de la Martinique, 1973), 105.

36. See Pierre Dessalles, *La Vie d'un colon à la Martinique au XIXe siècle*, 4 vols. (1986), 4:41–42; Armand Nicolas, *La Révolution anti-esclavagiste de mai 1848 à la Martinique* (Fort-de-France: 1967), 25–26.

37. Malenfant, *Des colonies et particulièrement de Saint-Domingue* (Paris, 1814), cited in Métral, *Histoire*, 40.

38. Vanony-Frisch, "Les Esclaves," 134–35; Gaspar, *Bondmen and Rebels*, 181; Higman, *Slave Populations of the British Caribbean*, 389; Patterson, *Sociology of Slavery*, 260; Michael Craton, *Testing the Chains: Resistance to Slavery in the British West Indies* (Ithaca, N.Y.: Cornell University Press, 1982), 61; Gautier, *Soeurs de solitude*, 236.

39. Meillassoux, "Female Slavery," 49–65; Fatou Sow, "Femme africaine, emploi et division internationale du travail," *Présence africaine* (Paris), no. 141 (1987): 199–205.

40. Gautier, *Soeurs de solitude*, 237; Patterson, *Slavery and Social Death*, 113; Vanony-Frisch, "Les Esclaves," 135; Fouchard, *Marrons*, 285.

41. Gazette de la Guadeloupe, December 4, 1788, 195; *Gazette de la Martinique,* October 28, 1803, 339; *Gazette de la Martinique,* September 4, 1804, 680.

42. *Gazette de la Guadeloupe,* December 4, 1788, 195; *Gazette de la Martinique,* October 28, 1803, 339; October 8, 1805, 194; November 1, 1805, 525; January 8, 1806, 44; March 19, 1806, 132; December 27, 1806, 472.

43. Joseph France, *La Vérité et les faits ou l'esclavage à nu dans ses rapports avec les maîtres et les agents de l'autorité* (Paris: Moreau, 1846), 98–99; Gautier, *Soeurs de solitude,* 159.

44. Bruleaux et al., *Deux siècles,* 91; Vanony-Frisch, "Les Esclaves," 133–36; Gautier, *Soeurs de solitude,* 229–37; *Gazette de la Guadeloupe,* September 25, 1788, 162; July 31, 1817, 4; January 5, 1826, 1; *Gazette de la Martinique,* March 12, 1803, 73; May 17, 1806, 213; August 13, 1809, 322.

45. *Gazette de la Martinique,* August 2, 1803, 236; July 10, 1804, 611; June 26, 1805, 322; *Gazette de la Guadeloupe,* August 10, 1810, 6.

46. Fouchard, *Marrons,* 289; Gautier, *Soeurs de solitude,* 228–30; *Gazette de la Martinique,* July 15, 1803, 217; November 8, 1805, 536; May 10, 1806, 200; September 6, 1806, 374.

47. Du Tertre, *Histoire,* 3:179; Gabriel Debien, "Le Marronage aux Antilles françaises au XVIIIe siècle," *Caribbean Studies* 6, no. 1 (1966): 4; Léo Elisabeth, "Résistance des esclaves aux XVIIe et XVIII siècles dans les colonies françaises d'Amérique, principalement aux Iles du vent," in *Les Abolitions de l'esclavage de L. F. Sonthonax à V. Schoelcher 1793, 1848,* ed. Marcel Dorigny (Paris: UNESCO, 1995), 78; ANSOM, Fonds généralités, carton 631, dossier 2737, November 23, 1821; ANSOM, Fonds généralités, carton 631, dossier 2737, Circulaire, Basse-Terre, December 8, 1821; Moreau de Saint-Méry, *Lois et constitutions,* 1:136: Arrêt du consul de la Martinique touchant les nègres marrons, March 2, 1665.

48. Fouchard, *Marrons,* 550.

49. ANSOM, Guyane 129, P2 (08), Commandeur et administrateur de la Guyane française, September 2, 1822; ANSOM, Fonds généralités, carton 630, dossier 2737, n.d.

50. *Code Noir,* 47.

51. Fouchard, *Marrons,* 409; Gautier, *Soeurs de solitude,* 237; Gaspar, *Bondmen and Rebels,* 155; *Gazette de la Martinique,* July 5, 1803, 40.

52. AN Col., C 8A 33, F276, October 8, 1724; AN Col., C 8A 34, F89, June 18, 1725; Abénon, *Guadeloupe,* 2:66–67.

53. ANSOM, Martinique 33, 281, "Arrêt du Conseil supérieur de l'isle Martinique," Fort-Royal, November 30, 1815.

54. Tanc, *De l'esclavage aux colonies,* 39.

55. ANSOM, Guyane 107, K7 (03), July 14, 1827.

56. See, for example, Lacour, *Histoire,* 3:120.

57. Gwendolyn Mildo Hall, *Social Control in Slave Plantation Societies: A Comparison of Saint-Domingue and Cuba* (Baltimore: Johns Hopkins University Press, 1971), 69.

58. Lacour, *Histoire,* 3:120; Satineau, *Histoire,* 285; Debien, *Plantations,* 56, 61; Labat, *Nouveau voyage,* 4:198, 307.

59. Satineau, *Histoire,* 289.

60. Tardo-Dino, *Le Collier de servitude,* 234.

61. AN Col., C 8A 18 F297, May 24, 1712.

62. Abénon, *Guadeloupe,* 1:256.

63. Yvan Debbasch, Le Crime d'empoisonnement aux îles pendant la période esclavagiste," *Revue française d'histoire d'outre-mer* 50 (1963): 146–47.

64. Satineau, *Histoire,* 289, cited in David, *Les Origines,* 82.

65. Satineau, *Histoire,* 289; Gabriel Debien, *Les Esclaves,* 400.

66. Satineau, *Histoire,* 289–90; Debien, *Les Esclaves,* 400; David, *Les Origines,* 82; AN Col., F3 88 210, "Mémoire sur les poisons qui règnent à St. Domingue," 1762; AN Col., F3 88

210, "Observations sur l'ordonnance de MM. de Reynaud et de Brasseur, concernant les poisons," 1780; ANSOM, Guyane 129 P2 (20), "Ordonnance contre l'empoisonnement des rivières," March 5, 1818.

67. Cited in Abénon, *Guadeloupe,* 1:255

68. Debien, *Les Esclaves,* 401; Debbasch, "Le Crime d'empoisonnement," 150.

69. Debien, *Les Esclaves,* 400–401.

70. Debien, *Les Esclaves,* 405, 408; Debien, *Plantations,* 63, 67.

71. Debbasch, "Le Crime d'empoisonnement," 141–52; Poyen de Sainte-Méry, *De l'exploitation des sucreries,* 22.

72. David, *Les Origines,* 96.

73. AN Col., C 8A 18 F297, May 24, 1712; C 8A 32 F266, November 17, 1723; C 8A 36 F204, September 17, 1726.

74. Debien, *Les Esclaves,* 408.

75. Labat, *Nouveau Voyage,* 3:446–47.

76. Lacour, *Histoire,* 3:339–404; Adélaïde-Merlande, *Delgrès,* 162; Lara, *Histoire,* 170–72.

77. Métral, *Histoire,* 75.

78. AN Col., C 8A 18 F297, May 24, 1712; C 8A 112 F210, June 9, 1806; C 8A 114 F176, June 10, 1806.

79. ANSOM, Martinique 42 348, Report of the Directeur Général de l'Intérieur, August 4, 1827; ANSOM, Martinique 42 348, Directeur Général de l'Interieur to governor, Fort-Royal, June 22, 1827.

80. ANSOM, Guyane 129 P2 (11), Extrait du registre des procès-verbaux des délibérations du conseil privé de la Guyane française, July 14, 1831.

81. ANSOM, Guyane 129 P2 (11), Extrait du registre, July 14, 1831.

82. Unidentified and undated newspaper clipping (Cour d'Assises de Cayenne) found in ANSOM, Guyane 107 K7 (7), 1843; ANSOM, Guyane 107 K7 (11), Cour d'Assises de la Guyane française—Traitements barbares et inhumains exercés par un régisseur sur la personne de plusieurs esclaves, November 23, 1843.

83. AN Col., C8 A 18 F364, September 3, 1712; ANSOM, Guyane 107 K7 (15) Affaire Paguenaut, March 167, 1848; Tanc, *De l'esclavage,* 5–6.

84. Gabriel Debien and Françoise Thésée, *Un Colon niortais à Saint-Domingue* (Niort: Imbert-Nicolas, 1975), 123.

85. Ibid.

86. Gabriel Debien, "A Saint-Domingue avec deux jeunes économes de plantation, 1774–1788," *Notes d'histoire coloniale,* no. 7 (1945): 3–19.

87. ANSOM, Fonds généralités, carton 207, dossier 1517, Extrait du registre de punitions infligées aux détenus du dit atelier pendant le mois de Janvier, 1848, January 27, 1848; Debien, *Les Esclaves,* 182.

88. ANSOM, Fonds généralités, carton 207, dossier 1516 (undated).

89. ANSOM, Guyane 107 K7 (7), Cayenne, June 12, 1843; ANSOM, Guyane 107 K7 (10), Cayenne, September 9, 1843; ANSOM, Guyane 107 K7 (10), January 16, 1844.

90. Yvan Debbasch, "Les Associations serviles à la Martinique au XIXe siècle," in *Études d'histoire du droit privé,* ed. Pierre Petot (Paris: Éditions Montchrestien, 1959), 124; Jacques Adélaïde-Merlande, "Problématique d'une histoire de l'esclavage urbain: Guadeloupe, Guyane, Martinique (vers 1815–1848)," *Bulletin de la Société d'histoire de la Guadeloupe,* nos. 65–66, 3–4 trimester (1985): 19–20.

91. Gautier, *Soeurs de solitude,* 223–24.

92. Bruleaux et al., *Deux siècles,* 185–86.

93. Debbasch, "Associations," 125.

8. Women and Manumission

1. Ivan Debbasch, *Couleur et liberté: Le Jeu de critère ethnique dans un ordre juridique esclavagiste*, 2 vols. (Paris: Dalloz, 1967), 1:22–27.

2. *Code Noir*, 33–34, 51, 55.

3. See Baude, "*L'Affranchissement*," 19–23; Debien, *Les Esclaves*, 377; Dessalles, *Histoire*, 3:416.

4. AN Col., C 8A 19 F80, Phélypeaux to Minister, April 6, 1713; AN Col., C 8A 20 F63, September 10, 1714; Mumford, *Black Ordeal*, 3:739–40; Léo Elisabeth, "Europe, Afrique, Nouveau Monde: Femmes d'antan aux origines de la femme créole," *Bulletin de la Société de la Martinique*, no. 27 (1988–91), 81; Peytraud, *L'Esclavage*, 420; Edward Cox, *Free Coloreds in the Slave Societies of St. Kitts and Grenada* (Knoxville: University of Tennessee Press, 1984), 21.

5. AN Col., C 8A 18, F18, June 3, 1711; ANSOM, Fonds généralités, carton 666, dossier 2845, July 12, 1832; *Bulletin des Actes Administratifs de la Martinique*, 1st ser., vol. 4 (1832): 95.

6. Durand-Molard, ed., *Code de la Martinique*, 5 vols. (St. Pierre, 1807), 2:557.

7. Durand-Molard, *Code de la Martinique*, 2:558–59; *Gazette officielle de la Martinique*, July 5, 1803, 88.

8. Durand-Molard, *Code de la Martinique*, vol. 4, Ordonnance de MM. le Général et Intendant concernant les soit-disant libres et les libertés non-registrées, September 10, 1789; Géraud Lafleur, *Saint-Claude: Histoire d'une commune de Guadeloupe* (Paris: Karthala, 1993), 80.

9. *Gazette de la Martinique*, March 26, 1803, 91–93; "Arrêté qui donne la vérification des titres dont se trouvent porteurs les gens de couleur libres du 15 mars, 1803"; *Bulletin des actes administratifs de la Martinique*, 4 vols. (Saint-Pierre, 1829–32) 1st ser., vol. 4 (1832): 94–96.

10. ANSOM, Fonds généralités, carton 372, dossier 2191, 1847, 7. See also Augustin Cochin, *L'Abolition de l'esclavage* (1861; reprint, Fort-de-France: Désormeaux, 1979), 41.

11. Dessalles, *Histoire*, 5:39; Baude, *L'Affranchissement*, 94.

12. Fallope, *Esclaves*, 298.

13. *Gazette de la Guadeloupe*, July 20, 1832, 1; Peytraud, *L'Esclavage*, 418; Gautier, *Soeurs de solitude*, 170.

14. Lafleur, *Saint-Claude*, 75.

15. Ibid., 79.

16. Gautier, *Soeurs de solitude*, 175–77; Debien, *Les Esclaves*, 376–77.

17. John Garrigus, "Blue and Brown: Contraband Indigo and the Rise of a Free Colored Planter Class in French Saint-Domingue," *The Americas* 50, no. 2 (October 1993): 257.

18. Debien, *Les Colons*, 275; Schoelcher, *Colonies*, 10; Josette Fallope, "Les Affranchissements d'esclaves à la Guadeloupe entre 1815 et 1848," *Annales de l'Université d'Abidjan*, 1st ser., vol. 6 (1978): 10.

19. Debien, *Les Esclaves*, 385–86.

20. Ibid., 383.

21. Fallope, "Les Affranchissements," 12–13.

22. *Bulletin des actes administratifs de la Martinique*, 1st ser., vol. 4 (1832): 137–50; Fallope, *Esclaves*, 290; Schoelcher, *Colonies*, 305–307.

23. Fallope, *Esclaves*, 296; Schoelcher, *Colonies*, 308; Moreau de Jonnès, *Recherches*, 17–22; Curtin, *Atlantic*, 78.

24. *Journal officiel de la Martinique*, April 19, 1834, 1; *Gazette officielle de la Guadeloupe*, January 5, 1832, 2; *Notice statistique sur la Guyane française*, 55–56; Moitt, "In the Shadow of the Plantation."

25. Schoelcher, *Histoire*, 2:43.

26. Ibid., 2:46–52; *L'Abolitionniste français*, nos. 10–12 (October–December 1845): 649–52.

27. Ibid., 651; Gautier, *Soeurs de solitude*, 147.

28. Schoelcher, *Histoire*, 2:55–62.

29. *Journal officiel de la Martinique*, April 8, 1848, 1; Rouvellat de Cussac, *Situation*, 148–49; Victor Schoelcher, *Les Magistrats des colonies depuis l'ordonnance du 18 juillet 1841 par Maxmillen Just* (Paris: Pagnerre, 1847), 5–72.

30. ANSOM, Fonds généralités, carton 40, dossier 316, "Rapports, débats, correspondances diverses concernant les lois des 18 et 19 juillet, 1845, Paris, July 18, 1845; *Journal officiel de la Martinique*, May 26, 1847, 1.

31. See "Compte rendu des lois des 18 et 19 juillet, 1845 sur le régime des esclaves, la création d'établissements agricoles par le travail libre," *Journal officiel de la Martinique*, May 26, 1847, 1; *Journal officiel de la Martinique*, May 15, 1847, 1; *Journal officiel de la Martinique*, May 12, 1847, 1; *Journal officiel de la Martinique*, May 26, 1847, 1; Fallope, *Esclaves*, 292; Schoelcher, *Histoire*, 2:19–26.

32. Schoelcher, *Histoire*, 2:19.

33. ANSOM, Fonds généralités, carton 40, dossier 316, July 19, 1845; *Journal officiel de la Martinique*, May 26, 1847, 2; Fallope, *Esclaves*, 293.

34. *Journal officiel de la Martinique*, May 26, 1847, 2; Fallope, *Esclaves*, 293.

35. *Journal officiel de la Martinique*, February 9, 1848, 1; *Journal officiel de la Martinique*, April 14, 1847, 1; *Journal officiel de la Martinique*, March 6, 1847, 2; Fallope, *Esclaves*, 293; Baude, *L'Affranchissement*, 96.

36. *Journal officiel de la Martinique*, June 19, 1847, 2.

37. *Journal officiel de la Martinique*, May 26, 1847, 1; Tomich, *Slavery*, 83.

38. *Journal officiel de la Martinique*, May 26, 1847, 3.

39. ANSOM, Fonds généralités, carton 372, dossier 2197, 1848, 4–16.

Conclusion

1. Stampp, *The Peculiar Institution*, 34.

2. Jacqueline Jones, *Labor of Love, Labor of Sorrow: Black Women, Work and the Family, from Slavery to the Present* (New York: Vintage, 1986), 14.

3. Hilary Beckles, *Centering Woman: Gender Discourses in Caribbean Slave Society* (Princeton: Markus Wiener, 1999), 179.

4. Jones, *Born a Child of Freedom*, 11–36.

Bibliography

PRIMARY SOURCES

Archives Consulted

Archives Départementales de la Guadeloupe, Basse-Terre, Guadeloupe (A D-M, Guadeloupe)
Archives Départementales de la Martinique, Fort-de-France, Martinique (A D-M, Martinique)
Archives Nationales Colonies, Paris, France (AN Col.)
Archives Nationales, Section D'Outre-Mer, Aix-en-Provence, France (ANSOM)

Official Publications

Bulletin des actes administratifs de la Martinique. 4 vols. Saint-Pierre, Martinique, 1829–32.
Durand-Molard. *Code de la Martinique.* 5 vols. Saint-Pierre, Martinique, 1807–14.
Le Code Noir ou recueil des règlements rendus jusqu'à présent. 1685. Reprint, Basse-Terre: Société d'histoire de la Guadeloupe, 1980.

Newspapers

L'Abolitionniste français
Le Courrier français
Gazette de la Martinique
Gazette des Tribunaux (Paris)
Gazette de la Guadeloupe
Gazette officielle de la Guadeloupe
Gazette officielle de la Martinique
Havre
Journal officiel de la Guadeloupe
Journal officiel de la Martinique
Moniteur général de la partie française de Saint-Domingue

SECONDARY SOURCES

Abénon, Lucien. *La Guadeloupe de 1671 à 1759.* 2 vols. Paris: L'Harmattan, 1987.
Adélaïde-Merlande, Jacques. *Delgrès ou la Guadeloupe en 1802.* Paris: Éditions Karthala, 1986.

——. "Demography and Names of Slaves of Le Moule, 1845 to May 1848." *Bulletin de la Société d'histoire de la Guadeloupe* 22, no. 2 (1974).

——. "Problématique d'une histoire de l'esclavage urbain: Guadeloupe, Guyane, Martinique (vers 1815-1848)." *Bulletin de la Société d'histoire de la Guadeloupe* 65-66, nos. 3-4 (1985).

Anderson, Karen. *Teaching Gender in U.S. History.* Washington, D.C.: American Historical Association, 1997.

Banbuck, C. A. *Histoire politique, économique et sociale de la Martinique sous l'Ancien Régime (1635-1789).* Paris: Librairie des sciences politiques et sociales, 1935.

Bangou, Henri. *La Guadeloupe.* 3 vols. Paris: L'Harmattan, 1987.

Barrey, M. Phillipe. *Les Origines de la colonisation française aux Antilles.* Le Havre: H. Micaux, 1918.

Baude, Pierre. *L'Affranchissement des esclaves aux Antilles françaises: Principalement à la Martinique du début de la colonisation à 1848.* Fort-de-France (Martinique): Impr. du gouvernement, 1948.

Beckles, Hilary. *Afro-Caribbean Women and Resistance in Barbados.* London: Karnak, 1988.

——. *Centering Woman: Gender Discourses in Caribbean Slave Society.* Princeton: Markus Wiener, 1999.

——. *Natural Rebels: A Social History of Enslaved Black Women in Barbados.* New Brunswick, N.J.: Rutgers University Press, 1989.

——. "Sex and Gender in the Historiography of Caribbean Slavery." In *Engendering History: Caribbean Women in Historical Perspective,* ed. Verene Shepherd et al., 125-40. New York: St. Martin's Press, 1995.

Blackburn, Robin. *The Making of New World Slavery: From the Baroque to the Modern, 1492-1800.* New York: Verso, 1999.

Bourgeois, Jean-Baptiste. *Opinion de Jean-Baptiste Bourgeois, habitant planteur de S. Domingue sur les moyens de rétablir les colonies.* Paris, 1794.

Boutin, Raymond. "Les Esclaves du Moule au XIXe siècle (naissances, mariages et décès)." *Bulletin de la Société d'histoire de la Guadeloupe,* nos. 75-78 (1988).

Brereton, Bridget. Review of *Slave Women in Caribbean Society 1650-1838,* by Barbara Bush. *Journal of Caribbean History* 24 (1992): 115-20.

——. "Searching for the Invisible Woman." *Slavery and Abolition* 13, no. 2 (1992): 86-96.

——. "Text, Testimony and Gender: An Examination of Some Texts by Women on the English-speaking Caribbean from the 1770s to the 1920s." In *Engendering History: Caribbean Women in Historical Perspective,* ed. Verene Shepherd et al., 63-93. New York: St. Martin's Press, 1995.

Bruleaux, Anne-Marie, Régine Calmont, and Serge Mam-Lam-Fouck, eds. *Deux Siècles d'esclavage en Guyane française, 1652-1848.* Paris: L'Harmattan, 1986.

Buffon, Alain. *Monnaie et crédit en économie coloniale: Contribution à l'histoire économique de la Guadeloupe, 1635-1919.* Basse-Terre: Société d'histoire de la Guadeloupe, 1979.

Bulletin des actes administratifs de la Martinique. 1st ser., vol. 4 (1832).

Bush, Barbara. *Slave Women in Caribbean Society, 1650-1838.* Bloomington: Indiana University Press, 1990.

Castelli, Pierre Paul. *De l'esclavage en général et de l'émancipation des Noirs.* Paris, 1844.

Cauna, Jacques. *Au temps des isles à sucre.* Paris: Karthala, 1978.

Césaire, Aimé. *La Tragédie du roi Christophe.* Paris: Présence africaine, 1963.

Chauleau, Liliane. *Dans les Isles du Vent: La Martinique (XVIIe–XIXe).* Paris: L'Harmattan, 1993.

———. *La Société à la Martinique au XVIIe siècle, 1635–1713.* Caen: Ozanne, 1966.

Cochin, Augustin. *L'Abolition de l'esclavage.* 1861. Reprint, Fort-de-France: Désmoreaux, 1979.

Cox, Edward. *Free Coloreds in the Slave Societies of St. Kitts and Grenada.* Knoxville: University of Tennessee Press, 1984.

Craton, Michael. *Empire, Enslavement and Freedom in the Caribbean.* Princeton: Markus Wiener, 1997.

———. *Searching for the Invisible Man: Slaves and Plantation Life in Jamaica.* Cambridge, Mass.: Harvard University Press, 1977.

———. *Testing the Chains: Resistance to Slavery in the British West Indies.* Ithaca: Cornell University Press, 1982.

Craton, Michael, and James Walvin. *A Jamaican Plantation: The History of Worthy Park.* Toronto: University of Toronto Press, 1970.

Curtin, Philip D. *The Atlantic Slave Trade: A Census.* Madison: University of Wisconsin Press, 1969.

———. *Economic Change in Precolonial Africa.* Madison: University of Wisconsin Press, 1975.

Daget, Serge. *La Traite des Noirs: Bastilles négrières et velléités abolitionnistes.* Rennes: Éditions Ouest-France, 1990.

David, Bernard. *Les Origines de la population martiniquaise au fil des ans 1635–1902.* Fort-de-France: Société d'histoire de la Martinique, 1973.

Davies, K. G. *The Royal African Company.* New York: Atheneum, 1970.

Davis, David Brion. *Slavery and Human Progress.* New York: Oxford University Press, 1984.

Dazille. *Observations sur les maladies des nègres, leurs causes, leurs traitements et les moyens de les prévenir.* Paris: Didot, 1776.

———. *Observations sur le tétanos.* Paris: Planche, 1788.

Debbasch, Yvan. "Les Associations serviles à la Martinique au XIXe siècle." In *Études d'histoire du droit privé,* ed. Pierre Petot. Paris: Éditions Montchrestien, 1959.

———. *Couleur et liberté: Le Jeu de critère ethnique dans un ordre juridique esclavagiste.* 2 vols. Paris: Dalloz, 1967.

———. "Le Crime d'empoisonnement aux îles pendant la période esclavagiste." *Revue française d'histoire d'outre-mer* 50, no. 2 (1967): 137–88.

Debien, Gabriel. "Un Colon niortais à Saint-Domingue: Jean Barre de Saint-Venant (1737–1810)." *Bulletin de la Société d'histoire de la Martinique,* no. 19 (1977).

———*Les Colons des Antilles et leur main d'oeuvre à la fin du XVIIIe siècle.* Paris: Annales historiques de la Révolution française, 1955.

———. "Comptes, profits, esclaves et travaux de deux sucreries de Saint-Domingue, 1774–1778." *Notes d'histoire coloniale* (Cairo, Egypt), no. 6 (Oct. 1944), 1–60.

———. "Destinées d'esclaves à la Martinique (1746–1778)." *Bulletin de L'Institut français d'Afrique noire,* series B, vol. 22, nos. 1–2 (Jan.–April 1960): 1–91.

———. *Les Engagés pour les Antilles (1634–1715).* Paris: Société de l'histoire des colonies françaises, 1952.

———. *Les Esclaves aux Antilles françaises, XVIIe–XVIIIe siècles.* Basse-Terre: Société d'histoire de la Guadeloupe, 1974.

————. *Lettres de colons.* Dakar: Publications de la Section d'histoire, Université de Dakar (now Université Cheikh Anta Diop), 1965.

————. "Le Marronage aux Antilles françaises au XVIIIe siècle." *Caribbean Studies* 6, no. 3 (1966): 3–43.

————. *Plantations et esclaves à Saint-Domingue.* Dakar: Publications de la Section d'histoire, Université de Dakar (now Université Cheikh Anta Diop), 1969.

————. "Les Premières Femmes des colons des Antilles, 1635–1680." *Revue de la Porte Océane,* France: nos. 89–90 (1952): 7–17.

————. "A Saint-Domingue avec deux jeunes économes de plantation, 1774–1788." *Notes d'histoire coloniale* (Cairo, Egypt), no. 7 (Port-au-Prince: 1945).

————. "La Société coloniale aux XVII et XVIIIe siècles: Les Engagés pour les Antilles (1634–1715). *Revue d'histoire des colonies* (Paris), nos. 1–2 (1952).

————. "Sucrerie Bréda de la Plaine-du-Nord (1785)." *Notes d'histoire coloniale* (Cairo, Egypt), no. 100 (1966).

Debien, Gabriel, and Françoise Thésée. *Un Colon niortais à Saint-Domingue.* Niort: Imbert-Nicolas, 1975.

Deerr, Noel. *A History of Sugar.* London: Chapman and Hull, 1949–50.

"Description d'un navire négrier." N.p. [1780? 1790?]. Pamphlet found among unclassified papers, file 027, at the Bibliothèque des Frères de Saint-Louis de Gonzague, Port-au-Prince, Haiti.

Dessalles, Pierre. *Histoire des Antilles.* 5 vols. Paris: Libraire-Éditeur, 1847.

————. *La vie d'un colon à la Martinique au XIXe siècle.* 4 vols. 1986.

Diop, Abdolaye Bara. *La Société wolof.* Paris: Karthala, 1981.

Dugoujon. *Lettres sur l'esclavage dans les colonies françaises.* Paris, 1845.

Dunn, Richard S. *Sugar and Slaves: The Rise of the Planter Class in the English West Indies, 1624–1713.* Chapel Hill: University of North Carolina Press, 1972.

Du Tertre, Jean-Baptiste (Père). *Histoire générale des Antilles habitées par les Français.* 4 vols. 1671. Reprint, Fort-de-France: Éditions des horizons caraïbes, 1973.

Elgersman, Maureen G. *Unyielding Spirits: Black Women and Slavery in Early Canada and Jamaica.* New York: Garland, 1999.

Elisabeth, Léo. "Europe, Afrique, Nouveau Monde: Femmes d'antan aux origines de la femme créole." *Bulletin de la Société d'histoire de la Martinique,* no. 27 (1988–91).

————"Résistance des esclaves aux XVIIe et XVIIIe siècles dans les colonies françaises d'Amérique, principalement aux Iles du vent." In *Les Abolitions de l'esclavage de L. F. Sonthonax à V. Schoelcher 1793, 1848,* ed. Marcel Dorigny. Paris: UNESCO, 1995.

"État nominatif et général des citoyens et les habitations de la Martinique, 1664–1764." Archives Départementales de la Martinique, série MI, 5mi. 89.

Fage, J. D. "The Effect of the Export Slave Trade on African Populations." In *The Population Factor in African Studies: The Proceedings of a Conference Organised by the African Studies Association of the United Kingdom, September 1972,* ed. R. P. Moss and R. J. A. Rathbone, 15–23. London: University of London Press, 1975.

Fallope, Josette. "Les Affranchissements d'esclaves à la Guadeloupe entre 1815 et 1848." *Annales de l'Université d'Abidjan,* series 1, vol. 6 (1978).

————. *Les Esclaves et citoyens: Les Noirs à la Guadeloupe au XIXe siècle dans les processus de résistance et d'intégration (1802–1910).* Basse-Terre: Société d'histoire de la Guadeloupe, 1992.

Fick, Carolyn. *The Making of Haiti: The Saint-Domingue Revolution from Below.* Knoxville: University of Tennessee Press, 1990.

Fouchard, Jean. *Les Marrons de la liberté.* Paris: Éditions de l'école, 1972.

Fox-Genovese, Elizabeth. *Within the Plantation Household: Black and White Women of the Old South.* Chapel Hill: University of North Carolina Press, 1988.

France, Joseph. *La Vérité et les faits ou l'esclavage à nu dans ses rapports avec les maîtres et les agents de l'autorité.* Paris: Moreau, 1846.

Fyfe, Christopher, and David McMaster, eds. *African Historical Demography.* 2 vols. Edinburgh: Centre of African Studies, University of Edinburgh, 1981.

Garrigus, John. "Blue and Brown: Contraband Indigo and the Rise of a Free Colored Planter Class in French Saint-Domingue." *The Americas* 50, no. 2 (Oct. 1993): 233–63.

Gaspar, David Barry. *Bondmen and Rebels: A Study of Master-Slave Relations in Antigua.* Baltimore: Johns Hopkins University Press, 1985.

Gaston-Martin. *Histoire de l'esclavage dans les colonies françaises.* Paris: Presses universitaires de France, 1948.

Gautier, Arlette. *Les Soeurs de solitude: La Condition féminine dans l'esclavage aux Antilles du XVIIe au XIX siécle.* Paris: Éditions Caribéennes, 1985.

Geggus, David Patrick. "Sex Ratio, Age and Ethnicity in the Atlantic Slave Trade: Data From French Shipping and Plantation Records." *Journal of African History* 30 (1989): 23–44.

———. *Slavery, War and Revolution: The British Occupation of Saint-Domingue, 1793–1798.* London: Oxford University Press, 1982.

———. "The Slaves of British-Occupied Saint-Domingue: An Analysis of the Workforces of 197 Absentee Plantations, 1796–1797." *Caribbean Studies* 18 (April–July 1978): 5–41.

Geracimos, Ann. "A Mystery in Miniature: An Enigmatic Button Once Decorated the Uniform of Haitian Liberator Toussaint Louverture." *Smithsonian* 30 (January 2000): 20–22.

Girod, François. *Une Fortune coloniale sous l'Ancien Régime: La Famille Hecquet à Saint-Domingue, 1724–1796.* Paris: Annales littéraires de l'Université de Besançon, 1970.

Girod-Chantrans, Justin. *Voyage d'un Suisse dans différentes colonies d'Amérique pendant la dernière guerre, avec une table d'observations météorologiques faites à Saint-Domingue.* Paris: Neufchâtel, 1785.

Gisler, Antoine. *L'Esclavage aux Antilles françaises XVIe–XIXe siècles.* Paris: Karthala, 1981.

Goveia, Elsa. *Slave Society in the British Leeward Islands at the End of the Eighteenth Century.* New Haven: Yale University Press, 1965.

———. *The West Indian Slave Laws of the Eighteenth Century.* Bridgetown: Caribbean Universities Press, 1970.

Granier de Cassagnac, Bernard Adolphe. *Voyage aux Antilles françaises, anglaises, danoises, espagnoles: À Saint-Domingue et aux États-Unis d'Amérique.* 2 vols. Paris: Dauvin et Fontaine, 1842–44.

Hall, Douglas. *In Miserable Slavery: Thomas Thistlewood in Jamaica, 1750–1786.* London: Macmillan, 1989.

Hall, Gwendolyn Mildo. *Social Control in Slave Plantation Societies: A Comparison of Saint-Domingue and Cuba.* Baltimore: Johns Hopkins University Press, 1971.

Handler, Jerome S., Frederick W. Lange, and Robert V. Riordan. *Plantation Slavery in Barbados: An Archaeological and Historical Investigation.* Cambridge, Mass.: Harvard University Press, 1978.

Higman, Barry. *Slave Population and Economy in Jamaica, 1807–1834.* Cambridge: Cambridge University Press, 1976.

———. *Slave Populations of the British Caribbean, 1807–1834.* Baltimore: Johns Hopkins University Press, 1984.

Inikori, Joseph E. Introduction to *Forced Migration: The Impact of the Export Slave Trade on African Societies,* ed. Joseph E. Inikori. New York: Africana Publishing Company, 1982.

———. "Underpopulation in Nineteenth Century West Africa: The Role of the Export Slave Trade." In *African Historical Demography,* ed. Christopher Fyfe and David McMaster, 2 vols., 2:283–313. Edinburgh: Centre of African Studies, University of Edinburgh, 1981.

James, C.L.R. *The Black Jacobins: Toussaint Louverture and the San Domingo Revolution.* New York: Vintage Books, 1989.

Jones, Jacqueline. *Labor of Love, Labor of Sorrow: Black Women, Work and the Family, From Slavery to the Present.* New York: Vintage, 1986.

Jones, Norrece T., Jr. *Born a Child of Freedom, Yet a Slave: Mechanisms of Control and Strategies of Resistance in Antebellum South Carolina.* Middletown, Conn.: Wesleyan University Press, 1990.

Kiple, Kenneth F. *The Caribbean Slave: A Biological History.* London: Cambridge University Press, 1984.

Klein, Herbert S. "African Women in the Atlantic Slave Trade." In *Women and Slavery In Africa,* ed. Claire C. Robertson and Martin A. Klein, 29–38. Madison: University of Wisconsin Press, 1983.

Klein, Martin A. "Women in Slavery in the Western Sudan." In *Women and Slavery in Africa,* ed. Claire C. Robertson and Martin A. Klein, 67–92. Madison: University of Wisconsin Press, 1983.

Knight, Franklin W. *The Caribbean: The Genesis of a Fragmented Nationalism.* New York: Oxford University Press, 1990.

Labat, Jean-Baptiste (Père). *Nouveau Voyage aux isles de l'Amérique.* 6 vols. Paris: Guillaume, 1722.

Lacharière, André. *De l'affranchissement des esclaves dans les colonies françaises.* Paris: Eugène Penduel, 1836.

Lacour, Auguste. *Histoire de la Guadeloupe.* 4 vols. Basse-Terre: Éditions de diffusion de la culture antillaise, 1976.

Lafleur, Géraud. *Saint-Claude: Histoire d'une commune de Guadeloupe.* Paris: Karthala, 1993.

Lara, Oruno. *La Guadeloupe dans l'histoire.* Paris: L'Harmattan, 1979.

Lasserie, Guy. *La Guadeloupe, étude géographique.* 2 vols. Bordeaux: CNRS, 1961.

Lavollée, M. P. *Notes sur les cultures et la production de la Martinique et de la Guadeloupe.* Paris: Ministère de la Marine et des Colonies, 1841.

Leti, Geneviève. *Santé et société esclavagiste à la Martinique (1802–1848).* Paris: L'Harmattan, 1998.

Lewis, Gordon K. *Main Currents in Caribbean Thought.* Baltimore: Johns Hopkins University Press, 1983.

Lewis, Matthew Gregory (Monk). *Journal of a West India Proprietor.* London: John Murray, 1834.

Lovejoy, Paul E. *Transformations in Slavery.* New York: Cambridge University Press, 1983.

———. "The Volume of the Atlantic Slave Trade: A Synthesis." *Journal of African History* 23 (1982): 473–501.

Ly, Abdoulaye. *La Compagnie du Sénégal.* Paris: Présence africaine, 1968.

Manning, Patrick. *Slavery and African Life: Occidental, Oriental, and African Slave Trades.* New York: Cambridge University Press, 1990.

Martineau, Alfred, and Louis-Phillipe May. *Trois Siècles d'histoire antillaise: Martinique et Guadeloupe de 1635 à nos jours.* Paris: Société d'histoire des colonies françaises, 1935.

Mathurin-Mair, Lucille. *The Rebel Woman in the British West Indies during Slavery.* Kingston: Institute of Jamaica, for the African-Caribbean Institute of Jamaica, 1975.

———. "Recollections of a Journey into a Rebel Past." In *Caribbean Women Writers,* ed. Selwyn Cudjoe, 51–60. Wellesley: Calaloux Publications, 1990.

Meillassoux, Claude. "Female Slavery." In *Women and Slavery in Africa,* ed. Claire C. Robertson and Martin A. Klein, 49–66. Madison: University of Wisconsin Press, 1983.

Métral, Antoine. *Histoire de l'expédition des Français à Saint-Domingue.* Paris: Éditions Karthala, 1985.

———. *Histoire de l'insurrection des esclaves dans le nord de Saint-Domingue.* Paris: F. Sceref, 1818.

Mettas, Jean. *Répertoire des expéditions négrières françaises au XVIIIe siècle.* 2 vols. Paris: Société française d'histoire d'Outre-Mer, 1978–1984.

Mims, S. L. *Colbert's West India Policy.* New Haven: Yale University Press, 1912.

Moitt, Bernard. "Behind the Sugar Fortunes: Women, Labor and the Development of Caribbean Plantations during Slavery." In *African Continuities,* ed. Simeon Chilungu and Sada Niang, 403–26. Toronto: Terebi Publications, 1989.

———. "In the Shadow of the Plantation: Women of Color and the *Libres de Fait* of Martinique and Guadeloupe." Unpublished paper.

———. "Slavery and Emancipation in Senegal's Peanut Basin: The Nineteenth and Twentieth Centuries." *International Journal of African Historical Studies* 22, no. 1 (1989): 27–50.

———. "Transcending Linguistic and Cultural Frontiers in Caribbean Historiography: C.L.R. James, French Sources, and Slavery in San Domingo." In *C.L.R. James: His Intellectual Legacies,* ed. Selwyn R. Cudjoe and William E. Cain, 136–60. Amherst: University of Massachusetts Press, 1995.

———. "Women, Work, and Resistance in the French Caribbean." In *Engendering History: Caribbean Women in Historical Perspective,* ed. Verene Shepherd, Bridget Brereton, and Barbara Bailey, 155–75. New York: St. Martin's Press, 1995.

Moreau de Jonnès, Alex. *Recherches statistiques sur l'esclavage colonial et sur les moyens de le supprimer.* Paris, 1842.

Moreau de Saint-Méry, M.L.E. *Description de la partie française de l'isle Saint-Domingue.* 3 vols. Paris: Société d'histoire des colonies françaises, 1958.

———. *Lois et constitutions des colonies françaises de l'Amérique sous le vent, de 1625 à 1785.* 6 vols. Paris, 1785–1790.

Morrissey, Marietta. *Slave Women in the New World: Gender Stratification in the Caribbean.* Lawrence: University Press of Kansas, 1989.

Mumford, Clarence J. *The Black Ordeal of Slavery and Slave Trading in the French West Indies, 1625–1713*. 3 vols. Lewiston, N.Y.: Edwin Mellen Press, 1991.

Nègre, André. *La Rébellion de la Guadeloupe, 1801–1802*. Paris: Éditions Caribéennes, 1987.

Nicolas, Armand. *Histoire de la Martinique*. 2 vols. Paris: L'Harmattan, 1996.

———. *La Révolution antiesclavagiste de mai 1848 à la Martinique*. Fort-de-France: 1967.

Nicolas, Maurice. *L'Affaire de la Grand'Anse*. Fort-de-France: Théodore Marchand, 1960.

Northrup, David. *Indentured Labor in the Age of Imperialism, 1834–1922*. New York: Cambridge University Press, 1995.

"Notice statistique sur la Guyane française." In *Notices statistiques sur les colonies françaises*. Paris: Société d'études, 1843.

Olwell, Robert. "'Loose, Idle and Disorderly' Slave Women in the Eighteenth-Century Charleston Marketplace." In *More Than Chattel: Black Women and Slavery in the Americas*, ed. David Barry Gaspar and Darlene Clark Hine, 97–110. Bloomington: Indiana University Press, 1996.

Pago, Gilbert. *Les Femmes et la liquidation du système esclavagiste à la Martinique, 1848–1852*. Pointe-à-Pitre: Ibis Rouge Editions, 1998.

Palmer, Colin. *Human Cargoes: The British Slave Trade to Spanish America 1700–1739*. Urbana: University of Illinois Press, 1981.

Patron, Félix. *Des Noirs et leur situation dans les colonies françaises*. Paris, 1831.

Patterson, Orlando. *Slavery and Social Death: A Comparative Study*. Cambridge, Mass.: Harvard University Press, 1982.

———. *The Sociology of Slavery*. London: Granada Publishing, 1973.

Peyreleau, Eugène-Edouard Boyer. *Les Antilles françaises, particulièrement la Guadeloupe*. 3 vols. Paris, 1825.

Peytraud, Lucien. *L'Esclavage aux Antilles françaises avant 1789*. Paris: Hachette, 1879.

Poyen de Sainte-Marie, M. *De l'exploitation des sucreries ou conseil d'un vieux planteur aux jeunes agriculteurs des colonies*. Basse-Terre: Imprimerie de la République, 1792.

Reddock, Rhoda. *Women, Labor and Politics in Trinidad and Tobago*. Highlands: Zed Books, 1994.

———. "Women and Slavery in the Caribbean: A Feminist Perspective." *Latin American Perspectives* 12 (Winter 1985): 63–80.

Reible, Marcel. "Les Esclaves et leurs travaux sur la sucrerie Lugé à Saint-Domingue (1788–1791)." *Notes d'histoire coloniale*, no. 173 (1976).

Robertson, Claire C., and Martin A. Klein. "Women's Importance in African Slave Systems." In *Women and Slavery In Africa*, ed. Claire C. Robertson and Martin Klein, 3–38. Madison: University of Wisconsin Press, 1983.

Rodney, Walter. *How Europe Underdeveloped Africa*. Washington, D.C.: Howard University Press, 1974.

———. *West Africa and the Atlantic Slave Trade*. Cambridge, Mass.: Africa Research Group, 1974.

Roget, Jacques Petit Jean. "Saint-Christophe, première des îles françaises d'Amérique." *Bulletin de la Société d'histoire de la Martinique*, no. 24 (1981): 3–20.

———. "La Société d'habitation à la Martinique: Un Demi Siècle de formation, 1635–1685." 2 vols. Ph.D. diss., Université de Lille III, 1980.

Romalet du Caillaud, Joseph. *Voyage à la Martinique fait en 1770–1773*. Paris, 1804.

Roumain, Jacques. *Gouverneurs de la rosée.* Paris: Les Éditeurs français réunis, 1946.

Rouvellat de Cussac, Jean-Baptiste. *Situation des esclaves dans les colonies françaises: Urgence de leur émancipation.* Paris: Pagnerre, 1845.

Sala-Molins, Louis. *Le Code Noir ou le calvaire du Canaan.* Paris: Presses universitaires de France, 1987.

Satchell, Veront. "Early Use of Steam Power in the Jamaica Sugar Economy, 1768–1810." *Transactions of the Newcomen Society* 67 (1995–96): 222–30.

Satineau, Maurice. *Histoire de la Guadeloupe sous L'Ancien Régime, 1635–1789.* Paris: Payot, 1928.

Schnakenbourg, Christian. *Histoire de l'industrie sucrière en Guadeloupe: La Crise du système esclavagiste (XIX–XX siècles).* Paris: L'Harmattan, 1980.

Schoelcher, Victor. *De l'abolition de l'esclavage: Examen critique du préjugé contre la couleur des Africains et des sangs-mêlés.* Paris: Pagnerre, 1840.

———. *Des colonies françaises: Abolition immédiate de l'esclavage.* 1842. Reprint, Basse-Terre: Société d'histoire de la Guadeloupe, 1976.

———. *Histoire de l'esclavage pendant les deux dernières années.* 2 vols. Paris: Pagnerre, 1847. Reprint, Pointe-à-Pitre: Émile Désormeaux, 1973.

———. *Les Magistrats des colonies depuis l'ordonnance du 18 juillet 1841 par Maxmillen Just.* Paris: Pagnerre, 1847.

Schwarz, Philip J. *Slave Laws in Virginia.* Athens: University of Georgia Press, 1999.

Schwarz-Bart, Simone. *Pluie et vent sur Télumée Miracle.* Paris: Éditions du seuil, 1972.

Shepherd, Verene, ed. *Women in Caribbean History.* Kingston: Ian Randle, 1999.

Shepherd, Verene, Bridget Brereton, and Barbara Bailey, eds. *Engendering History: Caribbean Women in Historical Perspective.* New York: St. Martin's Press, 1995.

Sheridan, Richard. *Doctors and Slaves: A Medical Demographic History of Slavery in the British Indies.* London: Cambridge University Press, 1985.

"Slavery No Oppression or, Some New Arguments and Opinions against the Idea of African Liberty." London: Lowndes and Christie, n.d. Pamphlet found among unclassified papers, file 027, at the Bibliothèque des Frères de Saint-Louis de Gonzague, Port-au-Prince, Haiti.

Sow, Fatou. "Femme africaine, emploi et division internationale du travail." *Présence Africaine* no. 141 (1987): 199–205.

Stampp, Kenneth. *The Peculiar Institution.* New York: Random House, 1984.

Stein, Robert Louis. *The French Slave Trade in the Eighteenth Century: An Old Regime Business.* Madison: University of Wisconsin Press, 1979.

———. *The French Sugar Business in the Eighteenth Century.* Baton Rouge: Louisiana State University Press, 1988.

———. "Measuring the French Slave Trade, 1713–1792/3." *Journal of African History* 19, no. 4 (1978): 515–21.

Tanc, Xavier. *De l'esclavage aux colonies françaises et spécialement à la Guadeloupe.* Paris, 1832.

Tardo-Dino, Frantz. *Le Collier de servitude.* Paris: Éditions Caribéennes, 1985.

Thomas, Clive. *Plantations, Peasants and State: A Study of the Mode of Sugar Production in Guyana.* Los Angeles: Center for Afro-American Studies, 1984.

Thornton, John. *Africa and Africans in the Making of the Atlantic World, 1400–1680.* New York: Cambridge University Press, 1992.

———. "The Demographic Effect of the Slave Trade on Western Africa, 1500–1850." In *African Historical Demography,* ed. Christopher Fyfe and David McMaster, 2 vols., 2:691–720. Edinburgh: Centre of African Studies, University of Edinburgh, 1981.

———. "Sexual Demography: The Impact of the Slave Trade on Family Structure." In *Women and Slavery in Africa,* ed. Claire C. Robertson and Martin A. Klein, 39–48. Madison: University of Wisconsin Press, 1983.

———. "The Slave Trade in Eighteenth-Century Angola: Effects on Demographic Structures." *Canadian Journal of African Studies* 14 (1980): 417–27.

Tomich, Dale. *Slavery in the Circuit of Sugar.* Baltimore: Johns Hopkins University Press, 1990.

Vanony-Frisch, Nicole. "Les Esclaves de la Guadeloupe à la fin de l'Ancien Régime d'après les sources notariales, 1770–1789." *Bulletin de la Société d'histoire de la Guadeloupe,* nos. 63–64 (1985).

Vassière, Pierre de. *Saint-Domingue: La Société et la vie créoles sous l'Ancien Régime (1629–1789).* Paris: Perrin, 1909.

Williams, Eric. *Capitalism and Slavery.* Chapel Hill: University of North Carolina Press, 1944.

Wimpffen, Baron de. *Voyage à Saint-Domingue pendant les années 1788, 1789 et 1790.* Paris, 1797.

Zay, E. *Histoire monétaire des colonies françaises d'après les documents officiels avec 278 figures.* Paris: 1892.

Index

Page references to tables are in italics.

BERNARD MOITT is an associate professor in the History Department at Virginia Commonwealth University in Richmond, Virginia. Previously, he taught at the University of Toronto and at Utica College of Syracuse University. Educated in Antigua (where he was born) and in Canada and the United States, he has published numerous articles and book chapters on aspects of francophone African and Caribbean history, with particular emphasis on gender and slavery.